DELAY, DENY, DEFEND

DELAY, DENY, DEFEND

Why Insurance Companies Don't Pay Claims and What You Can Do About It

Jay M. Feinman

Delden Press

Published by Delden Press
www.delaydenydefend.com
DeldenPress@gmail.com

Publisher's Note:
This publication is designed to produce accurate and authoritative information in regard to the subject matter covered. It is sold with the understanding that the publisher and author are not engaged in rendering legal advice or other professional services. If you require legal advice or other professional services, you should seek the advice of a competent professional.

ISBN 978-0-9895017-0-5

Manufactured in the United States of America

Contents

DELAY, DENY, DEFEND

Prologue

YOU ARE DRIVING down the highway when suddenly the left rear wheel falls off your car and the car jolts to the ground, causing an injury to your back. A month later you have surgery for a herniated disk. Although you have no medical insurance, you are confident that your medical bills will be paid. You bought an auto insurance policy from a company that promised to be your good neighbor, and the policy includes a promise to pay for medical expenses caused by an accident. That doesn't happen. Six months after the accident, when your bills total $11,000, your insurance company sends you a check for $1,662.18. You have to undergo a second surgery; the hospital won't let you have physical therapy after the surgery because you can't pay the hospital bill. You hire a lawyer, get more doctors' reports, and finally, three years after the accident, the insurance company pays you what it owed in the first place. It happened to Cindy Robinson—her story is told in Chapter 7—and it could happen to you.

A pipe breaks in the attic of your house, soaking walls, ceilings, carpets, and cabinets throughout the house. You need money to make repairs, and you expect that your insurance company, which sold you a "Deluxe Homeowners Policy" and promised that you would be in good hands, will come through for you. Instead, the company fails to adequately investigate the damage, looks for reasons to deny the claim, and refuses to pay for obviously needed repairs like the replacement of sagging, moldy drywall. Eventually the company offers you a check for less than you need to pay for the repairs, take it or leave it. You have to hire a lawyer and sue the company and, eventually, five years after the water leak, you recover enough to pay for your loss. It happened to Thomas Anderson—his story is told in Chapter 8—and it could happen to you

Consumers buy car insurance and homeowners insurance to be protected from financial disaster in situations like these. If you are injured in a car accident, you will suffer physical pain and emotional distress. If your house is inundated by water, you will undergo aggravation and inconvenience. No one can do anything about that. But if you have insurance, at least your insurance company will protect you from the financial consequences of the unfortunate events. That is why you buy insurance: to cushion the blow of accidents and injuries. Your insurance company pays for your medical bills, the repairs to your house, and the other expenses you are entitled to under your insurance policy.

Too often, however, it doesn't work that way. The insurance company you trusted will delay paying for your loss, deny payment of part or all of your claim, and aggressively defend the lawsuit you are forced to bring to make the company live up to its promise. The reason is simple: The less the insurance company pays out in claims to you and people like you, the more it makes in profits.

Delay, deny, defend is a violation of consumers' reliance on their insurance companies. It hurts people when they are at their most vulnerable and it erodes the trust that all of us put in insurance. This book explores where and how delay, deny, defend occurs, why it has increased, and what can be done to stop it.

Introduction

INSURANCE IS THE great protector of the standard of living of the American middle class. A good job provides the means to acquire a home, a car, a college education for the children, and a comfortable retirement, and insurance secures those things against the uncertainties of life. Houses will burn, but homeowners insurance furnishes funds to rebuild. Cars will crash, but auto insurance pays medical bills and repair costs and guards against potentially massive liability to other people who are injured. Illness, injury, and death will occur, but health insurance, disability insurance, and life insurance remove the burden of cost and replace the lost earnings of the breadwinner.

Insurance has come a long way in five thousand years, from the time when Babylonian merchants found investors who agreed to accept the risk of cargo lost at sea in return for a payment, a transaction that would develop into marine insurance.[1] Today insurance in the United States is a trillion-dollar industry, with 2,700 property/casualty insurance companies collecting $440 billion in premiums and paying $250 billion in claims each year. (Property/casualty insurance mostly protects against property damage and liability to others; "personal lines property/casualty" is largely auto and homeowners insurance, the subjects of this book.) State Farm, the industry's giant, has forty-two million policies in force and processes over twelve million claims each year.

Insurance is the great protector of the standard of living of the American middle class, but only when it works. Purchasing an insurance policy is less like buying a product and more like receiving a promise. In return for the policyholder's payment of a premium, the insurance company promises to accept the risks of financial loss that the policyholder otherwise could not bear. As a formal matter the promise to indemnify the insured against loss is embodied in the policy document, often fifty pages of eight-point type that is seldom read and less often understood, but the real promise is to provide security against loss. Long before the GEICO gecko promised to save you 15 percent or more on car insurance, the iconic slogans of insurance company advertising expressed that real promise: "Like a good neighbor, State Farm is there." "You're in good hands with Allstate."

Insurance doesn't work when the insurance company fails to honor the terms of the policy and its promise of security through the strategy that has become known as "delay, deny, defend." The company delays payment of a claim, denies all or part of a valid claim, or aggressively defends litigation the policyholder is forced to bring to get what he is rightfully owed. When insurance doesn't work, the consequences are more severe than when any other kind of company fails to keep its promise. If a homeowner hires someone to paint his house and the painter never shows up, the homeowner can take his money and hire someone else. If the insurance company refuses to pay a claim, it is too late to go elsewhere for another policy; no company will write a policy that will pay for fire damage that has already occurred.

Insurance didn't work for Kim Zilisch, who was in an accident that killed her fiancé and permanently injured her. After she filed a claim with State Farm, her insurance company, the response was to delay. State Farm's claims adjuster knew her injuries were permanent yet waited four months for a copy of a doctor's report he knew didn't exist. The adjuster then concluded without sufficient evidence that Zilisch's injuries were not that serious, waited another four months to make an offer to settle her claim, then changed the offer without regard to the facts. A year after her claim was filed Zilisch was awarded $387,500 by an arbitration panel, at which point State Farm finally paid the policy limit of $100,000.[2]

Insurance didn't work for Terry Buttery. When his home was burglarized he called the police and his insurance company, Hamilton Mutual.

Buttery completed the claims forms he was given within twenty-four hours but that was only the beginning. Even though he supplied three more statements, receipts for stolen items, repair estimates, and five years worth of tax returns, and gave testimony to Hamilton under oath four separate times, Hamilton still did not pay. So Buttery sued and won. But Hamilton delayed payment even after Buttery's judgment was upheld by the Kentucky Supreme Court, hoping that his precarious financial position would force him to settle for less than he was owed.[3]

Delay, deny, defend violates the rules for handling claims that are recognized by every company, taught to adjusters, and embodied in law. Within the vast bureaucracy of insurance companies, actuaries assess risks, underwriters price policies and evaluate prospective policyholders, and agents market policies. The claims department's only job is to pay what is owed, no more but no less. A classic text used to train adjusters, James Markham's *The Claims Environment,* states the principle: "The essential function of a claim department is to fulfill the insurance company's promise, as set forth in the insurance policy. . . . The claim function should ensure the prompt, fair, and efficient delivery of this promise."[4]

Beginning in the 1990s, many major insurance companies reconsidered this understanding of the claims process. The insight was simple. An insurance company's greatest expense is what it pays out in claims. If it pays out less in claims, it keeps more in profits. Therefore, the claims department became a profit center rather than the place that kept the company's promise.

A major step in this shift occurred when Allstate and other companies hired the megaconsulting firm McKinsey & Company to develop new strategies for handling claims. McKinsey saw claims as a "zero-sum game," with the policyholder and the company competing for the same dollars. No longer would each claim be treated on its merits. Instead, computer systems would be put in place to set the amounts policyholders would be offered, claimants would be deterred from hiring lawyers to help with their claims, and settlements would be offered on a take-it-or-litigate basis. If Allstate moved from "Good Hands" to "Boxing Gloves," as McKinsey described it, policyholders would either take a lowball offer from the good hands people or face the boxing gloves of extended litigation.

How widespread is delay, deny, defend? How often is it that insurance doesn't work? There are two answers: too widespread and too often, and no one knows.

Too widespread and too often. As the new claim strategies have been implemented there have been an increasing number of cases in which companies have delayed payment, denied valid claims, and unnecessarily defended litigation. Minor auto accidents have become the source of major litigation as companies routinely and systematically deny claims. Homeowners can no longer be assured of receiving enough from their insurance companies to rebuild their homes and their lives. When mass disasters strike, things get even worse. After Hurricane Katrina struck in 2005 policyholders who believed they were treated unfairly by their insurance companies complained to the Louisiana Department of Insurance at the rate of twenty thousand a month during the first six months after the storm. Thousands of policyholders sued their insurance companies; more than 6,600 suits were filed in federal court in New Orleans alone, and many cases are still pending.

Nor is delay, deny, defend restricted to auto and homeowners insurance. All insurance companies have an incentive to chisel their customers in order to increase profits. Unum, the largest seller of disability and long-term care insurance in the United States, became notorious for failing to pay what it owed to sick or injured workers. Numerous courts castigated the company for unscrupulous tactics, nonsensical legal arguments, and lack of objectivity amounting to bad faith in denying claims. Employees who were especially aggressive in denying claims were recognized with the company's Hungry Vulture Award. Under a settlement with insurance regulators in all the states, Unum was forced to review claims denied between 1997 and 2004, and it reversed its decisions in 42 percent of the cases, paying out $676 million in additional benefits. Almost everyone who has health insurance has a story about an arbitrary or incomprehensible denial of a claim. In 2009 New York attorney general Andrew Cuomo concluded that the databases used by insurance companies to calculate the "reasonable and customary" fees they would pay for out-of-network treatment were part of a scheme to defraud consumers by systematically lowballing the fees. UnitedHealth, Aetna, Guardian, and other companies agreed to stop using the faulty databases and contribute to the creation of a new independent database. The story of delay, deny, defend by property/casualty companies is part of the failure of insurance as a whole.

No one knows how widespread delay, deny, defend is because part of this story is the failure of state insurance regulators to police insurance companies' conduct. Insurance is the most heavily regulated industry in the United States. Every state has an insurance commissioner who licenses companies and agents, sets financial standards, requires regular reports, and examines the operations of companies. Most of the regulatory effort is devoted to making sure insurance companies have the resources to honor their promise to pay claims, and that effort works well; when insurance giant AIG collapsed in September 2008, its financial products division was a shambles, but regulators reported that its property/casualty insurance company subsidiaries were sound. Making sure companies actually do honor their promise has received much less attention. Insurance commissioners generally do not even collect, analyze, and publish comprehensive figures on the payment and denial of claims.

Consumers certainly do not know how widespread delay, deny, defend is for the industry as a whole or for individual companies. Consumers have little to go on when making one of their most important purchases—auto and homeowners insurance—to secure their standard of living. The average American homeowner pays $804 each year for homeowners insurance, about what she might pay for a new television set. Yet someone buying a television has many more sources of information about the product's performance and reliability than does the purchaser of homeowners insurance. *Consumer Reports* tests TVs in its labs and surveys hundreds of thousands of its subscribers so a shopper can learn that a Sony TV has better picture quality than a Westinghouse and is about three times less likely to need a repair, but the insurance shopper has little accurate information on whether Allstate or State Farm is more likely to pay a claim. And information is even more important when buying insurance; if a TV is unreliable it can be repaired or replaced, and the owner is at worst out the price of the set, but if an insurance company fails to pay a claim after a loss occurs, the consumer is out of luck.

The story of delay, deny, defend is easy to understand but hard to discover and document. It is easy to understand that insurance companies make more money when they pay less out in claims, and as with other industries, from chain restaurants to Internet sales, they have become more systematic about the ways in which they make money in recent decades. But while insurance companies like to shape the public's perception of them through advertising, they are notoriously unwilling to disclose information about their internal workings, especially information that shows they do not always deliver on their promises. Companies spend a great deal of money on advertising that they will fulfill their promise to provide security for their policyholders, but they also spend a great deal of money on lawyers to mask the times when that security fails.

News articles, trade journals, industry groups, academic studies, and an increasing number of Web sites and blogs cover insurance companies and their claim practices. But this book depends on three special kinds of sources that insurance companies go to great length to keep under wraps or discredit. The first are insider accounts provided by former insurance company employees who have become whistle-blowers. The second is information revealed in litigation against insurance companies. And the third is the documentary evidence of the redesign of claims practices to increase profits at the expense of policyholders and victims. Much of the evidence in this book is about well-known companies, State Farm and Allstate in particular, but it is not an attack on them; they are just the largest players in the industry and the companies whose involvement with McKinsey & Company in the transformation of claims is the best documented.

Traditionally, claims adjusters were taught to follow a simple maxim: "We pay what we owe." The adjuster's job, to determine what the claimant was entitled to under the insurance policy, carried independence to exercise judgment and an obligation to assist policyholders in their time of need. As the claims department became a profit center, and delay, deny, defend increased, the adjuster's job changed, diminishing the obligation to the claimant in favor of an increased obligation to the company's bottom line. For many adjusters the change was disheartening. Robert Dietz, a fifteen-year veteran of Farmers Insurance, described the shift: "My vast experience in evaluating claims was replaced by values generated by a computer. More often than not, these values were not representative of what I had experienced as fair and reasonable."[5]

Many adjusters adapted to the new system and kept their jobs or were replaced by "claims representatives"—the customer-friendly term now preferred by the industry—who were trained in the new normal. Some, like Dietz, left their employers and revealed what was happening. The companies' response has been, predictably, to try to silence or discredit the whistle-blowers. Dietz became an expert consultant on claim practices, and Farmers sued to obtain a gag order to prevent him from sharing his knowledge with lawyers representing policyholders. (Farmers eventually abandoned the attempt to silence Dietz.)[6] Other former employees have faced similar attempts to restrict them, but former insurance adjusters have become important sources for information about claims practices.

Usually, when an insurance company delays, denies, or underpays a claim that is the end of the story. The claimant might not understand that he has been shortchanged, or he may not believe that there is anything he can do about it, or he may just want to get on with his life. In some cases, however, the claimant sees that he has been wronged and believes that it is worthwhile to get a lawyer and fight for what he is entitled to. In the course of those cases, attorneys have discovered a great deal of information about insurance company behavior in the individual cases being litigated and about their general claims practices. Documents produced in discovery, testimony at trial, and reported judicial opinions provide major sources of information about how insurance companies organize and conduct their business and how it affects their claimants. Because litigation often drags on it can take years for this information to come to light, and when it does, the companies disingenuously attack it as outdated.

This evidence is seldom produced willingly; on the contrary, insurance companies expend considerable effort and lawyer time to limit the information produced and to keep what is produced out of the hands of those who should know about it. In numerous cases they have quibbled, equivocated, concealed, and sometimes even defied the legal processes that aim to produce an informed adjudication of disputed cases. When company executives and claims supervisors are deposed, they are often unresponsive or difficult; an Oklahoma trial judge described State Farm's witnesses as "obstructionist" when holding the company in contempt for discovery abuse in 2007.[7] In a Nevada case in 2002, State Farm tried to block a policyholder's lawyers from introducing documents that the company argued were confidential—though they came from the public records of the Washoe County court clerk's office.[8]

Even when a plaintiff's lawyer discovers damaging evidence about claims practices the company has a simple way to prevent it from ever becoming public: settle the case. In any case in which the plaintiff's lawyer discovers evidence that would be damaging in future cases, the company may conclude that it makes long-term sense to settle the case, on the condition that the plaintiff's lawyer agrees to keep confidential any discovery material. The attorney is forced to agree because he must accept a settlement that is favorable to his client, even if it injures future claimants and the public at large by keeping the bad practices secret.

In a case that is not settled, the company can still apply to the court for a protective order under which the plaintiff's lawyer can use the evidence in the current litigation but not reveal it to anyone else; in particular, he cannot give the evidence to a lawyer representing a policyholder in another suit against the company in which it might be used to prove that the company consistently violates fair claims practices. If the court grants the protective order, as unfortunately happens too often, it is harder and more expensive for the policyholder in the second case to prove what may already have been established in the earlier one.

Allstate went to especially great lengths in its attempt to prevent the release of the PowerPoint slides, notes, and training manuals prepared by McKinsey & Company when it was hired to redesign Allstate's claims processing in the 1990s. For critics of the industry, the McKinsey documents are the smoking gun that describes in detail how the claims process shifted from customer service to profit center. Allstate in turn contends the documents demonstrate its effort to make sure that each claim is promptly and fairly evaluated on its own merits.

The documents were the subject of a seven-year odyssey through the courts that began in an ordinary lawsuit. Santa Fe, New Mexico, lawyer David J. Berardinelli, who would become Allstate's principal antagonist over the McKinsey documents, represented José and Olivia Pincheira in a suit against the company and its agents for bad faith denial of an insurance claim. After considerable procedural wrangling, Allstate gave Berardinelli a copy of the slides with an overlay that prevented them from being photocopied. Following two years of more motions and appeals, the appellate court upheld the trial judge's order to Allstate to produce the documents, and Berardinelli returned the overlaid slides and requested a legible copy. The company refused to give him one, essentially asking to be held in contempt of court so it could further challenge the trial judge's order on appeal.

Lawyers in other cases sought to have Allstate disclose the documents, and it continued to resist, with varying degrees of success. (One Kentucky judge responded to Allstate's trade secrets claim by concluding that "the material sought does not rise to the level of the Colonel's secret recipe.")[9] Because McKinsey had also consulted with State Farm, plaintiffs' lawyers sought similar documents in actions against that company too. The most remarkable case turned out to be a suit brought in Missouri by Dale Deer, who had been injured in an auto accident by Allstate-insured Paul Aldridge. The company was ordered to produce the McKinsey documents and, when it refused, Judge Michael Manners held the company in contempt and fined it $25,000 per day beginning on September 4, 2007. Despite accruing fines eventually totaling $2.4 million, Allstate continued to refuse.

The denouement of the saga came in Florida. On October 16, 2007, Florida insurance commissioner Kevin McCarty exercised his regulatory authority to direct Allstate to produce the McKinsey documents. When Allstate refused, McCarty suspended Allstate from selling new insurance policies in the state. When the courts upheld McCarty's authority, on April 4, 2008, Allstate immediately posted on its Web site 150,000 pages of the McKinsey documents that it long had argued were confidential trade secrets and essential to its business.[10]

The point of view in this book is proconsumer but it is not anti-insurance. Insurance is essential to our economic security. But if insurance is to maintain its role as the great protector of the standard of living of the American middle class, prompt and fair claim handling has to be the rule. This book explores why that doesn't always happen, and why it is even less likely to happen today than fifteen or twenty years ago.

1

How Insurance Works

THE WORLD IS an uncertain place. Bad things happen to good people, and to bad people too. Houses burn down, cars crash, hurricanes devastate the coastline, pedestrians slip on ice-covered sidewalks, and, in other ways actual and metaphorical, lightning strikes. The bad things are usually unexpected, in part because people often assume or at least hope that bad things only happen to other people, not to them.

In the language of insurance, the bad things that can happen (and sometimes the people or things they can happen to) are known as "risks." The universally understood elements of risk are uncertainty and loss—the risk might or might not come to pass, but if it does, someone will suffer a financial loss.[1]

The purpose of insurance is to ameliorate the financial consequences of risk by transferring the risk from an individual to a group and sharing the cost of the risks that come to pass among the members of the group. In this way every insurance company essentially operates on the same premise as the oldest extant insurance company in the United States, the Philadelphia Contributionship for the Insurance of Houses from Loss by Fire. The contributionship was founded in 1752 by a group of volunteer firefighters led by Benjamin Franklin. The risk of destruction by fire in colonial America was immense, so Franklin and his colleagues adopted the model of the Amicable Contributionship of London, founded in 1696, in which subscribing homeowners contributed specified amounts to be paid to those unfortunate ones whose houses burned.[2] The risk of fire loss was transferred from the individual homeowner to the Contributionship and shared among its members by their financial contributions.

The Contributionship illustrates the concept of insurance in operation. A person is willing to exchange a small, certain loss (the payment of a premium) to avoid the potential of an uncertain but potentially larger loss (the cost of rebuilding a house). On the other end of the transaction is the insurance company, which is willing to accept the risk of the large, uncertain loss in exchange for the small, certain payment, because it pools many such payments. This simple description encapsulates every insurance transaction, whether it is the everyday purchase of a homeowners insurance policy or the acquisition of multibillion-dollar commercial policies by Larry Silverstein, who, with exquisitely bad timing, acquired a ninety-nine-year lease on the World Trade Center in July 2001.*

The process by which the company assesses risks and accepts their transfer from policyholders begins with the accumulation of information about the incidence of losses. Before it issues auto policies, for example, a company wants to know, for a given year (using 2007 figures), that: 515 out of 10,000 drivers will have claims for property damage; there will be 21 fatalities in motor vehicle accidents for every 1,000 licensed drivers; a driver age 21–24 is almost three times as likely to be involved in a fatal crash while legally intoxicated than a driver 55–64 years old; the average collision repair for all cars costs $3,131; the average collision repair on a Ford Focus costs 17 percent more than on a Honda Civic Hybrid; and so on. Actuaries sift and process this mass of statistical data to evaluate and

*The attack on 9/11 generated a dispute between Silverstein and his insurers. Was there a single "occurrence" of a coordinated attack on both towers, which would have limited his recovery to $3.5 billion, or were there two occurrences of one plane striking each tower, in which case the payment would have been $3.5 billion per occurrence, or $7 billion? After litigation involving armies of lawyers, courts came to different results under the language of different policies.

define what kinds of risks the company might insure and at what rates; drivers are classified and rated separately by age, gender, marital status, and driver training experience. Once the types of risks that will be insured are defined, underwriters establish the kinds of insurance policies that will be offered and the limitations on those policies: what will be covered, for what amounts, and to whom the policies will be sold. Then the marketers and agents go to work, advertising and selling the product, with the underwriters evaluating applications as they come in to ensure that they fit within the established guidelines.

As is typically the case with corporate America, the economics that make this system work are simple in concept but rococo in application. To remain solvent and to turn a profit, the insurance company wants to pay out less than it takes in. It takes in premium dollars from policyholders. It pays out on claims. The ratio between these two figures is known as the "pure loss ratio." The property/casualty industry as a whole in 2007 earned $451 billion in premiums and paid out $251 billion in claims, for a loss ratio of 56. In other words, the insurance industry paid out to policyholders and tort victims fifty-six cents of every dollar the policyholders paid in. The industry's pure loss ratio has been improving over time, if "improving" is measured from the company's perspective. The loss ratio in 1987 was 67 and in 1997 was 61, which means that it has paid out a nickel less for every premium dollar compared to ten years ago and a dime less compared to twenty years ago.

But paying out claims is not costless. Adjusters' salaries have to be paid, computers have to be bought, and offices have to be rented. All of these costs are considered "loss adjustment expense" (LAE), or expenses that are directly related to paying claims. These costs are added to pure losses—the direct payouts—to get, obviously, the "loss and loss adjustment expense ratio." For the property/casualty industry, LAE in 2007 was $54 billion, for a loss and loss adjustment expense ratio of 67. Then add to this all the other expenses the company has—salaries and expenses of the underwriting department, commissions to agents, the cost of the call center and gecko ads, and overhead such as the IT department and the executive dining room—to achieve the "combined ratio." In 2007 these other expenses were $121 billion, yielding a combined ratio of 95.

A combined ratio of less than 100 is good for the company. Considering all expenses, the company is taking in more than it is paying out. But even a combined ratio over 100 is not necessarily bad, because the company is taking in something else: investment income. The company pools policyholders' premiums to pay losses and expenses, but it does not simply hold the money until it needs to pay it out; it invests the money in the meantime, which is why insurance companies have been described as "investment companies that raise the money for their investments by selling insurance."[3] The time lag between taking in premiums and paying out claims (the "float") and the income earned in that time is a major source of profit; in 2007, industry investment profits totaled $58 billion. As Warren Buffett, whose Berkshire Hathaway owns GEICO and other insurance companies, has said, float is the great thing about the insurance business, because it is "money we hold that is not ours but which we get to invest."[4] A company that can take advantage of float and also produce an underwriting profit (a combined ratio less than 100) has the best of both worlds; Buffett trumpeted in his folksy 2009 letter to shareholders that "we were *paid* $2.8 billion to hold our float in 2008. Charlie [Munger, Buffett's longtime partner] and I find this enjoyable."[5]

In this way an insurance company is like a bank, which takes in customers' money as deposits and lends that money out at a higher interest rate than it pays on depositors' accounts. The difference between the rate on loans and the rate on deposits, less the bank's expenses, are a bank's profit. Insurance companies have an advantage over banks, though, because their loss ratio can be less than 100. The bank depositor always gets back 100 percent of the amount deposited, plus interest. The insurance company with a pure loss ratio of 50 is only paying its customers fifty cents on the dollar. Even with higher expenses than the bank, with a combined ratio less than 100 the insurance company is ahead of the game even before its investment earnings.

At some point one of the unfortunate events that constitute the risks that were transferred from the insured to the company will occur—a car will crash, a house will burn—and an insured will file a claim. At that point the fundamental truth about the claim process should come into play: When a loss occurs that is within the coverage of the insurance policy, the policyholder has already paid for the loss. The risk has been defined, priced, transferred from the insured to the insurance company, and shared by the company among its policyholders and investors, so all that is legitimately left to be done is to pay the claim. From the policyholder's point of view, the covered event should now be risk free—that is, free of the risk that the company will fail to pay what it owes. The actuary's job is to evaluate risk characteristics, the underwriter's job is to evaluate potential insureds, and the executive's job is to manage the whole process, but the claims adjuster's only job is to decide if a loss falls within the policy, determine the extent of the loss, and pay the claim.

Under life insurance policies, keeping the company's promise and paying what is owed usually is easy. The family sends in a death certificate, so the adjuster knows the insured is dead. The adjuster knows how much to pay from the face amount of the policy. All that's left to do is cut the check. Only in the most unusual cases is anything else involved. Rare are situations like that of Helen Golay and Olga Rutterschmidt, the "hit-and-run grannies," two elderly ladies who took out dozens of life insurance policies, worth a total of $2.8 million, on homeless men Kenneth McDavid and Paul Vados and then murdered them in staged hit-and-run accidents to collect the insurance.[6]

The claim process in property/casualty policies, on the other hand, can be more complicated. The definition of coverage under the policy can be byzantine; a homeowners policy covers all risks of sudden physical loss to the property, an exception excludes coverage for damage caused by water, and an exception to the exception includes coverage for water damage caused by sewers backing up. The facts that trigger coverage can be unclear; how much of the damage to a house struck by Hurricane Katrina was due to wind (covered) and how much to water (not covered)? If an event is covered, the amount due may not be fixed; uninsured motorist coverage pays for noneconomic damages such as pain and suffering, but there is no simple monetary measure of how much suffering a claimant has endured.

No matter how complex in an individual case, a set of simple rules of the road of claim adjusting control the process. These standards are subscribed to by every insurance company: "Allstate's goal remains the same:

to investigate, evaluate and promptly resolve each claim based on its merits," according to spokesman Michael Siemienas.[7] Even when being sued by their policyholders, insurance companies acknowledge the rules. In a California case arising out of the Northridge earthquake of 1994, State Farm acknowledged "its claim obligation is to operate its claim service in a manner so as to ensure that insureds receive all that they are owed consistent with the facts of the loss and the language contained in its policies."[8] The National Association of Insurance Commissioners (NAIC) has promulgated minimum, legally enforceable standards in its Model Unfair Claims Settlement Practices Act, a version of which is in effect in nearly every state, and judicial decisions in every state adopt and amplify the standards.

The most basic rule is that in adjusting a claim, the company must not put its own interests above the interests of its policyholder. When a policyholder files a claim, she is invoking the promise of the insurance company to accept the risk and to provide security in the event of loss. That promise means that the company will not try to increase its own profit at the expense of the policyholder or to take advantage of the insured precisely at the moment when she is most vulnerable.

Giving adequate consideration to the policyholder's interests means that the company must act promptly and must fully pay all legitimate claims. The NAIC Model Act requires a company to promptly and fairly settle claims in which liability is reasonably clear, to make its decisions about coverage within a reasonable time, to give reasons if it denies a claim, to maintain standards for investigating claims, and to be objective in investigating claims. It explicitly prohibits companies from making lowball settlement offers that force policyholders or accident victims to sue to recover the amounts they are entitled to. Industry standards and the law require companies to interpret provisions of the policy that establish coverage broadly and to interpret provisions that exclude coverage narrowly. In case of uncertainty, all doubts are resolved in favor of the policyholder and against the company, which wrote the policy and had the ability to draft it in a way that removed doubt.

The company's obligation is even greater than being an independent adjudicator; the company has an affirmative obligation to help the insured with its claim. Insurance companies tout this role of aiding their policyholders; the State Farm Web site quotes Karman Drake, an auto claims adjuster, who says, "I approach each customer's claim as if it were my own."[9] That is, of course, what a good neighbor should do. The company must tell the policyholder about all the benefits and conditions of the policies; she should not have to hunt through the policy to find out what she is covered for and what pieces of paper she has to file to establish her claim within what time periods.

A fair claim process is central to the insurance relationship because the policyholder is not just buying a run-of-the-mill product or entering into an ordinary contract—she is obtaining security against an uncertain world. The Utah Supreme Court summed it up in the course of an opinion castigating State Farm for denying policyholders the benefits to which they were entitled: "Insureds buy financial protection and peace of mind against fortuitous losses. They pay the requisite premiums and put their faith and trust in their insurers to pay policy benefits promptly and fairly when the insured event occurs. Good faith and fair dealing is their expectation. It is the very essence of the insurer-insured relationship."[10]

The insurance company's promise of security has real value, and people often understate its value. In a classic commentary in 1849, insurance entrepreneur D. R. Jacques wrote with respect to premiums: "The afflicted finds his money spent to some purpose; and only the fortunate part with it for nothing."[11] But that is wrong. The fortunate—those whose risks never come to pass and therefore never collect a penny from their insurance companies—spent their money for the purpose of security and peace of mind.

Insurance companies market this feeling of security as much as they market individual policies.* "You're in good hands with Allstate." "Nationwide is on your side." "Like a good neighbor, State Farm is there." "At Liberty Mutual, it's responsibility." A good neighbor is not a stickler for legal technicalities. A good neighbor picks up your newspapers while you are on vacation and doesn't complain if you don't return the cup of sugar

*At least traditionally. Today more of the advertising emphasis is on price. See Chapter 4.

you borrowed. More to the point, a good neighbor shovels the snow off your sidewalk if you are elderly and brings you soup when you are sick. Like good neighbors, your insurance company and you are bound by ties that law and profits cannot define.

The insurance policy is a detailed contract, not just a vague promise of security, but it is a contract of a distinctive kind. Insurance lawyers sometimes speak of the "four-corners rule"—the scope of coverage and the company's responsibilities are defined within the four corners of the paper on which the policy is printed. But courts have recognized that the relationship of the parties involved in an insurance contract is not fully captured in the printed words because it arises in a context and contains expectations created by advertisements, the sales pitches of agents, and common understandings of the role of insurance in providing security. Indeed, some courts disregard the express terms of the policy when they conflict with the reasonable expectations of the policyholder. In a famous case articulating this principle, the Iowa Supreme Court rejected the policy definition of the burglary of a store as requiring visible marks of forced entry on an exterior door, preferring instead an understanding held by the reasonable policyholder that "burglary" meant anything other than an inside job.[12]

The insurance contract is also different from most ordinary contracts because it requires sequential performance. In a typical contract, if one party doesn't perform, the other party can procure a substitute performance and sue for any added cost. If a homeowner hires a contractor to renovate his house and the contractor fails to show, the homeowner can refuse to pay, hire another contractor, and, if he pays the second a higher price, sue the first contractor for the extra. But if the homeowner has a fire and his insurance company fails to pay the claim, it's too late for the homeowner to buy alternate insurance. The best the homeowner can hope for is to sue the company for the coverage that should have been paid. But even that is not an effective remedy; the lawsuit does not give the homeowner the money needed to rebuild until the litigation is concluded, perhaps years later, during which time the homeowner has lost the security and peace of mind for which he contracted. Accordingly, courts hold insurance companies to a higher standard and subject them to special remedies if they fail to honor their promises.

The promise of security extends beyond the relationship between an insurance company and an individual policyholder. For a long time insurance in America was a community project, starting with the Philadelphia Contributionship. The original "Deed of Settlement" creating the Contributionship, still on display at its offices in Philadelphia, is a forty-four-foot-long parchment scroll containing the signatures and property descriptions of the original 1,774 subscribers, starting with Pennsylvania lieutenant governor James Hamilton and the first private subscriber, Benjamin Franklin.

Beginning shortly after Wisconsin received statehood in 1848, several local insurance companies were formed to provide security for small-town residents, just like the Contributionship, and to promote development in individual towns: Germantown Mutual, City of Waukesha Mutual, Cedarburg Mutual, Lakeland Mutual, and Menomonee Mutual. Various lumbermen's insurance companies came several generations later. The Indiana Lumbermens Mutual Insurance Company was founded in 1895 by the Indiana Retail Lumber Dealers Association to provide fire insurance to its members at reasonable rates; eastern lumberyard owners formed the Pennsylvania Lumbermens Mutual Fire Insurance Company the same year for the same purpose. Lumbermens Mutual Casualty Company was organized in 1912 on behalf of lumber companies to provide the newly mandated workers compensation insurance and to keep rates low by promoting safer workplaces; its first manager was James S. Kemper, who would later give his name to the Kemper Insurance companies of which Lumbermens became a part.

Because these companies were formed by businesses and individuals to share losses, they were keenly aware of their responsibility to pay claims. Hartford Fire Insurance Co. was founded by a group of Hartford, Connecticut, merchants in 1810, when fire posed a major threat to homes and businesses. After the Great New York Fire of 1835 destroyed hundreds of downtown buildings, including the New York Stock Exchange, twenty-three of twenty-six insurance companies in the city went bankrupt. Hartford's president, Eliphalet Terry, met his responsibility by driving a horse-drawn sleigh from Hartford to New York to personally pay policyholders' claims.[13]

Even today, The Doctors Company Insurance Group promotes itself as "founded by doctors, for doctors." With some forty-three thousand physician members, the company writes $700 million of premiums each year. Beyond its primary function of providing liability insurance, it rewards participation with its Tribute Plan that accrues funds based on a member's premiums and pays benefits on retirement, disability, or death. The company also promotes the collective interests of its members by lobbying for proposals to limit malpractice liability and working to promote electronic medical records.

What is striking about all of these efforts is that they are collective activities among groups of like-minded people and firms for their mutual benefit—thus the origins of the term "mutual" insurance company. These are not transactions between a self-interested insured and a distant corporate entity. They are, rather, joint enterprises among Philadelphia homeowners, Waukesha residents, Indiana lumber dealers, or practicing physicians. In that respect they share origins and purposes with traditional savings and loan societies (think of the Bailey Building and Loan Society from *It's a Wonderful Life*, not the S&L debacle of the 1980s), *landsmanschaften* and other immigrant aid groups, and fraternal organizations that provide financial support for their members. In these entities, participation in insurance is a social activity that involves protecting oneself against calamity and a social responsibility, as a member of the community, to contribute for the benefit of fellows who might suffer a loss.

Today, of course, most insurance is purchased through large companies rather than local organizations of coventurers. For collective activities conducted on such a large scale the company is the necessary vehicle. Thousands or millions of insureds are involved, so a bureaucratic apparatus and the incentives of executive bonuses and shareholder profits are necessary to fund and motivate the enterprise. The core of the activity remains the same, however: collective action of all against the possibility of loss by some. The company acts as a fiduciary for the premiums pooled by all insureds and other like-minded people. The company profits from the transaction—that is necessary to motivate it to act at all—but it owes the insured a duty to act to protect the insured's security. More broadly, insurance provides a social safety net for individuals and businesses, particularly for the middle class. Most Americans are only a car accident, a fire in the home, a lawsuit, or an injury away from having the wealth, the comfort, and the lifestyle accumulated over a lifetime of work wiped out. Insurance does not remove all of the consequences of a catastrophic loss, but it can make it something other than a catastrophe.

2

How Insurance Doesn't Work

INSURANCE WORKS WHEN the insurance company honors a simple promise: When a policyholder files a claim, the company will pay what it owes, no more but no less, and will do so promptly and fairly. Insurance doesn't work when the company breaks its promise in order to increase its profits.

Insurance doesn't work when companies delay, deny, defend. When they delay payment of claims to wear down claimants and to increase their investment income, flat-out deny some valid claims in whole or part, and defend against valid claims in litigation to back up the delays and denials, they break their basic promise.

Processing claims without delay is one of the basic claim practices required by law, stated in industry texts, and touted by every insurer. But delay helps the company's bottom line. The company keeps the premiums paid for longer and gets to invest those premiums and keep the investment earnings—Warren Buffett's crowing about the magic of float. Every dollar and every day that the insurance company fails to pay means more profits on the investment side of the ledger. Even a few dollars held for a few days on each claim add up when the company has thousands or millions of claims each year. More important, many claimants are vulnerable and need to be paid. An injured accident victim needs money for doctor bills and may be out of work. A homeowner after a fire wants to rebuild his house. Delay increases the pressure on the claimant to take what the insurance company offers so that she can meet her immediate financial needs and get on with her life. The longer the delay, the greater the pressure.

Sometimes delay in paying a claim is simply stalling. Kim Zilisch, an Arizona accountant insured by State Farm, was a victim twice, first of an auto accident and then of State Farm's delay.[1] After three exhausting days taking her CPA licensing exam, Zilisch was returning home from a Billy Joel concert with her fiancé, Jeff Rosinski. While Rosinski drove, Zilisch dozed off—and awoke two days later in a hospital. A teenage drag racer had run through two red lights before smashing into the driver's side of the car, killing Rosinski instantly and crushing Zilisch against the console and window of the car, injuring her permanently.

Zilisch recovered $146,500 from the drag racer's insurance company, but that amount was not enough to compensate her for her injuries. Fortunately, she thought, she also had her own insurance policy from State Farm that promised to pay her up to $100,000 if she was injured by a driver who did not have enough insurance to pay for all of her losses (called "underinsured motorist" coverage, typically paired with "uninsured motorist"—UM/UIM—coverage to pay losses caused by a driver who has no insurance). State Farm's response was delay. A month after Zilisch filed her claim, which included all of her medical and employment records, State Farm's claims adjuster, Scott Chan, met with her and then reported to his superiors on the severity of her permanent injuries. Chan then requested an additional report from a neuro-ophthalmologic surgeon with whom she had met, Dr. William Hoyt, who had not written a report because Zilisch only saw him for a consultation. Nevertheless, Dr. Hoyt talked to Chan and confirmed that Zilisch's injuries were permanent. Chan then waited for Dr. Hoyt's nonexistent report for four months despite having talked to him, received reports from four other physicians, and consulted another neurologist who agreed with Dr. Hoyt's diagnosis. Dr. Hoyt subsequently provided a written report, but

Chan still concluded that Zilisch's injuries had been fully compensated by the payment from the drag racer. State Farm required Zilisch to be questioned under oath by State Farm's lawyers and ordered her to undergo another medical exam by its own doctor. Nevertheless, it made no settlement offer for nearly a year and never offered to pay the full policy limit of $100,000. A year after her claim was filed, Zilisch was awarded $387,500 by an arbitration panel, and State Farm finally paid the policy limit of $100,000. Zilisch then brought a suit against State Farm for bad faith in processing her claim, and the jury awarded her $460,000 in compensatory damages and $540,000 in punitive damages.

At other times companies delay by investigating a claim excessively—by pursuing more and more information that is not really needed for resolving the claim, dragging things out, and often exasperating the claimant into submission. Theodore Price's tortuous saga with his insurance company is an example. While at work on August 30, 1995, he was struck by a car driven by Howard Wanderman. Because Wanderman's company ultimately denied coverage, on February 12, 1998, Price's attorney notified his insurance company, New Jersey Manufacturers, that he would be pursuing an uninsured motorist claim. On March 18, 1998, NJM asked for information about the accident and Price's workers' compensation claim. Fair enough. Then the delaying tactics began. In May 1998, NJM asked for more information about the workers' compensation claim. On October 8, 1998, NJM asked for Price's medical bills. On April 20, 1999, NJM demanded that Price be examined by a doctor of its choosing, which took place on September 14, 1999. On January 15, March 1, and April 5, 2001, Price's attorney sent NJM medical reports, employment records, a workers' compensation lien letter, and a medical authorization form. On August 21, 2001, NJM asked for Price's complete workers' compensation file, the original MRI pictures dated December 20, 1996, February 12, 1998, and November 20, 1998, and information on his employer's insurance policy. On September 20, 2001, October 1, 2001, March 27, April 23, and September 27, 2002, Price's lawyer sent more documents to NJM. Finally, on November 22, 2002, Price and his lawyer had had enough and filed suit seeking to compel NJM to arbitrate the claims. Too late, said NJM, because the statute of limitations expired six years after the accident, on August 30, 2001. The court saw through the delay strategy, however, and held that NJM's strategy had "lulled" Price into a false sense of security that the frequent contacts were enough to constitute filing a claim. As is always the case, that resolution did not come without its own delay; NJM's argument was rejected by the New Jersey Supreme Court and ordered to arbitration on March 10, 2005, almost ten years after the accident.[2]

Homeowners filing claims can suffer similar fates. When Terry Buttery's home was vandalized and burglarized, he immediately called the police and then his insurance company, Hamilton Mutual.[3] Buttery completed and returned the claim forms Hamilton gave him within twenty-four hours. But that was not enough; eventually, Buttery submitted what the court described as "a vast amount of paper work and documentation," including three proof of loss statements, all his receipts for the stolen or destroyed items, written estimates that he had obtained for the cost of repairs to his house, and his tax returns for the previous five years. He also gave testimony under oath to Hamilton four times and offered to have his accountant testify too. After a year of delay by Hamilton, Buttery sued, and the court awarded him $58,000. Hamilton then appealed to the Court of Appeals and then the Kentucky Supreme Court; both upheld the verdict, but Hamilton still refused to pay. Not until Buttery threatened to proceed against the bond Hamilton was required to post to appeal the case did it eventually pay what the court said it owed, nearly four years after the loss. In Buttery's subsequent suit for Hamilton's bad faith delay, the reason for its conduct became clear: The investigation was not aimed at determining the amount of the loss but at ways of avoiding payment. Hamilton had closely monitored Buttery's financial position, hoping his struggles and its delay would create leverage to make him take less than he was owed. And knowing that it was acting in bad faith, it intended to refuse to pay anything on the claim until Buttery released the company from future liability for its wrongdoing.

Except in extreme cases like Buttery's, delay doesn't last forever. At some point a decision has to be made on a claim. Fair claim practices require that the decision be made based on the facts of the individual claim measured against the promises made in the insurance policy, independent of any considerations of financial benefit to the company. But as the *New York Times* editorialized, many insurance companies "have turned denying valid claims into an art form."[4] Denying valid claims in whole or in part is the logical successor to delay and the precursor to defense of litigation. After a company has delayed a decision on a claim, grinding the victim down and increasing investment profits in the meantime, the company's denial of payment of the amount owed forces the victim to either give up or be subjected to more delay, as the company can resort to an aggressive and extended defense of the claim in court.

Tactics of denial have been colorfully referred to as "lowballing" and "stonewalling." James Nelson, an attorney with extensive experience in insurance cases, testified in a 2008 Oregon case and defined lowballing as "making minimal settlement offers to signal that the insurance company is willing to fight the claim and to lower the claimant's expectations" and stonewalling as "refusing to negotiate settlement because claimants often have very limited resources and mounting medical and legal bills; 'stonewalling' puts psychological and financial pressure on such claimants."[5]

In lowballing and stonewalling claims, companies may resort to unreasonable interpretations of the terms of the policy. Kristen Dhyne was struck by a car driven by an uninsured motorist and suffered a broken pelvis, nerve damage, and kidney failure.[6] Her initial expenses were covered by workers' compensation, but she contacted her auto insurer, State Farm, to claim benefits for other losses under her uninsured motorist coverage. Brandon Hill, State Farm's adjuster, told her that most of her claim was not covered (which was not true), that if State Farm paid her anything she would only have to reimburse the workers' compensation insurer anyway (also not true), and, to boot, if she filed a claim, her insurance premiums would rise (which was not a great concern in the circumstance, since any potential increase in her premiums would be overshadowed by the amount of her lost wages of $26,603 and medical bills of $13,373). Soon after, State Farm's lawyer told adjuster Hill that Dhyne was covered under her policy, but still State Farm did not pay. When Dhyne sued for her policy coverage, State Farm again simply denied liability despite its own attorney's advice.

Companies may also resort to unreasonable interpretations of the facts to lowball and stonewall. Reagan Wilson was injured when a drunk driver made a left turn directly in front of her car. She suffered arm, neck, and back injuries and was treated in an emergency room, and she was later examined by her own physician and an orthopedist. After examining her and ordering X-rays and an MRI, the orthopedist concluded, "A young woman involved in a high speed motor vehicle accident with changes now in the cervical spine which are atypical for a patient of her age and are almost certainly due to the history of trauma. She probably has degenerative disk changes as a result of occult disk injury at the levels in the neck from her high speed motor vehicle accident." Paul Le, the adjuster for her insurance company, 21st Century (formerly owned by AIG, since sold to Farmers, which is itself a subsidiary of Zurich Financial Services), entertained a different opinion, for which he had no medical basis. In a memorandum to his supervisor asking for and receiving approval to deny her uninsured motorist claim, Le wrote that Wilson "has a pre-existing condition pertaining to scolosis [*sic*], MRI shows no encroachment of a neural structure, it is unlikely that the 2mm bulge was produced by this accident." Only after Wilson's doctors recommended surgery did 21st Century order an examination by a doctor it selected, which confirmed the initial diagnosis and forced 21st Century to pay—two years after she had initially filed her claim.[7]

And when there are no facts to justify the denial, insurance companies may go looking for them. Investigation can take strange turns, even to what the popular InsureBlog calls "Stupid Carrier Tricks" or "Insurers Behaving Badly."[8] Leandra Pitts was injured in a car accident near Atlanta and suffered a brain injury that affected her balance, memory, and speech. Because the other driver had only low limits on his policy, Pitts filed an uninsured motorist claim with Progressive, her own insurer. Because of the severity of the case Progressive hired a private investigator, Merlin Investigations, to help determine whether Leandra's injuries really were severe. Standard tactics might include observing Leandra in public places to see if she exhibited the symptoms she was claiming continuously. Merlin went further. James Purgason, Jr., and Paige Weeks, Merlin's investigators, posed as a married couple and began to attend Southside Christian Fellowship, the church to which the Pittses belonged. The phony married couple pretended to be interested in joining the church and were invited to attend support sessions for church members held in the basement of the home of Ken King, a member and ordained minister. The sessions included confessionals about drug and alcohol addiction, abortion, sexual orientation issues, and other matters far removed from the question of Leandra's injuries, but Purgason and Weeks secretly recorded the sessions. They did not discover any evidence that Leandra was faking her injuries, so Progressive eventually paid her claim. When the company's investigative tactics came out, the Pittses and other church members were devastated; Progressive CEO Glenn Renwick refused interview requests but posted an apology online stating, "What the investigators and Progressive people involved in that case did was wrong—period. I personally want to apologize to anyone who was affected by this incident. We know that we were wrong in this situation and we take full responsibility for the mistakes that were made." Full responsibility had its limits, however. When Bill and Leandra sued for the invasion of their privacy, Progressive denied responsibility.

Pursuing an insurance claim is like running a marathon or an obstacle course, and for those few who do not drop out, or are diverted, along the way, the final obstacle is a program of litigation that can wear down and defeat all but the hardiest. By forcing claims to litigation and aggressively defending it, insurance companies backstop the delay and denial of claims.

The battle cry of the tort reform movement, in which insurance companies have played a prominent role, has been that there are too many frivolous lawsuits brought by too many greedy plaintiffs and too many ambitious lawyers. In fact, one reason there is a lot of litigation is because insurance companies force claimants to sue in response to delay, deny, defend. When claims are not paid promptly at their fair value, litigation is the only avenue for claimants to get what is owed to them, but it is not an easy path. For each claimant, having to resort to litigation increases the delay, cost, and aggravation of getting what she is entitled to. For all claimants, the knowledge that companies aggressively defend litigation provides a powerful deterrent to suing at all and increases the costs to victims and their lawyers. Forcing litigation brings the game to the insurance companies' home court; for a policyholder, bringing a lawsuit is likely to be a unique and trying (no pun intended) event, but an insurance company, as Liberty Mutual once acknowledged, is "a professional defender of lawsuits."[9] (It should know; Chief Judge Edward Nottingham of the federal district court in Colorado described Liberty Mutual as "a major league team" in the game of "hardball litigation.")[10]

Acronyms tell much of the story. For some claims the insurance company offers little or nothing, either because it contests liability or argues there is no damage. This is particularly likely for MIST—Minor Impact, Soft Tissue—claims, or what the industry likes to deride as whiplash claims. In auto crashes at slow speeds (minor impact), passengers are suddenly thrust back and forward, causing injuries that do not result in broken bones or other obvious trauma that readily appear on X-rays but that can cause significant neck and back pain (soft tissue). Insurance companies often deny that a minor-impact accident can cause a serious injury and either pay nothing or offer small amounts on a take-it-or-leave-it basis. MIST claims, discussed at greater length in Chapter 6, are particularly ripe for the defend strategy because the amounts involved are relatively small—typically a few thousand dollars—but the expense of litigating the case, including hiring medical and biomechanical experts, can be substantial. The company often will spend much more in attorney fees and expert witness fees to defend a MIST case than it would cost to settle it at the fair value. If the insurance company refuses to settle, few attorneys are willing to invest the time and money in a case in which their fee is not likely to justify the expense, so the injured victim cannot pursue the claim.

In MIST and other denial cases the insurance companies' key concept is SFXOL: Settle For X [amount] Or Litigate, where X is likely to be the amount set for the plaintiff's claim by a computer system. The company will not depart from X, the predetermined amount, so if it is not a fair offer then the claimant has no choice but to litigate. Realistically, as claimants' attorneys usually say, the acronym stands for "Settle For X Or eLse," with the "else" being the threat of litigation.

And litigation in this context can be even more painful, protracted, and expensive than the ordinary lawsuit. The approach is DOLF—Defense

Of Litigated Files—which means defend to the teeth, with protracted and intrusive discovery, an extended pretrial process, occasionally a settlement on the courthouse steps but just as often an expensive trial.

Stonewalling in litigation—refusing to pay what is owed in the hope that better facts will emerge or the claimant will be ground down by delay and will accept less than a fair settlement—is the logical complement to stonewalling in the denial of claims. Consider the strategy used by Farmers Insurance against the estate of Marc Goddard in a 2008 case from Oregon. Goddard was killed when his car collided with a truck driven by John Munson and owned by Helen Foley. Munson made a left turn into a parking lot and collided with Goddard's car, which was in its proper lane and had its headlights on. Foley and Munson told the police officer at the scene that he had permission to drive her truck. Munson's blood alcohol level was twice the legal limit, which was not surprising since, as he later admitted to Farmers' adjuster, he had had eight to ten beers before the accident.

Both Munson and Foley were insured by Farmers Insurance.[11] Sellers, the Farmers representative, concluded that Munson's liability for the collision was clear, but he suggested, "I feel we should let things 'ripen' a bit before making any settlement talk." Ripen they did; even as Munson was convicted of manslaughter, Farmers received an accident reconstruction report confirming that Goddard had been going at the speed limit when Munson turned in front him without using a turn signal, and the state police confirmed that Goddard's headlights were on at the time of the accident. Throughout, Goddard's family's lawyer offered to settle the case for the policy limits. Farmers' refusal to settle surprised even Munson's criminal lawyers, in light of Munson's "manifest criminal liability" and the possibility of a verdict beyond the policy limits, for which Munson personally would be responsible. A month after Munson was convicted of manslaughter the attorneys hired by Farmers for the civil action filed an answer in court denying that Munson had been drunk and that he had caused the collision.

Farmers refused to settle for the $200,000 in part because it believed only one of the policies applied to the accident, a position that was ultimately vindicated. Subsequently the plaintiff's lawyers offered to settle for the $100,000 coverage under the applicable policy, but Farmers continued to offer only $30,000. Shortly before trial Farmers' lawyers hand-delivered to Farmers a letter concluding that "the case has a reasonable jury value between $75,000 and $150,000 for non-economic damages plus punitive damages." Strangely, later that day, perhaps in anticipation of a bad faith claim, the lawyers retrieved that letter and replaced it with a letter that deleted the amounts $75,000 and $150,000 and substituted a much lower range of exposure—$35,000 to $60,000—for noneconomic damages. Both estimates were low; the jury returned a verdict for $188,274 in economic damages, $425,000 in noneconomic damages, and $250,000 in punitive damages—a total of $863,274. Then came the suit against Farmers for its bad faith stonewalling of the claim. In that litigation, based on expert testimony that Farmers' stonewalling violated fair claim practices standards, Farmers was found liable for punitive damages of $2.7 million.

Beyond stonewalling is the full-court press of delay, deny, defend, what the United States Court of Appeals for the Fourth Circuit called the "fight-and-delay approach" in a case brought against Kentucky National Insurance Company.[12] Leslie Joe Nance was driving his employer's tractor trailer on U.S. Route 25 in Barbourville, Kentucky, when Lisa Cordell ran a stop sign and pulled out directly in front of him. Nance slammed on his brakes and swerved to the left trying to avoid Cordell, but his tractor trailer jackknifed. Police officers arrived on the scene within four minutes, and their investigation concluded that Nance was traveling at the speed limit of fifty-five miles per hour (as confirmed by his truck's onboard computer) and was without fault in causing the accident, but Cordell's car windows were covered with frost that prevented her from seeing Nance's truck and she failed to yield the right of way.

Because of the accident Nance suffered serious injuries to his head, neck, shoulder, back, and brain. His injuries required back surgery and other extensive treatments, and they left him out of work and unable even to do chores around his farm or enjoy family activities. Cordell was uninsured, so Nance filed a claim under his uninsured motorist coverage with Kentucky National.

Nance's attorney faxed the police report establishing Cordell's liability to Kentucky National. Nevertheless, it refused to pay on the policy and instead created what the federal court described as "bogus issues" in an effort to delay payment, deny liability, and eventually defend against Nance's suit. Kentucky National claimed, without any evidence, that the brakes on the tractor trailer were defective at the time of the accident. Also without evidence, the company accused Nance of speeding, an accusation that it gave up when the truck's onboard computer proved otherwise. The company hired an accident reconstruction expert to demonstrate that Nance caused the accident, but even that expert agreed that Nance was blameless.

Nance had been treated by over twenty doctors and had voluminous medical records, but Kentucky National forced Nance to undergo a medical examination by its own doctor. Nance asked that the company use a doctor close to his home because his medical condition made travel difficult, but the company insisted that he be examined by a doctor in Lexington, Kentucky, a two-and-one-half-hour drive from his home. After the two-and-a-half-hour trip, Kentucky National's designated doctor examined him for all of eight to ten minutes.

As Nance and his wife, Debra, left the doctor's office, they realized that someone was following them and became frightened. At trial Debra testified about the events: "Well, we had parked in a parking garage, and when we pulled out of the parking garage, we just looked back in the mirror and we noticed there's a guy, the car behind us, has a video camera up to our car, and we thought, that's kind of weird, you know, a guy in a parking garage filming somebody. So we pull out of the parking garage. The guy proceeds to pull out with us. We make a right, he makes a right. He has still got that video camera. Me and Joe start to think there's something weird—something is weird about this. So we had to get on 64 to come home. So we get on 64, this brown car gets on to 64. The guy is still filming us. We change lanes, he changes lanes. We get faster, he gets faster." At trial their suspicions were confirmed. The guy was a private investigator hired by Kentucky National.

After a year and a half of discovery, during which Kentucky National refused to discuss settling the case, Nance's attorney tried to move the case toward trial. Kentucky National instead asked the court to schedule a mediation session. What followed was not mediation but more harassment. Nance, his wife, and his lawyer traveled over three hours to attend the mediation session, but Kentucky National refused to make a settlement offer and unilaterally cut the session short.

Experts valued Nance's claim at between $750,000 and $1.3 million, but Kentucky National did not make a settlement offer until three years after Nance filed suit against them, two weeks before the trial date, and then only for $25,000. A week later it raised the offer to $35,000, and then to $50,000. On the eve of trial Kentucky National raised its offer to $60,000, and Nance was forced to capitulate. Kentucky National's tactics had put the Nances in dire straits. They had had to remortgage their house, sell farm equipment and even their hunting dogs, drain their personal savings accounts and their son's college fund, and hold yard sales to make ends meet. As Nance said in accepting the offer, Kentucky National "had finally beat me down."

And it turned out that Kentucky National's treatment of Nance was not an isolated case but part of a pattern by the company. Kentucky National policyholder James Garland was injured when his car was struck by another car driven by a drunk driver who had just stolen gas from a convenience store and was speeding down a busy street and crossing the center line. As with Nance, Kentucky National denied the underinsured motorist claim, fabricated an argument that Garland was at fault, and offered to settle only on the eve of trial. Joe Holstein was a passenger in a car crashed in a single-vehicle accident by a Kentucky National insured who was speeding. Kentucky National offered Holstein substantially less than even his documented medical bills to settle his claim, forced him to file suit, and finally offered to settle only on the eve of trial. Based on this pattern, when Nance sued Kentucky National again, this time for violating the claims practices rules of the road, the court imposed punitive damages of $850,000 on Kentucky National.

Delay, deny, defend is so common that lawyers have plenty of stories to tell. One plaintiff's lawyer described a case in which the insurance company claims representative announced that "even if a verdict higher than the [multimillion]-dollar offer was returned, [the company] could delay payment indefinitely with the appellate process, and there was no telling when our client would ever see any money." Another reported on "something weird happening" at a major national insurance company, in that it was "almost impossible to settle cases with them, forcing litigation in almost every case."

One might expect these tales from plaintiffs' lawyers, but even defense lawyers report this type of behavior among their insurance company clients. Professor Herbert Kritzer interviewed many of them. One insurance defense lawyer, he writes, "expressed frustration to me after a no-fault arbitration hearing about handling cases where the insurer had no good defense. The lawyer believed that the insurer had made a business decision to fight such cases as a means of deterring certain classes of claims even though the insurer should have known that the claimant who persisted with such a claim would prevail." Another lawyer described a case the insurance company required him to defend as a "virtual sure loser."[13]

Delay, deny, defend is so frequent that it is even possible for a policyholder to buy insurance against the risk that the insurance company will deny a claim. Insurance broker Swett & Crawford offers "Claims Dispute Insurance" on behalf of NAS Insurance Services and Lloyd's of London. "We know that wrongful coverage denials occur in our industry," said Swett & Crawford managing director Jason White. Insurance against wrongful denials is needed because businesses that are wrongfully denied coverage by their insurers often cannot find lawyers to take their cases; even simple cases can cost fifty thousand dollars to litigate and complicated cases twice that, making litigation financially impractical.[14]

These examples could be multiplied from litigated cases and media reports. ABC News's *Primetime*, NBC's *Dateline*, the *CBS Evening News*, *Bloomberg Markets* magazine, the *Detroit Free Press*, the *New Orleans Times-Picayune*, *Kiplinger* magazine, *Money* magazine, and others have done exposés of bad faith claim practices. The industry, of course, dismisses the cases described as exceptional and decries media reports as biased and unreliable. When *Bloomberg Markets* magazine exposed State

Farm's use of the delay, deny, and defend strategy the response from the company's public relations spokesman was predictable: The evidence was "nothing more than anecdotes and a handful of lawsuits, most of which are routinely peddled by the trial bar to the news media."[15]

The problem is bigger than that. It is not just a handful of lawsuits and, even more important, claims that should turn into lawsuits but do not. But how much bigger than that, no one knows. More precisely, no one knows except the insurance companies, and they're not telling.

One obstacle to knowing the true extent of delay, deny, defend is the process that sociologists cleverly call "naming, blaming, and claiming." If a consumer is chiseled, stonewalled, or otherwise mistreated by her insurance company, she has to identify herself as the victim of a wrong (naming), attribute that wrong to the insurance company (blaming), and then do something about it (claiming). Most of the time that does not happen. The consumer may not realize that an event is covered by her insurance policy. If she does and contacts her insurance company, the company's behavior may seem normal or appropriate, so she will not think to file a complaint or bring suit. An auto policyholder files a claim for car damage caused by an accident. The company pays the costs of repair but does not advise the policyholder that she is entitled to be compensated for a rental car. The company-affiliated repair center bases the estimated cost of repair on a visible inspection but doesn't do sufficient investigation to reveal hidden damage to the frame. The company takes a long time to pay. Or the company offers the policyholder less than the full value of the claim, asserting that that is all the claim is "worth." In all of these cases the insured may not know the company has breached its obligation under the policy and violated the law, so she accepts the insurance company's decision.

Even if the policyholder feels that the insurance company has acted improperly, she may not know that redress is available through the state insurance department or the courts. If she does know, she may believe that it's too much trouble or unlikely to be worthwhile. Often companies are not required to advise insureds of their right to file a complaint, and it may not occur to consumers on their own. And in many cases the policyholder will not consult a lawyer, particularly in smaller cases or where insurance companies actively discourage insureds from asserting their rights.

A few policyholders make it over these hurdles and complain to their state's insurance department. Some insurance departments and the National Association of Insurance Commissioners (NAIC) publish figures on complaints filed, but they fail to portray an accurate picture of the problem; law professor and NAIC consumer representative Daniel Schwarcz accurately characterizes the data as "over-lapping, confusing, and ambiguous."[16] The states and the NAIC define categories that are impenetrable; there are "complaints" by consumers that are different than mere "inquiries." Some complaints are "confirmed" by the department and others are "justified" or just "closed." Sometimes the company takes "corrective action" and sometimes there are "other outcomes." With these definitions it is impossible to make much sense out of the numbers that are published. In 2008, for example, the California insurance department rated State Farm, the largest auto insurer in the state, as having the sixth-best complaint ratio in the state, with just under 1 justified complaint for every 100,000 vehicles insured. (Kemper Independence Insurance topped the list with no justified complaints, and Lincoln General Insurance was at the bottom with 17.6 justified complaints per 100,000 vehicles.) That sounds good for State Farm, but there is more. Beyond the 28 justified complaints, it had a total of 669 closed complaints. "Corrective action," including a compromise settlement by the company, was required in 97 more cases, and 307 had "other outcomes." But the appropriate baseline for measuring the volume of complaints is not the number of insureds but the number of incidents of loss; a driver who never has an accident has no reason to complain. About 1 out of 100 drivers in a year files a claim involving bodily injury, and 5 out of 100 file a claim for damage to the car. Five percent of State Farm's 3 million insured drivers in California means 150,000 policyholders filed a claim. If there were 669 complaints, State Farm's ratio of complaints drops to 1 in 224 who made it through all the filters to complain to state regulators.

One thing that is clear from the numbers is that when consumers complain, their most common complaints are about improper claim practices. Nationally, of all complaints filed with insurance departments, delays in processing claims account for 19 percent of the complaints, denials for 18 percent, and unsatisfactory settlements or offers to settle for 14 percent.

The ultimate step in claiming is suing an insurance company, and a measure of the incidence of delay, deny, defend is the number of times policyholders and others are forced to sue companies to get the benefits to which they are entitled. Insurance companies certainly are frequently sued for violating fair claim practices, but they closely guard data on those suits. A rare instance in which one was forced to reveal how often it was sued was in an Oklahoma case against State Farm, the country's largest property/casualty insurer, in 2001. Its lawyers were required to produce a list of all cases pending against it for violation of fair claim practices. What was unusual about the disclosure was that it was not subject to a protective order or confidentiality agreement; ordinarily insurance companies disclose such information grudgingly and then only if the plaintiff agrees or the court orders that the information not be communicated to anyone else. The result was a computer-generated list four inches thick, with 807 pages of six-point type. It includes 4,706 causes of action brought by 3,237 separate policyholders and claimants, most filed within the year or two before but some dating back seven years and more. The number of cases brought varied widely from state to state, depending on the number of policies State Farm had in force and the strength of the state's laws protecting policyholders. Texas, for example, saw suits by 1,163 policyholders, California had 258, West Virginia had 162, and Pennsylvania, 159.

The reported figures of consumer complaints, and the even more rare numbers on suits filed—limited and unreliable though they are—indicate there is a problem. It would be easy to get better figures, and the best evidence of the problem of delay, deny, defend is that better figures are not available. Companies could report on how many claims are filed with them, how long it takes to process the claims, how many claims are denied, how many policyholders have to resort to suing the companies to have their claims satisfied, and how those suits turn out. They could report the information to state regulators or use it in their advertising.

Then the scope of the problem nationally would be easy to determine, and consumers would know who the worst offenders are.

In fact, some states require insurance companies to report these numbers, and the NAIC has begun to collect the data. But the reporting and collection are secret, at the insistence of the insurance companies. If they wanted to refute the existence of delay, deny, defend, they could do so. Their silence speaks louder than any numbers.

3

Moral Hazard, the Bottom Line, and the Origins of Delay, Deny, Defend

INSURANCE WORKS WHEN insurance companies pay claims promptly and fairly. But there always has been a problem with this principle, the problem economists label as "moral hazard." In the nineteenth century insurers began to label as moral hazards those in which the occurrence or magnitude of a risk was increased by people of bad character. In the 1960s neoclassical economics adapted the concept to fit with its emphasis on incentives. While studying the role of insurance in health care, Nobel Prize–winning economist Kenneth Arrow used it when he hypothesized that people with insurance would be more likely to consult doctors and more likely to use expensive medical procedures, increasing the cost of insurance and health care.[1] Other economists criticized Arrow's use of the value-laden term, arguing that moral hazard has little to do with morality but instead was a rational response by the individual to the presence of insurance, even if it would have detrimental effects for the community as a whole.[2] But Arrow, in a lesson that insurance companies could take to heart, argued that morality and economically rational behavior are not independent. "Judas turned a profit by betraying Jesus, but even economists could argue that the behavior was blameworthy. . . . One of the characteristics of a successful economic system," according to Arrow, "is that the relations of trust and confidence between principal and agent are sufficiently strong so that the agent will not cheat even though it may be 'rational economic behavior' to do so."[3]

In a principal and agent relationship, one party has freedom to act in a way that will affect the other. The steps an insured takes to avoid or minimize a loss, or not to do so, affects the insurance company. On the other hand, how the company responds to a claim affects the insured. When the insured submits a claim the insurance company has an incentive to delay, diminish, or deny the claim for the simple reason that it gets to keep the money unless and until it has to pay the insured. Therefore, the company is subject to moral hazard too.

The history of insurance demonstrates regular instances of insurance companies succumbing to the moral hazard of not paying valid claims. In the nineteenth century, life insurance companies often refused to pay death benefits, arguing that the insured had misrepresented his physical condition when applying for the policy, which rendered the policy void. The companies required voluminous but vague disclosures on the application for insurance to set up the misrepresentation argument. In the 1870s, among the sixteen questions Connecticut Mutual Life Insurance Company asked its potential insureds were the following:

> Have you ever had any of the following diseases? Answer (yes or no) Apoplexy, paralysis, insanity, epilepsy, habitual headache, fits, consumption, pneumonia, pleurisy, diphtheria, bronchitis, spitting of blood, habitual cough, asthma, scarlet fever, dyspepsia, colic, rupture, fistula, piles, affection of liver, affection of spleen, fever and ague, disease of the heart, palpitation, aneurism, disease of the urinary organs, syphilis, rheumatism, gout, neuralgia, dropsy, scrofula, small-pox, yellow fever, and cancer or any tumor.
>
> Have you had any other illness, local disease, or personal injury; and if so, of what nature, how long since, and what effect on general health?
>
> Is there any fact relating to your physical condition, personal or

> family history, or habits which has not been stated in the answers to the foregoing questions, and with which the company ought to be made acquainted?[4]

If any of the answers were incomplete or incorrect the company later would assert that the misrepresentation voided the policy and the company didn't have to pay. August Baumgart, for example, was presented with a similar application that inquired about thirty-seven diseases. He failed to disclose that he had been treated once for diarrhea and, apparently, "piles," a listed disease. The failure was understandable; the trial judge found that Baumgart never knew he had piles. No matter, said the Wisconsin Supreme Court, and no matter that the illness did not contribute to his death from pneumonia. The insurance company could seize on the unknowing error to refuse to pay.[5]

As a result of these abuses, some companies began offering policies with incontestability clauses. After a period of time when the policy was in force, the policy would become "incontestable" for mistakes or misrepresentations in the application; that is, the company could not refuse to pay because of the mistake or misrepresentation. The market advantage to these companies was insufficient to control the abuse, however, and state legislatures responded. Ohio enacted a statute in 1873 providing that after an insurer had received three premium payments it could no longer deny payment because of such misrepresentations. In 1906 New York's Armstrong Commission investigated widespread fraud and abuse by insurance companies and recommended modern incontestability legislation, and in 1946 the National Association of Insurance Commissioners recommended model legislation that was adopted in most of the states.[6]

Life insurance companies succumbing to the moral hazard of manufacturing misrepresentations to avoid paying claims was common but ultimately obvious and easily controlled. Delay, deny, defend is different. It arose as a strategy in the mid-1990s because of unusual pressure on insurance companies' profits from the insurance "underwriting cycle" and a number of catastrophic events. Then it was fed by the new corporate culture that worshiped growth and profit, and by intense price competition. At its core it involves more than cheating customers here and there; it transforms the claims process into a profit center.

People in business are supposed to act rationally in pricing and selling their products. Insurance companies don't. In alternating cycles over time they sell a lot of their product at low prices and then sell less of their product at high prices; the high prices attract competition that drives prices down, starting the cycle over again. In a "soft market" companies compete to sell more insurance. They relax underwriting standards and cut premium rates, so they sell more policies and riskier policies at lower prices. The inevitable result is that even though total premiums increase, claims rise too, and as claims rise, profits decline. When profits decline the shortfall has to be made up from the companies' capital surplus, so the capital needed to back up new policies is depleted. To compensate, the companies tighten underwriting standards and raise rates, so less insurance is available but loss results are better (a "hard market"). Profits rise and new capital is attracted by the higher profits, so the capacity to underwrite more policies increases, starting the cycle over again.[7]

The pressure to cut premium rates would be peculiar but understandable even if lower premium rates produced lower profits, but the fact that underwriting losses are not the whole story makes the behavior more logical. Premium dollars collected become funds for the insurance company to invest, and the expected return on those investments helps determine how much it is worth to accumulate those dollars, even at the expense of higher claims costs. When investment returns are high, companies engage in "cash flow underwriting," or underwriting designed less to produce a gain on the ratio of premiums to claims and more to produce funds to be invested. Most insurers invest the bulk of their assets in bonds—for property/casualty insurers as a whole, about two thirds of their investments. (Industry giant State Farm and GEICO, the investments of which are managed by Warren Buffett as part of Berkshire Hathaway's portfolio, are the exceptions, with twice as much of their assets in stocks as most insurers.)[8] Therefore, interest rates affect returns greatly. Higher rates mean greater returns, and that fewer assets have to be set aside now to cover claims to be paid in the future. Conversely, when interest rates fall, the lure of more premiums is less attractive, and there is less incentive to cut prices to grow revenue.

Insurance underwriting cycles usually follow four-to-six-year patterns. Starting in 1988, however, the pattern was broken by an unusually extended soft market that ran from 1988 until 2000. Underwriting losses for the industry were $10.2 billion in 1987 and $11.8 billion in 1988, then nearly doubled in 1989 and 1990, jumped to $36.3 billion in 1991, and never fell below $17.1 billion for the next five years. This extended soft market put company profits under unusual pressure.

The pressure was particularly pronounced in auto insurance.[9] The All-Industry Research Advisory Council (now the Insurance Research Council) conducted an extensive study of auto claims in 1987 and concluded that the cost of injuries rose 140 percent over the previous decade. That was more than half again the rate of inflation, with much of the increase driven by rising medical costs.

At the same time that the underwriting cycle and rising medical costs were cutting profits, Mother Nature intervened and made things worse. A series of natural disasters increased losses and therefore decreased profits and depleted capital in a dramatic way. Hurricane Hugo in 1989 and Hurricane Andrew in 1992, the San Francisco earthquake in 1989 and the Northridge earthquake in 1994, and wildfires in Santa Barbara County, California, in 1990, Oakland, California, in 1991, and Orange County and Los Angeles in 1993 imposed losses for which companies had inadequate reserves.

Each of these catastrophes was devastating, and each had its effect on insurance companies and the insurance market. Hurricane Andrew was, until Hurricane Katrina in 2005, the costliest natural disaster on record in the United States. Andrew swept ashore near Homestead, Florida, with sustained winds of about 150 mph; the peak winds could not be measured because they destroyed the measuring devices. The hurricane was blamed for 40 deaths, it destroyed over 120,000 homes, and its economic cost totaled $30 billion. The effects on the insurance industry were devastating. About $16 billion of the total loss was covered by insurance, more than 600,000 claims were filed, and a reported one fourth of the nation's insurance adjusters converged on the hurricane zone to handle the claims. Allstate suffered a $2.7 billion loss, and State Farm, $2.1 billion. The volume of claims exceeded the funds the companies had set aside as reserves to cover losses; eleven companies were bankrupted and thirty others lost 20 percent or more of their surplus.[10]

The Northridge earthquake two years later also imposed huge burdens on the industry. The quake struck on January 17, 1994, with a magnitude of 6.7 on the Richter scale. Over 300,000 buildings were destroyed or damaged, and there was massive damage to autos and infrastructure. A total of 600,000 claims were filed, and the total covered loss exceeded $15 billion. The losses far exceeded the amount of premiums collected for earthquake coverage. State Farm, for example, paid $3.5 billion on 117,000 claims, having collected $1.2 billion in premiums; Farmers paid $2 billion on 36,000 claims, four times the amount it had collected in premiums.

The soft market of the late 1980s and early 1990s and the shocks to profits and capital by the string of natural disasters during the same period spurred new corporate strategies. The response of Farmers was the most obvious. A. M. Best, the authoritative rating agency for insurance company financial stability, lowered Farmers' quality rating and, because Farmers' losses cut into its capital surplus and therefore its ability to reserve for potential losses, it needed to raise an additional $1.6 billion or cease writing new policies. Part of the loss was made up for by the sale of $375 million in preferred stock the year after Northridge, but the principal means of recovery was a program the company called "Bring Back A Billion." Leo E. Denlea, Jr., Farmers CEO, told employees, "We must each do our part to help restore surplus and ultimately improve our A.M. Best rating."[11] The mandate applied to all employees, including claim employees, who were asked to sign individual forms committing themselves to the goal. For claim employees the way to bring back a billion was to reduce costs, of which the largest portion was claims costs; each line of insurance was given its own goal for reducing its combined ratio.[12]

Allstate pursued a different path. Following the hard market of the mid-1980s Allstate embarked on an extreme soft market strategy of reducing underwriting standards and expanding its base of agents to increase its market share. The results showed dramatically in Allstate's book of business. Between 1985 and 1990, the company's share of private auto insurance sold grew from 10.4 percent to 12.4 percent, and its share of the homeowners market grew from 9.6 percent to 12.4 percent. All of this came at a cost to the bottom line and therefore to reserves, however; its pretax operating income fell from $415 million in 1988, when the last of the hard market profits were flowing, to $41 million the next year, and it suffered a loss of $380 million in 1990. The natural disasters imposed more losses; overall losses were almost $2 billion in 1992, the year of Hurricane Andrew, and $330 million in 1994, due in part to the Northridge earthquake.

Even more important was the decision to separate Allstate from its lifelong connection to Sears. Allstate began in effect as an adjunct of the Sears catalog. In 1930 insurance broker Carl Odell, while playing bridge with his neighbor Robert E. Wood, CEO of Sears, suggested that a low-cost way of selling insurance would be through direct mail and the Sears catalog. By the early 1990s, however, Sears decided to focus on its core retailing business and divest itself of its three financial services subsidiaries: Coldwell Banker real estate; the Dean Witter–Discover brokerage and credit cards; and Allstate. In 1993 Sears engaged in an IPO to sell 20 percent of Allstate, and in 1995 it distributed the remaining 80 percent to Sears shareholders. In part due to the influx of new capital, Allstate embarked on a period of increased profitability. Its operating income grew steadily for five years after 1994, the year of the Northridge earthquake, and it saw its profits range from $1.1 billion to $4.8 billion over the next decade, during hard and soft markets.

Lawyer and Allstate critic David Berardinelli notes another coincidence of events. After Allstate achieved its independence from Sears, the rewards to its executives under incentive compensation schemes would depend on its own profitability. It was just at this point that Allstate brought in management consultant McKinsey & Company to reengineer its claim practices to make them more profitable.

Allstate was not unique in its new emphasis on stock price and shareholder value. Looking back in 2001, Richard Stewart, former superintendent of insurance for New York and president of the National Association of Insurance Commissioners, described the shift in the industry as "from orientation toward policyholders to orientation toward stockholders . . . Securities analysts and corporate managements emphasized 'shareholder value' and, by stock options, the alignment of management's interests with those of stockholders." The effect on claim practices was direct: "Through dividends and appreciation, stockholders get the benefit of what is not paid out for claims."[13] Paul Hasse, CEO of reinsurer Centre Cat Ltd., commented, "In an industry that in the past has been dominated by dinosaurs, we are beginning to see some mammals evolving." "Mammals," according to a 1996 report on the industry in *Best's Review,* were marked by "financially oriented owners who will pay more attention to the bottom line." The report described "character" as the new key to success, but defined character in a particular, business school mentality way: the ability "to make the tough decisions necessary to improve profitability," where "cost cutting is the main driving force in the property/casualty industry today."[14] And as elsewhere in American business in the 1980s and 1990s, profitability in the long term is too long to wait, and financial results need to be measured here and now. (Multinational insurer Allianz has taken the logical step of feeding the demand for up-to-the-minute reports by providing news on financial information and share prices by text messages sent to investors' and analysts' cell phones.)

One indication of the shift in emphasis was the move through the 1980s and 1990s by dozens of insurance companies to demutualize, or to shift from being mutual companies to stock companies. Mutual companies are owned by their policyholders, so policyholders share in the company's profits through the payment of dividends on their policies, effectively a reduction in the premium rate. Stock companies are like any other corporations, owned by their shareholders to whom management is responsible and who reap the financial rewards if the company is profitable.

The attraction of demutualization was the access to capital markets. Mutual companies can only build the capital needed to sell policies through retaining profits in surplus, but stock companies can attract outside investment. When companies were capital-constrained in the 1980s and 1990s, conversion enabled them to build surplus quickly through the sale of stock. The presence of ownership shares also provides an easy means of compensating key executives by awarding stock or options through executive compensation programs, and it provides currency for the company to grow through corporate acquisitions.

Once a company demutualizes, though, it is subject to the discipline of the stock market. Mutual companies at least in theory serve only the interests of their policyholders, the owners of the company. The measure of value in a stock company is the price of the stock, and the company's principal obligation is not to its policyholders but to its shareholders.

Even those companies that remained mutuals increasingly focused on growth and revenue. Warren Buffett complained that State Farm, the largest property/casualty insurer and a mutual, was taking huge underwriting losses at the end of the long soft market of the 1990s to maintain its market share—about 18 percent compared to GEICO's 6 percent. Liberty Mutual has grown to become the sixth largest property/casualty insurer by acquiring other companies, including Ohio Casualty and Safeco; although as a mutual it has no investors, it does have an investor relations department.

State Farm's strategy exemplified the vicious war for market share, fought mainly through price cutting, that broke out in the 1990s in auto insurance, the largest segment of property/casualty insurance, and that exacerbated the financial pressure on companies.[15] The stage for price competition was set by a new flexibility in the setting of rates for premiums. From the rise of insurance in the nineteenth century through the U.S. Supreme Court's decision in the *South-Eastern Underwriters Association* case in 1944, insurance companies had formed cartels to fix premium prices, sometimes under the nominal supervision of state regulators, and the regulation of premiums "was neither vigorous nor effectual," as a leading insurance treatise gently described the situation.[16] When the Court held that insurance could be regulated by the federal government as a part of interstate commerce, the insurance industry and state regulators lobbied Congress to enact the McCarran-Ferguson Act, which allowed states to preempt federal regulation of insurance, making the insurance industry and Major League Baseball the only two industries exempt from the reach of the federal antitrust laws.

Within a half-dozen years nearly every state had done so in the area of rate regulation, typically by legislation that established rating bureaus. The bureaus allowed companies to collaborate in sharing information about risks and losses and in setting premiums, and therefore avoid price competition.[17]

Beginning in the late 1960s, pressure from the industry for more independence in rate setting, and dissatisfaction from consumers over high auto insurance rates, led to an opening up of the process of regulation. While some states continued to require approval of premiums, and even imposed special restrictions on rates for auto insurance, many others opted for open competition, in which companies could adopt new rates without prior approval from state regulators. In general there was more flexibility in setting rates and an attitude that price competition was valuable. Price competition then put increased pressure on claims, as cutting prices meant cutting costs, and the principal component of a company's costs is its loss expense.

The new flexibility in setting rates showed the increasing emphasis on price as a means of gaining new customers. The results of a survey announced at the 1996 annual meeting of the National Association of Independent Insurers showed that the key driver of sales was low cost, with satisfactory claims service far behind.[18] Top industry executives in the room, including CEOs Jerry Choate of Allstate and Thomas Crawford of Prudential Property and Casualty, professed to be "surprised" and "troubled" by the results, much, perhaps, as Captain Renault professed to be shocked to find gambling at Rick's Café in *Casablanca*.

New marketing strategies became the essential weapons in the war over price and customers. Insurance became more like a commodity, a standard item sold off the shelf for which price becomes a principal feature. (Progressive's television commercials gave life to the concept by portraying an insurance supermarket in which the perky salesclerk, Flo, helped consumers take policy packages off the shelf and to the cashier.) It is a commodity of an odd sort certainly, since policies vary greatly. Nevertheless, for many customers most of the policy terms are invisible, and the only things that matter are the amount of coverage and the cost of the premium.

Traditionally insurance was sold through agents, either independent agents who worked for themselves and sold the policies of several companies, or "captive agents," who sold the policies of only one company. A key to the success of State Farm has been its army of local agents, a tradition begun by company founder G. J. Mecherle in 1922. Dealing with an agent is attractive to buyers who have more complex needs, want personalized service, or are brand loyalists who prefer to have an ongoing relationship with a company and its agents. But treating insurance as a commodity, particularly a commodity sold through call centers and Web sites, made growth possible without such an army. If an insurance policy is a standard product, or if its options are standard, many prospective buyers will see little value in dealing with a middleman agent. Instead, purchasers can go directly to the company, and the company can both reach out to new markets and lower its cost of distribution at the same time.[19] Thus the modern industry maxim: Personal lines like homeowners and auto insurance compete on price, and commercial lines, which are more complex, compete on service.

Allstate's use of mail order and the Sears catalog was an early example of direct marketing, but the company that made the best use of the technique, and the one that would transform the entire industry in the 1990s and after, was GEICO. Originally the Government Employees Insurance Company, GEICO's strategy was to reduce costs and therefore premiums by marketing through the mail rather than through a sales force of agents. The problem in this strategy was that agents didn't just sell policies—they also evaluated and screened clients to make sure the risks were appropriate to the premiums. If direct marketing produced undesirable customers, the whole system would fall apart. GEICO's substitute for agents performing these functions was, as its original name suggests, to limit its clientele to government employees, who were presumed to be more responsible. Beginning in the time of World War II and its aftermath, when GEICO expanded greatly, government employees also were an appealing market because there were so many of them. The system was so attractive that in the fall of 1950 a young Warren Buffett sold three fourths of his investments to buy 350 shares of GEICO stock; decades later, he would acquire the entire company for Berkshire Hathaway, where the premiums it collected would be a major source of capital for Buffett's other acquisitions.[20]

Price competition and direct marketing caused upheavals in the industry. From 1995 to 1999, for example, the share of the private passenger auto insurance market held by the industry's perennially largest company, State Farm, fell from 21.6 percent to 18.9 percent, while direct marketers increased their share: GEICO from 2.5 percent to 4.1 percent, and Progressive from 2.6 percent to 4.8 percent. State Farm responded when its chairman, Ed Rust, Jr., announced "the big dog is off the porch."[21] It cut its rates and underwriting standards to regain market share, reducing auto premiums by $2.7 billion and paying out an additional $2.6 billion in dividends to policyholders (further reducing their premium costs), producing a loss ratio 14 percent higher than GEICO's, all at the expense of profitability. In the short term this competition squeezed profits for all; in the long term it was unsustainable and increased the pressure to cut costs, an effect that made low-cost companies the most likely to be successful, and therefore put pressure on claim practices.[22]

The industry recognized the changes. As Ted Kelly, CEO of Liberty Mutual, acknowledged, "Personal lines is now a merchandising business, and GEICO is doing it remarkably well."[23] In 1999, Allstate shifted its marketing strategy, aiming to reduce annual expenses by $600 million by cutting 12 percent of its workforce, expanding into call centers and Internet sales, and moving away from its historic reliance on company agents. In 2007 one out of twenty insurance company Web sites offered online purchasing; a year later one out of four did so, and nearly all at least offered online quotes. Even regulators got into the business of online quotes; in 2008 the Massachusetts insurance department, treating insurance as a commodity, established its own Web site that enabled consumers to shop for prices for car insurance by providing their ZIP code, the number of years they have been licensed, the type of vehicle, their driving record, and the coverage wanted.[24]

The shift to direct marketing and the growth of price competition to attract new customers spurred what former Allstate CEO Edward Liddy (later picked by the federal government to run AIG after the government's bailout of the insurance giant) called "an advertising arms race."

Insurance companies have always advertised, and through their advertising the companies have positioned themselves as much as their product. Much of the early and iconic insurance advertising focused on the security provided by the company, particularly with respect to the security of claim payments. In an ad in *Harper's Weekly* magazine on April 24, 1869, the Travelers' Insurance Co. of Hartford touted its claims record: "More than TEN THOUSAND Claims of Policyholders, for Death or Injury by Accident, HAVE BEEN PAID, showing the value of Accident Insurance," including, oddly, the payment to "Mr. Chas. M. Rogers, whose mysterious murder created such a sensation." (Price was not irrelevant, however; the ad also promised "A policy costs but little—try it.")[25]

Two of the most famous slogans in American advertising history emphasize insurance companies' promises to provide security: Allstate's "You're in Good Hands with Allstate" (with the image of cradling hands), created by Davis W. Ellis, Allstate's general sales manager, in 1950, and State Farm's "Like a good neighbor, State Farm is there" (with the clever jingle written in 1971 by a then little-known songwriter named Barry Manilow). More recently Allstate hired actor Dennis Haysbert, a warm, trustworthy presence from his portrayal of President David Palmer on the Fox television series *24*, to deliver the message that security and confidence are "Allstate's stand." Liberty Mutual's remarkably popular "responsibility" campaign is to the same effect, with a series of commercials on a pay-it-forward theme, with ordinary folks demonstrating random acts of kindness and caring echoed in the line: "When an insurance company does it, it's called Liberty Mutual." Even GEICO occasionally joins the trend, with real customers' stories about GEICO's claims service jocularly retold by celebrities from James Lipton and Phyllis Diller to Mrs. Butterworth.

Pioneered by GEICO, insurance companies increasingly position themselves as funky as well as secure. Through its geckos, cavemen, and mix of celebrities and "real people" GEICO has increased its ad awareness to more than nine out of ten shoppers, significantly more than State Farm or Allstate; increased new customer acquisition at a rate almost half again as high as other companies; and increased market share in private-passenger auto insurance from 5.1 percent to 7.2 percent from 2003 to

2007, moving into third place overall. GEICO's style also set a tone for attracting attention, a style that has been copied by such oddities as Esurance's animated commercials and Nationwide's "Life Comes at You Fast" campaign with such fifteen-minutes-of-fame wonders as Fabio, Kevin Federline, and *American Idol* antihero Sanjaya Malakar. Even staid State Farm has responded by hiring basketball superstar LeBron James to attract younger shoppers.

But the dominant focus of insurance advertising in recent years has been price. GEICO's "Fifteen minutes could save you 15 percent or more on car insurance" has become the new standard. Progressive advertises its comparison-shopping approach and frequent discounts. Esurance's pink-haired cartoon heroine, Erin, is the only one who can stop overpriced car insurance from taking over the world. Allstate touts that it will lower rates for avoiding accidents and will not raise rates after an accident. Only Chubb broke the industry norm and emphasized its strong record of paying claims and denigrated other companies' claims practices. It warned in one advertisement that "not all insurance companies treat you the same. If being treated fairly and paid quickly are important to you when you or your business has a loss, you want Chubb," and in another, quoted a *Worth* magazine article that reported, "Chubb's best feature is a three-decade history of paying claims that other companies might balk at."

Low prices don't come cheap, though, because only expensive advertising can sell the message of low price, particularly for direct marketers such as GEICO and Progressive. Television advertising is particularly expensive but particularly necessary. As Steve Sullivan, senior vice president for communications at Liberty Mutual, noted, aside from the ubiquity of television in American life, "Our business, insurance, doesn't have a tangible product, so what television does for us is allow us to establish an emotional connection with a consumer—sight, sound, emotion—and nothing else does that—yet."[26] Expenditures on advertising by the fifty largest insurers doubled in the five years between 2001 and 2006, from $1.28 billion to $2.48 billion, making insurance companies among the top spenders on advertising. On *Advertising Age*'s 2008 list of "megabrands," the biggest spenders of advertising dollars, GEICO stood at number thirteen, with $619 million; State Farm was number seventeen, with $436 million; and Allstate, number thirty, with $362 million. (The biggest spenders are communications companies, with Verizon at number one and AT&T at number two, with expenditures of $2.2 billion and $2.0 billion, respectively.)

4

McKinsey Redefines the Game: Claims as a Profit Center

THE EXTENDED SOFT underwriting market that began in 1988, the shocks of natural disasters in the late 1980s and early 1990s, the increase in medical costs and other claim sources, the growing importance of price competition, and the new mania for profits and growth set the table for the transformation of claim practices and the rise of delay, deny, defend. It was left to McKinsey & Company, the megaconsulting firm that redesigned much of the corporate world, to serve the meal. The main course: to violate the fundamental principle of claim handling by redefining the claim process as a profit center.

One of McKinsey's maxims is that the firm never sells; that is, it does not do what its business clients do, namely, advertise and promote their services to potential customers. The firm does, however, aggressively market itself by publishing a semischolarly journal, *The McKinsey Quarterly;* supporting an economics research center, the McKinsey Global Institute; publishing reports; and encouraging publicity through the press and word of mouth in the corporate community. With a remarkable lack of embarrassment, one of the firm's white papers on the insurance industry—*Factory and Firm: The Future of Claims Handling*—provides the best retrospective of the transformation of the claim process that increased delay, deny, defend and of McKinsey's own role in the change.

The story begins with the traditional claim process, in which claims adjusters had substantial autonomy in doing their work and authority in settling claims. "In the 70s," McKinsey states, "claims was seen largely as an art—with senior claims managers as craftsmen deserving of great freedom and latitude. Some believed that this posed little risk, because the result was really determined by the underwriting decisions made months or years earlier."

Claims managers deserved great freedom and latitude because the objective of the process was to arrive at a fair value for the claim, consistent with "the underwriting decisions"—the promise of indemnity the company made to the insured to pay the insured's full loss, within the limits of coverage. The company would be profitable, or not, because of the decisions made by underwriters and actuaries; the adjuster's job was to pay what was owed. But the financial situation presented a challenge to this model. "By the 80s, with costs growing rapidly, claims' status as an art came increasingly under fire. Management began looking to claims for more cost efficiency and, while the indemnity result was still largely seen as set by underwriting choices, the focus shifted toward managing the loss adjustment expense more aggressively." Good management takes hold as loss adjustment expense—the cost of processing claims—is cut, but not in a way that violates the nature of the insurance relationship and the promise the company makes to its policyholders, to pay for losses suffered.

Then came the key moment in the rise of delay, deny, defend.

> By the 90s, the pendulum began to swing back the other way. After years of squeezing the cost side, management recognized huge opportunities to rebalance and invested cautiously in LAE [loss adjustment expense] to capture indemnity savings. The concept of "leakage" or total economic opportunity came into vogue as firms, led by McKinsey, encouraged many in the industry to use closed file reviews (CFRs) to measure the trade-offs between LAE investments and indemnity accuracy. These projects frequently identified

> huge indemnity opportunities and, in some cases, under-resourced claims organizations. Many executives used CFR data to make new investments in claims and reaped substantial economic improvement as a result.

In the 1980s the emphasis was on cutting the cost of administering the claims department—monitoring adjusters' salaries, introducing technological efficiencies, and using fewer paper clips. The real money in claims, though, is in the amount paid out in claims and not in the expenses. In 1992, for example, for every premium dollar taken in property/casualty companies paid thirteen cents for the expense of running the claims department but paid out seventy-two cents in claims. So in the 1990s the focus shifted to leakage. McKinsey's *Factory and Firm* describes leakage as the falloff from indemnity accuracy, or how much more the company paid on claims than it should accurately pay. But the goal was smaller payouts, not accurate payouts. "Huge indemnity opportunities" and "substantial economic improvement" result only from paying less in claims, not more. "New investments in claims" processes could "capture indemnity savings." By spending a little more or a little more intelligently on the claims process, particularly by introducing computer systems to measure the value of claims and spending money on lawyers to fight them, companies could cut the amount paid to their insureds and their victims dramatically. "Substantial economic improvement" resulted as the claim process became a profit center for the company. The focus of the claim process was no longer on paying a fair amount promptly but on paying—or not paying—in amounts, at times, and under conditions that increase the company's profits.

McKinsey brings the story up-to-date.

> By the end of the 90s, the leakage story had grown more complicated. . . . While focusing largely on indemnity, some carriers have seen expenses on the LAE side creep up. Additionally, leakage measurement itself can be costly and difficult to sustain—some carriers have been searching for ways to measure leakage in a more cost effective/rapid manner, while sustaining objectivity. Others have

> wanted to add measures that focus more on the customer service components of claims handling. Finally, some managers believe that while leakage measures are very useful for guiding an organization, they want additional operational metrics that are tied to near-term outcomes.

In short, claims payouts need to be kept down, but claims costs are part of the story too. Both leakage and costs are important, as are "additional operational metrics," such as how many claims are disposed of how quickly.

McKinsey has been more than the chronicler of changes in claims practices; it was the architect of those changes to such an extent that the credit that it "led" the movement to bring leakage "into vogue" is a modest one. The firm was founded in 1926 by James O. McKinsey, formerly a professor of accounting at the University of Chicago.[1] The principal builder of the modern firm was Marvin Bower, who joined the firm in 1933. Bower, holder of a law degree and MBA from Harvard, spent three years at the prestigious Cleveland law firm of Jones, Day, Reavis & Pogue before joining McKinsey. His aim was to build a new type of management consulting firm on the model of the leading professional firms in law and accounting, which were characterized by high professional standards, ownership by active partners, and a lifelong career commitment.

For decades McKinsey was the gold standard in management consulting, with its advice sought by the world's largest corporations, its reputation burnished not only by the firm's A-list clients but also by the pronouncements of its executives and alumni, such as *In Search of Excellence,* the bestselling business book by former McKinseyites Thomas Peters and Robert Waterman. McKinsey claims to have served 147 of the world's 200 largest corporations, and its services come dear; annual fees routinely cost $10 million, with its largest clients paying $50 million a year and more.[2] Employment at McKinsey was prized by graduates of elite MBA programs; for a dozen years they scored it as the most popular place to work in Universum's IDEAL Employer Survey, until it was supplanted by Google in 2007.[3]

McKinsey's most famous engagement became more notorious than notable. Enron was headed by former McKinsey partner Jeffrey Skilling, who brought his reputation for analytical brilliance, McKinsey methods, and many McKinsey consultants to that ill-fated company. McKinsey consultants were part of Enron's transformation from a natural-gas pipeline company to a pipeline for impenetrable financial transactions. Prior to the firm's collapse the *McKinsey Quarterly* touted Enron's new "petropeneurs," who were able to "build a better mousetrap" and issue a "wake-up call" to the oil industry through "intermediation and risk management skills" and "deployment of off-balance-sheet funds."[4]

McKinsey deployed teams of intense MBAs on its engagements. The prospect of this kind of searching analysis was not always welcome down the management line. As *Fortune* magazine described the prospect of a McKinsey engagement, "[I]t begins as a rumor of impending destruction, the way a Category 5 hurricane first appears on a radar screen as a smudge off the west coast of Africa. 'I was in a meeting with Chuck,' somebody will say, eyes lowered to hide his expression, 'and he said something about McKinsey.'"[5] What McKinsey offered, however, was an analytical method that presumably enabled it to analyze and improve a company's businesses better than the people running the business on a day-to-day basis could.[6] By the turn of the twenty-first century, however, the allure of involving management consultants in every aspect of a corporation's business had faded, because of both the considerable expense and the questionable results; the notion returned that people actually involved in a business knew more about it than "a bunch of beefed-up MBAs with big egos who charge a lot to tell executives what they should already know," as one CEO put it.[7] As time went on the perception of limited value and great cost caught up with the consulting trade, and many clients cut back on engagements, and consultants in turn cut back on expenses and employees.[8]

The McKinsey approach that was brought to insurance claims begins by accumulating as many facts as possible about a company and its context from as many sources as possible, thereby allowing its consultants, who are outsiders to an industry, to compensate for their lack of experience. Then the consultants describe all of the issues potentially involved in the business and define the problem to be solved. Once the facts have been identified and the issues defined, the consultants generate an initial hypothesis. Oddly enough, McKinsey consultants, perhaps new to the industry and having done only a preliminary review of background facts and a definition of issues, propose the answer to the company's problem before they do most of the work on the engagement. The point is, as former McKinsey partner Ethan Rasiel explained it, "Figure out the solution to the problem before you start."[9] The initial hypothesis needs to be tested, possibly reformulated, perhaps even rejected, but it becomes the road map to solving the client's problem.

Every consulting problem is different, but no problem is entirely unique. McKinsey has a wealth of knowledge to draw on from prior engagements; it also employs a tool kit of techniques that were used with particular effect in its work for Allstate, State Farm, Farmers, Liberty Mutual, and other insurance companies. One is to identify the "key drivers," or the most important factors affecting the client's problem.* Another is the focus on "core process redesign," also called "business process redesign" or "re-engineering" (which would, in its Allstate iteration, become Claims Core Process Redesign, or CCPR). Core process redesign conceives of a business as composed of a small number of core processes (new product development or order generation and fulfillment, for example) rather than traditional functional units (research and development, manufacturing, and marketing) and then rethinks those processes to maximize the company's objectives.[10]

The final part of every consulting engagement is implementation, and McKinsey is rigorous about implementation of its ideas. Consultants sometimes are criticized for generating big ideas that cannot be put into practice. McKinsey typically insists that part of its obligation is to create a detailed plan for implementing its ideas, from buy-in and direction at top levels of management to the lowest possible level of detail; not just what should happen, but what will happen, how, and by whom. Projects differ in scope, of course, but a major redesign, such as McKinsey brought to Allstate and other insurance companies, is a multiyear

*Drivers became popular management-speak; Colossus, the artificial intelligence system used to assess personal injury claims, also focuses on the key drivers of the claim to determine how much should be paid. See Chapter 8.

project, the effects of which last for decades. "Immoderate redesign" is the goal; as a McKinsey article of that name argued, "Any redesign effort large enough to produce a significant bottom-line impact has to stir up and sustain a critical mass of change in an organization's culture. True redesign efforts are never really completed."[11]

In the 1980s McKinsey likely had consulted with a number of insurance companies, including State Farm, Hartford, and USAA (the United Services Automobile Association); consistent with the timeline in its *Factory and Firm* white paper, these engagements probably focused on achieving efficiencies in the cost of processing claims.[12] With that experience and a few months of fact gathering, McKinsey consultants applied their systems to redesigning Allstate's claim processes. They identified the core issues in descending levels of generality. The overall core process redesign objectives were: "1) Build customer-focused organization with service levels equal to or better than that of our competition. 2) Redesign activities and core processes to significantly improve Allstate's competitive economics over the intermediate and longer time period. 3) Develop a home office and field organization structure that yields competitive advantage, becoming a low-cost, broadly-based insurer for the selected level of service by customer segment."

At this level of generality the objectives seem unobjectionable and even laudable. A major company should strive to provide service "equal to or better than that of our competition." At least one court that looked at some of the McKinsey documents and Allstate manuals that drew on them concluded that "unless read in a way to give meanings to words that are rather far-fetched and improbable," they lacked a "sinister nature."[13] As McKinsey developed its hypothesis in more detail and implemented the redesign, its effects became more apparent.

The elements of the hypothesis for redesign were based on the drivers of value in the claim process, a hypothesis that was mapped out in detail early in McKinsey's engagement and would be borne out throughout the implementation of CCPR. McKinsey stated the basic principle: "Our change goal is to redefine the game . . . to . . . question, improve, and radically alter our whole approach to the business of claims." The game would be radically altered by making the claim process a key to increasing Allstate's profits, and at every step the focus would be on reducing the amounts paid to policyholders and accident victims. Every element of the claim process would be transformed. The accepted understanding had been that "severities" (the average paid on claims) were "the cost of doing business." The new approach: "We can and should manage specific components of severity to provide greater financial support to the company." Manage how? Among other ways, focus on paying less on the largest group of claims, because "our volume of small- to mid-sized claims actually offers the opportunity for greatest improvement." Discourage claimants from being helped by lawyers, and pay them less when they don't have lawyers to help, because "the way we approach claimants and develop relationships will significantly alter representation rates and contribute to lower severities."

In short, as summarized at a claim management conference in the spring of 1994: "We will win the economics game. . . . Winning will be a zero sum game. . . . We will win [the] game in two phases: Phase 1. Consistent execution of better plays and new game plans. Phase 2. Change rules and play a new game." Allstate's chairman, Jerry Choate, explained the new economics of claims to employees in 1997: "In the long run, if we don't win on the claim side of this business we don't win. Because that's where all the leverage is. Three-quarters of every dollar that leaves this company goes to pay claims. So we have to build a long-term, sustainable competitive advantage in claims. It's as simple as that."[14] A decade later the company could report that the goals of winning on the claim side remained the same and were being met: "The most important factors we monitor to evaluate the financial condition and performance of our company include . . . severity (average cost per claim) and loss ratio. . . . Our Property-Liability combined ratio [the ratio of claims payments and expenses to premiums] has been below 90 percent over the last two years—an underlying indication of our ability and commitment to shareholder value."[15]

CCPR was an ongoing process, designed to be built into Allstate's DNA and to continue to evolve over time, because "true redesign efforts are never really completed."[16] Although Allstate claims not to have kept all the McKinsey innovations, at least through 2007, Christine Sullivan, assistant vice president for claims in Allstate's home office, reported that "Allstate still uses . . . most of the claim-handling processes and procedures developed and implemented as part of CCPR for investigating, evaluating, handling and resolving automobile bodily injury claims, except that some of the processes and procedures have been modified since initial implementation."[17] Allstate's most recent automated claims system, Next Gen, "a technology and service platform that supports our reinvention of the consumer experience," has been described by industry analyst Paul Newsome as "round two, if not three, four, or five" of CCPR.[18]

McKinsey & Company installed similar plans at other companies. At State Farm, Claims vice president G. Robert Mecherle conveyed the goal to the company's divisional claims superintendents in 1986: "Especially in relation to the bottom line that I want to talk about and that is being better than the competition in everyday claim handling." Better how? "Really what I'm talking about is the loss ratio, because that's the difference between profit and loss. . . . And if our competition settles claims for less money than we do, we stand a good chance of being noncompetitive. . . . Now you all know losses are a function of frequency and severity. You can't do a whole lot about the frequency but severity is strictly in our ballpark."[19]

State Farm's initial program for revamping the claims process was known as ACE, for Advancing Claims Excellence.[20] But ACE was only one of several programs in operation at one time and over time. The different versions included Fire ACE for homeowners insurance, Auto ACE for auto bodily injury claims, and Estimatics ACE for auto property damage. Siblings included Total Evaluation And Claims Handling (TEACH) and others lacking in catchy acronyms such as Medical Management, Service First (also for auto damage claims), Auto Claims Reorganization (redesigning the organization), Quality Reviews (to track progress in achieving claims goals), and Business Process Improvement ("the way we handle claims from beginning to end, the various people who handle them, and the system that we have in place").

The point of ACE was the same as Allstate's CCPR. The ACE basic definitions included "Shortfall: Quality shortfall is the quantifiable difference between what was paid and what should have been paid to conclude a file." There was no comparable definition of "longfall" for cases in which too little was paid on a claim. As a program update reported by 2000, "Considerable opportunity exists in the area of loss payout. . . . If ACE determines that there is a 12% claims payment shortfall nationwide . . . and we are able to reduce the shortfall to 10%, we have recovered the $2 billion savings in expenses." Frank Comella, senior consultant in general auto claims and head of ACE, explained how ACE would implement its objectives: "When we get to the settlement of losses, questions arise, particularly about over-payment. . . . For example, you can have good trendings in average paid cost, but a close review of the files indicates we may be paying too much. Remember, our objective is to pay the appropriate amount." State Farm's objective is to pay the appropriate amount on claims, but questions arise about overpayment (not underpayment) when a review of files indicates the company is paying too much (never too little).

Comella's prediction was borne out in looking at the data. A closed file review in one region reported the percentage of "leakage" (payment of claims for more than they could have been paid) and "opportunities" (the amount by which State Farm profits could be enhanced by cutting payments): In bodily injury claims, 12.5 percent leakage, costing $30 million, 10.7 percent in personal injury protection (no-fault), costing $15 million, and 5.8 percent in property damage, costing $18 million.

For State Farm, as for Allstate and other companies, particular programs and their monikers came and went, but the changes they instituted were evolving and permanent. Frank Comella stated: "Long term, after we get through this learning curve, the goal of the ACE group that I'm part of is to work ourselves out of a job. Ultimately the success of this program is going to rest with the regionally assigned consultants. . . . ACE is here to stay."[21] The company's bullet-point introduction to ACE made clear that "ACE is an ongoing process. ACE will become a way of doing business in the future, and ACE as a term will most likely disappear."[22] And disappear it did, but its effects stayed. In 2003, five years after the formal termination of ACE, State Farm representative Steve Hassold testified that there were "initiatives as a result of the ACE program that we are still using. . . . [T]he ACE program is gone, but things that it did are still in place."[23] (Today State Farm claims "the ACE program was only used for a short period of time in the 1990s as a way to go after insurance fraud and we have not used it since.")[24]

Farmers Insurance competed with State Farm for the best acronym with its ACME program (Achieving Claims Management Excellence). The epigraphs of its ACME best practices manual were admirable: "We provide the best value for the money in the industry. We will do everything in our power to restore people's lives to order. We do the right thing . . . 'Whatever it takes.' . . . We pay what we owe, nothing more, nothing less." Then it got down to business. ACME provided a "methodology for determining best practice within our organization while identifying potential opportunities for overpayments or leakage. Through these efforts, we will improve customer service, control loss costs, maximize productivity, and identify training requirements." Loss costs would be controlled by focusing on leakage: "Overpayment or leakage is the indemnity and/or expense payment associated with incorrect or improper file management or untimely decisions. Overpayment/leakage is that amount above an acceptable disposition or in excess of an acceptable range." Translated: We pay what we owe, but determining what we owe focuses only on identifying overpayments and leakage not underpayments and, one supposes, overflow, and the aim was to control loss costs, not increase them.

For Farmers' ACME, as for Allstate's CCPR and State Farm's ACE, the McKinsey principles applied. The claims process would be radically altered. Traditionally companies pay what they should pay, with "should" defined by what the policyholder was owed. Transforming claims into a profit center would require focusing on leakage, or on where they paid more than they should, where "should" was measured by the goal of reducing costs and increasing profits. The solution was to reduce payments to policyholders and other claimants. The solution would be implemented by redefining every step of the claim process and creating a new, systematic claim process across auto and homeowners claims.

5

Mr. Incredible Goes to Work: The New, Systematic Claims Process

DRIVERS, HOMEOWNERS, VICTIMS of auto accidents, and other people who depend on insurance care about how well claims are handled but not much about the internal workings of the claims departments. Claims are handled well when insurance companies pay what they owe, promptly and without muss or fuss. When claims departments become transformed into profit centers and the job of claims adjuster is redesigned to be a contributor to corporate profits, however, how claims departments work affects how well they work. With a new, systematic approach to the claim process, claims departments work well for the companies but sometimes not so well for those who rely on them.

Once the key to the claim process was the front-line claims adjuster, who would investigate a claim; evaluate coverage under the policy, liability if it was in dispute, and damages; negotiate with the policyholder or accident victim; and, if the claim went to litigation, work with the lawyers. The adjuster was a "claims man," literally, likely to be an army veteran with some college background who drifted into insurance instead of accounting, teaching, or sales. Being an insurance adjuster was an attractive job that allowed initiative. As *Claims* magazine gushed about the top portrayal of a claims adjuster in a film, Edward G. Robinson's Barton Keyes in *Double Indemnity*, "One wonders how many young men returning home in 1944 and '45 chose their professions after hearing Keyes attempt to recruit Fred MacMurray's character, an insurance agent, to be his assistant with the speech."

> The job I'm talking about takes brains and integrity. It takes more guts than there is in 50 salesmen. It's the hottest job in the business.... To me, a claims man is a surgeon, that desk is an operating table, and those pencils are scalpels and bone chisels, and those papers are not just forms and statistics and claims for compensation. They're alive, they're packed with drama, with twisted hopes and crooked dreams.... A claims man is a doctor, and a bloodhound, and a cop, and a judge, and a jury, and a father, and a confessor all in one.[1]

As late as the 1970s most adjusters exercised a great deal of discretion. The adjuster saw his job as settling claims for a fair amount; the common understanding, as sociologist H. Laurence Ross reported in his study of adjusters, was "we close the case out with everybody happy" by paying "what the claim is worth." Fairness was the goal even in liability claims, when the claimant was not the policyholder. Ross quoted a typical sentiment: "We are not in business to chisel the public, I don't feel.... If we know it is worth $20,000 then let's pay $20,000."[2]

The claims man whose job demands brains, integrity, and guts is now much less in evidence, because most adjusters are more closely bound to office and computer, and are subject to elaborate systems that direct their work. Today's adjuster is less often an advocate for fair treatment of the consumer, because adjusters are often required to conform to the demands of the claim-processing system and are evaluated on their conformity to the system, including, explicitly or sub rosa, on the amount paid out, or not paid out, in claims. The contemporary cinematic portrayal of the adjuster comes from the animated satire *The Incredibles*. Bob Parr, the decaped superhero formerly known as Mr. Incredible, toils in the drudgery of an office subject to the berating of his penny-pinching supervisor, Gilbert Huph. Parr doesn't understand the adjuster's new role. When he explains his conception of the job—"We're supposed to help people"—his boss Huph corrects him: "We're supposed to help *our* people, starting with our stockholders, Bob." (Parr's escape from tedium, available only to movie superheroes, is to subvert the system by actually helping claimants, as Huph complains, in "exploiting every loophole, dodging every obstacle, penetrating the bureaucracy.")

Insurance adjusters are part of the armies of bureaucrats and office workers who staff modern corporations and government. Like soldiers in all armies, adjusters (or "claim representatives," as the industry would have it), have different functions and ranks. Some highly skilled, highly paid adjusters investigate and resolve multimillion-dollar claims involving fires at commercial buildings; others process routine claims coming from fender benders. The federal government's Bureau of Labor Statistics reports a total of 209,000 adjusters, claim examiners, and investigators of all types in private employment. Of these, 141,000 work directly for insurance companies, and most of the rest work for independent adjusting companies or for themselves, called on when insurers outsource claims processing or for large-scale catastrophes when their in-house resources are insufficient.

Today the key to the claim process is the system, not the adjuster. A highly organized, industrialized system for processing claims is the key to modern insurance adjusting. The model is the shift from individual craftsman as jack-of-all-trades to specialized production in which each worker in a factory produces a single product, over and over. As an article in *Claims* describes the scene, "Adjusters have less street experience than 30 years ago. Entire generations of claim staffs have spent their entire careers inside the office. . . . Computer processes in which time-study experts have removed precious keystrokes have also removed basic information gathering tools."[3] Claims are grouped and handled by type, by subtype, and by dollar amount. Auto claims are separated from homeowners claims; within auto claims, specialized units serve no-fault claims, property damage, minor personal injury, and major injuries. The Special Investigations Unit is separate still, to investigate possible fraud and to deal with a range of cases in which the company's liability can be contested. State Farm, for example, has units for Homeowner Fire, Homeowner Fire Large Loss, Homeowner Complex Casualty/Environmental, Auto Centralized Total Loss, Auto Complex Property Damage, Auto No-fault, Auto No-fault Litigation, Auto Uninsured/Underinsured Motorist, and more. And the claims units are increasingly centralized as well as specialized. In 2001, for example, Allstate began consolidating its offices that handle auto claims, with the result that about 40 percent of them are processed through three "Auto Express" centers, in Alabama, Indiana, and California.[4]

Because the adjuster has less discretion, she needs less training, and the training that is provided is focused on applying the system. According to a survey by *Claims*, more than a third of insurance companies provide new adjusters with two to four weeks of training, and one out of eight companies provide less than a week of training or no training at all.[5] Advanced training is provided for adjusters who specialize in more complex problems or larger cases, but always there is a point of view; an Allstate training seminar included basic information about fractures, provided by an orthopedist, and "red flags to watch for in a soft tissue injury" provided by a physical therapist.[6] The knowledge that is needed for processing claims is built into the system and therefore does not have to be held by the adjuster. Less of the adjuster's job is involved with developing facts relevant to a claim and more to receiving facts from others—the policyholder, medical providers, the policyholder's attorney, contractors, and body shops. Then the information is entered into the system, with accuracy and speed of data input essential.[7]

Adjusters have become less independent and more efficient from the company's point of view, with efficiency defined in terms of following the dictates of the claims systems.[8] A group of Allstate employees who brought age discrimination claims against the company complained that "CCPR [Allstate's McKinsey-led Claims Core Process Redesign] relegated them to nothing more than data input clerks." The employees reported that they could only determine liability in accident cases by adhering to a "liability matrix," they could only set reserves for claims after consulting a computer program, and they were limited in their ability to negotiate settlements by computer software and the CCPR manual.[9]

The diminution of the adjuster's role was exposed in a class action suit brought by adjusters for Farmers Insurance, in which they argued that Farmers improperly failed to pay them overtime to which they were entitled under California law.[10] Part of the evidence was Farmers' own characterization of their role in its *Regional Claims Manual,* which required that "questions of importance must be decided by the branch claims manager, and at a higher level by the regional claims manager" and only "routine and unimportant" tasks could be delegated to adjusters. The court further described the adjusters' role as clerks who processed information but did not make significant decisions, likening them to production workers in a factory: "On matters of relatively greater importance, they are engaged only in conveying information to their supervisors—again primarily a 'routine and unimportant' role. This characterization of their role in the company places the plaintiffs in the sphere of rank and file production workers."

The systems dictate process and results, and adjusters are evaluated on their adherence to the system. According to adjusters who testified in the Farmers overtime case, the company conducted quality assurance audits of adjusters' work to ensure that they complied with the procedures, what one described as "a do or die situation" with "no gray area in audits re: complying with policies and procedures—either you complied or you didn't. Deviation from stated objectives was cause for termination." Another adjuster, too much Barton Keyes and not enough Gilbert Huph, was "repeatedly and severely criticized for using discretion and judgment in evaluating and adjusting claims."[11]

The adjuster's new role, therefore, is less to be an experienced professional making an individual evaluation of each claim and more a clerk executing the demands of the system. From the company's and the adjuster's perspective this makes each claim much like every other claim, which generates efficient and predictable results. From the policyholder's or claimant's perspective, of course, that is not the point of the insurance policy; the point is prompt and fair processing of a unique loss.

The systems control the adjusters, and the systems are driven by information technology. An industry has developed to provide computerized systems to process the mass of information that adjusters deal with: estimate the cost of repairs to damaged property; check medical expenses; evaluate personal injury claims; store and report on a claimant's history; and do everything else a claims department needs to do. Insurance companies can choose among Claims Desktop, ClaimsOffice Suite, ClaimSearch, ClaimDirector, Claims Outcome Advisor, ClaimIQ (including Medical InjuryIQ and LiabilityIQ), and eClaim Manager, among others. Or they can develop their own systems. At an estimated cost of $125 million, Allstate has developed Next Gen, which earned it a place among the top 100 innovative users of technology in *Information Week*'s awards for 2008. Allstate hired Mike Jackowski, formerly a consultant with McKinsey & Company competitor Accenture, as Allstate's vice president of claims technology services to lead the development of Next Gen.[12] Next Gen's technological efficiencies reduce claim adjustment expenses and apparently also reduce Allstate's payouts to its customers. "People seem to be happier with less money right away, than more money after a lot of hassle," according to insurance industry analyst Paul Newsome of A. G. Edwards, commenting on the implementation of Next Gen.[13]

Two of the most widely used information systems are Colossus, which is designed to put a dollar value on bodily injury claims from car accidents, and Xactimate, which estimates the cost of repairs to damaged homes and other property. The immodestly named Colossus takes information about a claimant's injury, symptoms, trauma, treatment, and impairment, churns the information through more than ten thousand decision rules, measures the results against financial parameters input by the insurance company, and places a monetary value on an injured person's claim. Its moniker may not be immodest after all, because adjusters are often bound by the program's output; reportedly they can offer no more in settlement than Colossus allows, and they are evaluated on their ability to impose the program's dictates on claimants. Xactimate's name expresses similar hubris; it is software for estimating the extent of a loss and the cost of repairs that presumes to be exact. A property loss adjuster takes his Xactimate-loaded laptop and measures, records, and lists information about the damaged property, and the program produces a dollar amount that will be the basis of the insurance company's payment of a claim.

If Colossus was colossal and Xactimate exact, they would benefit insurance companies and claimants alike. Unfortunately, like HAL in *2001: A Space Odyssey* or other computers run amok in science-fiction movies, they can aspire to perfection free of human intervention but not attain it. Each permits considerable error by adjusters and each is subject to manipulation by insurance companies. Like other elements of the systematic approach to claims processing, they may favor efficiency and profits at the expense of accuracy and fairness. (There is more on Colossus in Chapter 7 and Xactimate in Chapter 8.)

Creating a new approach to claim processing and payment, with new structures and computer systems, is not enough unless it is implemented by front-line claim adjusters on a day-to-day-basis. In addition to training adjusters to conform to the system and putting them in front of computers that control much of their work, two principles are fundamental to this transformed claims process. First, as McKinsey & Company stated succinctly at a 1994 Claims Management Conference, "We get what we measure." Second, people respond to incentives. The principles are so basic that McKinsey's first presentation to Allstate management on September 28, 1992, emphasized the importance of measuring performance according to the company's objectives: "Measurement systems that track claim performance in economic terms are critical to successful implementation."

For a long time the primary measurements of adjuster performance were "pendings" (the number of claims an adjuster processed and the speed with which he did so) and expenses (the costs of processing claims). McKinsey recommended that it was more important to measure the parts of an adjuster's performance that contributed directly to increased profits. For auto personal injury claims, the principal measures were the proportion of claims closed without payment to the policyholder and the average cost of payments made. And that approach spread. The first nationwide study of claim vice presidents of insurance companies and adjusting firms, conducted in 2001 by trade groups and the Computer Sciences Corporation (CSC), found fewer than half of the companies still measured average time to close a claim, and the number one measure of costs was severity—the average paid per claim, measured by 85 percent of the firms.[14]

The point of measurement, of course, is not to measure but to use the results to advance the companies' objectives. Part of the redesign of the claims process was to use the new measurements to direct employees' behavior toward the corporate goal of increased profitability. As McKinsey stated, part of the new game plan was "mandatory standards and performance expectations." Each of the companies that adopted the new game plan set new expectations for employees and often used those expectations as a basis for incentives, positive and negative, in promotion, pay, and other rewards.

For actuaries, underwriters, managers, and other insurance company employees, measures that align the employees' incentives with company goals, including the goal of profitability, are perfectly appropriate. Not so for adjusters. The adjuster's job is to honor the company's promise to pay what is owed, no more but no less. Whether and how much an adjuster pays in a particular case or all cases should depend only on how much the company owes on the claims. If the adjuster's pay is tied to reducing severity, or cases closed without payment, the company has given the adjuster an incentive to violate accepted practices and break the promise the company made to its policyholders. As a survey of insurance personnel by ethics expert Peter Kensicki concluded, "[I]f the standard being established improves service to a stakeholder, it is ethically based. If it creates benefit for the employer at the expense of the rightful amount due a claimant, it is not."[15] Indeed, this standard is so fundamental that it is the law. A California statute, for example, prohibits insurance companies from paying adjusters any part of their compensation based on the amount for which they settle claims.[16]

Nevertheless, as one of Kensicki's respondents stated, "The practice of performance-based compensating is growing and we are hearing 'everybody's doing it' as a defense."[17] The redesign of measurement and incentives was central to McKinsey's Claims Core Process Redesign at Allstate. McKinsey emphasized the switch away from an old focus on how efficient adjusters were in moving claims along, and how much it cost them to do so, toward one more aligned with the new objectives of CCPR: "Current process[es] are incenting and reinforcing behavior that does not reward shareholders." "Currently we measure expenses and pending. The new measurement approach will be based on the processes and activities required to achieve the desired outcomes."

Merely measuring was not enough. Goals had to be set and behavior had to be rewarded and punished. McKinsey set goals that it described as "aggressive." One goal for minor impact auto claims with soft tissue injuries, to be met in the first year of CCPR and maintained thereafter, was that the "[a]verage claim settlement is equal to the amount established through the evaluation process." In other words, once Colossus or another system determined what the company was willing to pay for a claim, the adjuster's job was to make sure that the claimant got that amount and no more. To maintain an average settlement equal to the evaluated amount, for every dollar that one policyholder received above that amount adjusters had to extract a dollar from another policyholder's settlement.

Adjusters at Allstate received an evaluation by their supervisors—a performance development summary, or PDS—twice a year, and the supervisor would review the results with the adjuster. At these meetings supervisors always discussed goals that reflected the amounts of the claims paid, including the percent paid at the Colossus evaluated amount.

Adjusters were issued company "Big Blue" (presumably Allstate blue) Citibank credit cards to use for work-related expenses such as travel to attend training sessions away from their offices. Because the cards were not for everyday expenses, prior authorization was needed to use them. But the prior authorization would sometimes be used to give employees a bonus for meeting performance goals, including reducing claims payouts. Bonuses were small but frequent, consistent with an employee relations approach that frequent reinforcement is more important than the scale of the reward and, just as important, to avoid tax liability; the Recognition Program brochure advised that "[n]on-cash gifts or awards given on an occasional basis to employees which do not exceed $100 are not taxable."[18] One employee's voucher showed bonuses including $20 for a successful (that is, low) rate of claims in which the insured was represented by an attorney, $5 for promptly contacting insureds, and $50 in other bonuses (accompanied by chintzy desktop publishing certificates with sentiments such as "Congratulations! For your achievement in 3 day contact [of claimants] you may charge $5 on your Allstate Credit Card)."

State Farm took a different approach, generating measurements that affected claims payouts but avoiding documents that would demonstrate how they were used to put pressure on individual adjusters. Its official policy, as stated at a 1995 conference, was "numbers are not developed below division level" and "can't develop quality shortfall below 100 files so can't really take it down to claim rep level."[19] But that policy may have been a reaction to 1991 litigation in Alaska that exposed the details of its pay-for-performance process. Managers were warned not to state specific numerical goals on performance review documents and instead to discuss the numerical goals with adjusters during their quarterly and annual meetings. The unrecorded goals included some for severity, such as, according to former senior adjuster Grace Hess, the average amount paid on claims.[20] The leader of a training session for adjusters emphasized the point of the meetings: "The goal is to make sure Claim Reps leave the sessions understanding there will be consequences for the appropriateness of their Quality Claims Resolution. Consequences include positive and negative ones. They have never been evaluated in this manner before."[21]

Farmers Insurance had one of the most elaborate programs—actually, a series of measurement and incentive programs implemented over time—and one that has been the best documented in subsequent litigation. In 1992 Farmers inaugurated its Partners in Progress program, through which, employees were told, "you and your supervisor will set performance expectations tied to results that help meet the company's business needs." The Partners in Progress manual explained that the adjuster and supervisor would discuss the most important components of the adjuster's job and the weight to be accorded to each component, on a scale of "crucial, important, expected, and risk opportunity." Then, "[y]ou can expect that your individual performance ratings will play a key role in determining your pay level each year."

Individual performance review forms show how this worked in operation. One employee's "Critical" objectives included "Maintain indemnity costs at inflationary levels"; that is, don't pay out more in claims than you paid out last year, accounting for inflation. The measures were specific, showing that employee's figures for the year and the change from the previous year: "Average costs available are BI [bodily injury auto claims] $6,875 (114%), Collision $4,425 (+109%), Comprehensive $1,688 (-1.5%), PD [property damage] $1,092 (-29%) compared to last year's figures." A manager from Tucson was lauded for cutting payouts and reducing the number of claims in which claimants were represented by a lawyer: "Comparing overall costs as of 2nd Quarter 1995 vs. 1996, Tucson BCO has succeeded in decreasing our total indemnity costs by 28% in 1996. . . . This is an excellent result! . . . Attorney penetration for 2nd Quarter 1996 was 49.7% [a decrease]. These represent excellent accomplishments in light of our 'low impact' program."

Following the Northridge earthquake in 1994, Farmers' Bring Back a Billion program, discussed in Chapter 3, added urgency to measurement and adjuster incentives. William R. Hurst, a Farmers adjuster, testified that adjusters were told to "deny everything you can." Adjusters were "routinely evaluated based on the average amount we paid out in claims. . . . I was specifically told by my superior that even a low-level office adjuster, who was much, much less experienced than I, was doing a better job than I was, simply because his 'average amount paid per claim' statistics were lower than mine. I pointed out that I had much more major claims assigned to me than did this office adjuster, but this seemed to make no difference to my supervisor."[22]

In 1998 Farmers shifted again, naming its revised incentive program Quest for Gold. Initially it created bonus pools of cash and extra vacation days for offices that furthered the company's goals. The goals included normal business measures such as growth in premiums, but there was only one goal to which adjusters could contribute: "Personal lines combined ratio—Goal 98.54%." The combined ratio compares the amount paid out in claims plus the company's expenses to the premiums it takes in, and adjusters could contribute in only two ways. They could cut costs, say, by using fewer paper clips and making fewer copies, or by cutting what they paid out to Farmers' policyholders and other injured parties.

In its next iteration the focus on combined ratio became even more clear. In a memo to all company employees on April 11, 2001,

Farmers' top executives announced a new plan under which half of the company's cash profit sharing "will be tied to achievement of company-wide combined ratio results" and "Farmers Group employees will have their award tied to achievement of local combined ratio goals." John Lynch, executive vice president of Market Management, drove the point home:

> The number one priority, the number one goal, the number one objective for the year 2001 was to fix our combined ratio. We recognized that it would take the hard work of absolutely every member of the Farmers organization: claims, underwriting, policy processing, market management, agents, district managers, everybody that's in a leadership role in the Farmers organization.
>
> And I think there's no better way to reward people than to align what's really important for them, what are the things they really need to get done, what are the goals, what are the actions, what are the accomplishments?
>
> And you tie that together with compensation, and all of a sudden, you've got very solid alignment between our business goals, our actions, our accomplishments, and our compensation. So for 2002, we will be tying this kind of perhaps over simplistic, but very focused approach to your compensation.

The next year Michael L. Kent, vice president of human resources, again exhorted all the troops: "And now that 2001 is over, let's strive to do even better in 2002! *What's Important Now?* It can be summed up in two words: Combined Ratio. . . . Every Farmers employee has a stake in our results. Ask yourself, 'Where will my contribution be?'"

Farmers denied that these company goals, vigorously asserted over and over again by executives and addressed to all employees, would affect the performance reviews of individual employees. In a 2003 hearing, for example, Farmers claim manager for the Plains States region, James Keefe, was examined by leading bad faith lawyer James Abourezk. Keefe testified that there were no financial goals for individual claim representatives and, in Nixonian echoes, "it would be wrong" to have financial goals or expected results. When shown performance review documents that listed such goals, Keefe tried to explain: "Well, they're expected results. They're not necessarily goals. They're targets or they're—they can be—they can be a number of things. Goals may or may not be one of them."

The North Dakota Insurance Department examined Farmers's practices and reached a different and more definitive conclusion than Keefe. In 2004 it began a three-year investigation of Farmers's incentive practices, and in June 2007 it issued the report of its market conduct examination. The department had examined personnel files from the Bismarck office, over five thousand pages of documents produced in civil litigation against Farmers, and other affidavits, documents, videos, and company e-mails and memos. It had reviewed the company's Bring Back a Billion and Quest for Gold programs, among others. The report reached several conclusions.

> As early as 1990 and before, the management of Farmers Insurance Exchange set various goals for claims handlers and other employees in an effort to increase company profits and thereby grow company surplus.
>
> Employees were informed that their individual performance ratings would play a key role in determining their pay level each year.
>
> Many of the performance goals for individual claims employees were appropriate. However, goals that were arbitrary and unfair to policyholders and claimants were also identified. . . .
>
> The Bismarck branch claims office's PP&Rs [Performance Planning and Review forms] included unfair and arbitrary goals (1) to maintain an average cost claim, allowing for inflationary amounts, at the previous year's level or below, (2) to settle bodily injury claims within a predetermined range and maintain average medical payment amounts, . . . (4) to increase the number of fraud referrals, . . . (6) to close a set percentage of claims without payment, (7) to estimate the condition of damaged vehicles at or below the national average to minimize indemnity payments. . . . These goals were set

> without regard to the nature or merits of the individual claims that might be handled by the individual claims settlement personnel.

Farmers did not agree with the department's conclusions and argued that the company's leadership had changed in 2002, resulting in "an enhanced awareness among claims handling staff of the need to pay what is owed on a claim in a timely manner and a clear understanding of its incentive programs." Despite its disagreement, Farmers paid a fine of $750,000 and promised to "eliminate incentive plans that utilize goals relating to settling claims within certain ranges" and to "emphasize the importance of evaluating each claim on its own merit and to neither underpay or overpay claims."

The North Dakota regulator's findings were confirmed in litigation brought by Farmers adjusters seeking to be compensated for overtime. Federal judge Robert E. Jones found in 2004 that Farmers had "a settlement philosophy of 'we pay what we owe, nothing more, nothing less,'" and it conducted studies of closed claims "to ensure that CRs [claims representatives] are following best practices." But he also found that Farmers had "zero tolerance for overpayment" of claims, with apparently a greater tolerance for underpayment. The claims studies focused on "lost economic opportunity" to the company in failing to pay as little as possible on a claim. Farmers set goals for "leakage" or overpayment of 2 percent for auto property damage and liability, and slightly more than 2 percent for property claims; the goals were to overpay by no more than 2 percent, certainly not to overpay by no less than 2 percent.[23]

When policyholders or victims cannot be persuaded or coerced to take what the insurance company offers, it gears up to defend itself in litigation. The litigation may arise early and regularly, as in the strategy of denying minor impact, soft tissue claims, and forcing claimants to sue, or it may come only at the end of a more protracted period of investigation and negotiation over the value of a claim. The defense may be conducted by staff lawyers or by outside law firms. But just as war is too important to be left to the generals, for a systematic claim process litigation is too important to be left to the lawyers. Like adjusters, they need to be managed in order to maximize the insurance company's profits.

Just as the first step in redesigning the claim process focused on costs, at an early stage insurance companies recognized that they could increase profits by spending less on lawyers. In the late 1980s McKinsey analyzed two thousand claims at St. Paul Fire & Marine and concluded that litigation management, including auditing the bills submitted by outside lawyers, cut costs by 20 percent, or $50 million.[24] The conclusion was apparent. Lawyers retained by insurance companies are just another part of the claim-processing system, and they are, for the companies, just another outside vendor of services, like the companies that furnish janitorial services or office supplies. As such they should be subject to cost control systems, mostly put into place as part of the redesign of claim processing.

Cost control begins even before the lawyer is retained. Up until the 1990s outside lawyers were most often hired by insurance companies' local claims offices, often based on personal relationships between adjusters and lawyers. Hourly rates were negotiated based on the local market for legal services and the level of experience and expertise of the lawyers.[25]

Today that is seldom if ever the case. Allstate again was an innovator, although it took much criticism for one innovation in lawyer hiring. Beginning in 1999, it began to use an Internet-based bidding system for many routine cases. Outside law firms filled out a prequalification questionnaire indicating what types of cases they can handle and at what price. Allstate described anonymous cases on a Web site, and law firms bid for the cases on a modified flat-fee basis.[26]

Insurance companies also control legal costs by auditing law firm bills, often by using outside auditing agencies or, increasingly, auditing software. The auditing imperative was spurred in part by some high-profile cases, including one in 1996 in which a Miami Beach attorney was convicted of submitting $5 million in false bills to Lloyd's. The response was dramatic. As Atlanta lawyer Terence Sullivan described the situation, "These auditing companies come in with a stereotype—all lawyers cheat." Bills are audited to ensure that they conform to the rules established by the insurance company, and they are often reduced as excessive. Work must be done by the least expensive person qualified to do it, and multiple attorneys working on the same matter are closely scrutinized. Excessive photocopying is discouraged. Even meeting to discuss a case with colleagues may not be paid for.[27]

Traditionally defense lawyers would be paid on an hourly basis. Now it is much more common for small cases to be paid a flat fee, or a flat fee up to the point of trial; a typical flat fee is $2,500 to $3,000, much less than the lawyer would receive if paid on an hourly basis. Some companies in effect franchise their legal work, selecting one firm to do all cases of a certain kind in a city or area and paying a reduced hourly rate that includes all costs.[28]

Because the processing of litigation has become routine, insurance companies now require firms to submit bills using complex software that then organizes, audits, and reports on the company's legal costs. The American Bar Association's Litigation Section and the American Corporate Counsel Association, with the participation of major law firms and corporate purchasers of law firm services, have aided the process by developing the Uniform Task-Based Management System (UTBMS) litigation task code set that contains a digital code listing all the elements of all the tasks and activities associated with litigation. The Defense Research Institute (DRI) adopted Recommended Case-handling Guidelines. Together the two provide a uniform means for law firms to bill and insurance companies to evaluate their bills. CounselLink is advertised as enabling companies to "control your legal costs through enhanced billing compliance and greater understanding of your legal spending." Using natural language analysis instead of UTMBS codes, it "catches discrepancies to your billing guidelines and helps you identify greater cost saving opportunities."

All of this might have an inside-baseball quality to it; indeed, keeping legal costs down helps keeps premiums down. But there are two problems. First, in cases in which the insurance company hires an attorney to defend a policyholder in litigation arising out of an accident, the constraints imposed on the attorney may impinge the duties he owes to the policyholder. Second, it demonstrates how litigation management has taken hold to increase company profits at the expense of the policyholder, just like other elements of the claim process.

Litigation management was part of McKinsey's early strategy for Allstate, and McKinsey made clear that the goal of defending a claim is not necessarily to win the particular case but to maximize the company's profits. An August 8, 1994, briefing was entitled "Redesigning the Litigation Management Process to Enhance Allstate's Competitive Position." The value of "[e]nhanced organizational consistency and execution" in litigation management was predicted to be between $275 million and $400 million after expenses. "A key part of this process will be development of market-wide strategies to strengthen negotiation and litigation approaches. These strategies will include significantly higher levels of litigation to establish more consistent values." Allstate would contest more cases to set the bar lower for all claimants. For example, as discussed in Chapter 6, playing hardball with minor impact, soft tissue claims would produce "higher levels of litigation" over small claims. Although this strategy costs more in the short run—spending ten thousand dollars to fight a two-thousand-dollar claim is not unusual—in the long run it would increase profits, as claimants would be forced to take unfairly low offers because they knew that the expense of suing would exceed the reward.

Under this approach to litigation management, the attorney to whom the litigation is referred is little more than a superadjuster, the next step in the process of claim resolution. The amount for which the attorney is authorized to settle the case is equal to the amount of the last offer the company adjuster made, even if that amount is lower than the Colossus Evaluated Amount (EA) at which the company might otherwise be willing to settle. The financial effects of this consistent strategy were measured in early tests; when the adjuster sets the parameters for settlement, and those are followed when the case goes to the attorney, there was on average $4,100 less deviation from the EA than before the litigation management measures were instituted.

Cases that could not be resolved by the adjuster were referred to as DOLF, for defense of litigated files. These cases had been investigated, evaluated, and negotiated already by the adjuster without a conclusion; the referral is only necessary because "defense counsel provides the litigation expertise," according to McKinsey. The attorney's job, therefore, required "consistently achieving evaluated amount, impacting market value to reduce loss payout, [and] maintaining tight cost control." Performing that job well would result in "more trials," putting more policyholders and accident victims to the aggravation and expense of litigation to receive what they were owed.

To carry out a consistent strategy in each case, the insurance company sets a plan, and in many cases supervises the course of the litigation. Companies differ, and classes of cases differ. In MIST cases, for example, the attorney may follow guidelines set up by the company but will not require much hands-on supervision. In larger cases, the adjuster or "Litigation Consultant," may be more intimately involved in tactical decisions. Allstate's "Legal Matter Management and Billing Guidelines," for example, provided: "All work billed must conform to a Litigation Plan. The Plan will be jointly developed at the commencement of a matter, and revised and updated as appropriate. It should detail specific procedures to prepare the matter for trial or resolution. The Plan will establish objectives, designate specific activities related to these objectives and identify who will perform these procedures." Within the context of the litigation plan, specific advance approval was required for many of the normal steps in litigation, including preparing discovery or other motions, undertaking any major research project, retaining expert witnesses, preparing for trial, and taking an appeal.

Other companies followed similar protocols. Progressive's Claims Standards dictate that "each Business Unit must establish or adopt Defense Attorney Standards applicable to all defense work performed in its jurisdiction, . . . Progressive must be consulted before a motion or pleading (other than a standard answer) is filed, [and] claims management should be involved in all trial decisions."

Lawyers sometimes express frustration or resignation at the degree of control exercised by insurance companies. One defense lawyer interviewed by Professor Herbert Kritzer bemoaned the changes in insurance defense practice over the last decade:

> Oh man . . . much more oversight by the insurance companies. Much more concern with the bottom line. Much more control, or

> attempt to control the case, by the insurance companies, rather than to rely on my judgment. I feel like I'm being second-guessed a lot more. And it's getting to the point where it's almost an adversarial relationship. Adversarial isn't the right word. But it's like the companies who are hiring us to do the best job for their insureds don't trust us enough to do the best job. They have to second-guess what we're doing.[29]

Defense lawyers interviewed by Kritzer reported that the companies' control often is without legal foundation, or is ethically questionable. One company required its lawyer to refuse to turn over materials that it claimed was privileged, even though there was "no doubt" the plaintiff's lawyer could successfully bring a motion to compel the materials' production. Another company insisted that a claimant appear in person at an arbitration hearing rather than by telephone, even though (perhaps because) it would cost the claimant more to travel from his out-of-state home than the case was worth. A third company had made "a business decision" to fight no-fault cases even though it had no valid defense, to deter future claimants.

With this, the story of the new systematic claim process comes full circle. Claim adjusters once exercised considerable discretion in determining how much a claimant was fairly owed. Attorneys exercised considerable independent professional judgment about whether and how litigation should be conducted. Increasingly, they have become agents of a system of claim processing that aims to increase company profits rather than serve policyholders. The system affects anyone who files a claim under an auto or homeowners policy.

6

Lawyers, Claimants, and Into the MIST: Segmenting Automobile Claims

AUTO INSURANCE IS the largest component of noncommercial property/casualty insurance. Americans spend $160 billion a year for auto insurance, about one third of all property/casualty premiums and three times the amount spent for homeowners insurance. Claims under auto policies are proportionally larger as well; insurance companies pay $90 billion annually under them. As the largest area of personal lines insurance, it presents the largest opportunity for using a delay, deny, defend strategy to increase company profits. In the redesign of the claim process companies have recognized that profits can be increased by treating different types of claims differently, what the industry calls "segmentation."

Segmentation turns the long-standing approach to claim handling on its head. Under the traditional approach, each claim was different but all claims were alike. Although the facts of each accident differed—how the accident occurred, what injuries the claimant suffered, and, in cases in which liability was at issue, who was at fault and to what degree—the goal of the claim process was the same in every case: to fairly assess the individual facts of the claim and arrive at the dollar figure that compensated the claimant for her particular loss. With segmentation, each claim is not different and all claims are not alike. Claims are divided into categories, and all of the claims in a category are treated basically the same. But all claims are not treated alike, because the goal is not to honor the promise of indemnity based on the individual facts of the case but to treat cases in the different categories differently to increase company profits.

Segmentation was a basic principle of McKinsey's redesign of Allstate's claim process. In an early briefing, on January 14, 1993, McKinsey explained:

> Claims is not one homogenous portfolio where one winning formula can be applied across the board. A differentiated approach is required to capture the opportunity, and segmentation of claims into homogenous groups is required. Based on this, specific objectives, strategies, and actions can be tailored in separate claim processes for each segment.

A first division was between claimants who were represented by an attorney and claimants who were not. "Capturing the opportunity will require reducing the number of represented claimants and more aggressively managing the claims that do become represented," according to McKinsey. If a claimant comes in without an attorney, Allstate adjusters would make systematic efforts to make sure that he never gets one.

When a claimant has an attorney, two additional segments provide special opportunities to reduce payments. One is bodily injury and uninsured motorist/underinsured motorist (UM/UIM) coverage. Bodily injury claims are brought by someone injured by a policyholder in an accident. The insurance company is obligated under the policy to represent the policyholder and, even if the injured person sues the policyholder, the company is obligated to treat him fairly. UM/UIM claims are brought against the company by the policyholder after an accident in which the other driver is at fault but does not have enough insurance to pay all the policyholder's damages. The other segment is what McKinsey called "subjective injuries." These are the smaller cases, involving low-speed crashes that produce injuries other than broken bones or similar immediately apparent injuries, what have become universally known as MIST cases—minor impact, soft tissue.

McKinsey even quantified the benefit to Allstate's bottom line from segmenting claims and treating each one differently. After adding up how much payouts could be reduced in different segments, McKinsey estimated that Allstate's "opportunity" from "loss overpayment" was 15 percent of claims paid, with another 1 percent "opportunity" in reducing loss adjustment expenses, for a total of $550 million to $600 million.

In its initial attempt to segment auto claims in a hand-drawn chart for the January 14, 1993, briefing, McKinsey identified whether the claimant was represented by a lawyer as a key factor. In every segment in which the claimant was not initially represented, the stated objective is: "keep attorney out." That objective was supported by a number of studies McKinsey conducted that proved the obvious: Attorneys help injury victims recover higher amounts. One study of uninsured motorist claims concluded that represented policyholders recovered 90 percent more than those without lawyers. Another found that unrepresented MIST claimants recovered an average of $3,464 and MIST claimants represented by an attorney recovered $7,450. In general, represented claimants recovered two to five times as much as those without the aid of a lawyer. McKinsey's solution was obvious: "Focus on reducing the need for attorney representation."

One way to reduce the need for attorney representation, of course, is to raise the amounts paid to unrepresented claimants to the fair value levels paid to those who are represented. But that approach would decrease company profits. Instead, insurers have adopted a variety of techniques to prevent their policyholders and other claimants from consulting a lawyer and to take the lower amounts the company offers.

One method is to avoid mentioning the advantages of hiring a lawyer. Allstate's Web site, for example, outlines the stages a claim goes through. The steps are: "File your claim, gather the facts, resolve, and moving forward." Nowhere is the need or desirability of hiring an attorney mentioned. Instead, Allstate pledges: "If someone was hurt, we will handle the claim fairly and promptly." State Farm's Web site is similar, promising: "The auto claims process made simple"—which is made simpler still by no mention of an attorney.

The Allstate Claims Manual outlined a more developed strategy. The adjuster should "establish a trust-based relationship through extremely rapid initial contact to educate the claimants about Allstate's approach to fair claim settlement, anticipation and resolution of a broad range of claimant needs in a genuine and empathetic manner, [and] rapid liability investigation and amicable resolution of property damage issues to maintain rapport," among other steps.

Getting in touch with claimants early, being empathetic, maintaining contact, and resolving some issues sound like elements of good customer service, and they are. But they also benefit a company's bottom line because they keep claimants from hiring a lawyer, which would enable them to recover more of the benefits they are entitled to from the company. The emphasis on "amicable resolution of property damage" is an attempt to get the claimant to focus on the damage to the car, even in cases in which there is personal injury with the associated medical expenses and noneconomic loss, which are likely to far exceed the amount of property damage. If the property damages issues are handled quickly and to the claimant's satisfaction, it makes the claimant believe that the company is interested in a fair and favorable resolution, which means the company may be able to pay less on the larger personal injury damages. (Allstate's Web site pursues the tactic by describing the "Resolve" stage as focused entirely on repair of the car.)

An even more important tactic is to emphasize and even misstate the cost of hiring an attorney. This element was explained in the Claims Manual's "Recommended Attorney Economics Script": "Quite often our customers ask if an attorney is necessary to settle a claim. Some people choose to hire an attorney, but we would really like the opportunity to work directly with you to settle the claim. Attorneys commonly take between 25-40% of the total settlement you receive from an insurance company plus the expenses incurred. If you settle directly with Allstate, however, the total amount of the settlement is yours. At any time in the process you may choose to hire an attorney. I would, however, like to make an offer to you first. This way, should you go to an attorney, you would be able to negotiate with the attorney so his/her fees would only apply to amounts over my offer to you."

This is a clever tactic. The script advises the adjuster to tell the claimant that the attorney will take 25 to 40 percent of whatever the claimant receives from the insurance company. The adjuster is not advised to tell the claimant that the attorney will not just take part of the recovery but will earn it, because claimants who are represented by an attorney receive two to five times more money from the company. The advantage of having Allstate make an offer with the suggestion that the claimant negotiate for an attorney fee only above that offer is that it makes it practically impossible for the claimant to get a lawyer, an example of McKinsey's suggestion that Allstate "exploit the economics of the practice of law." Personal injury lawyers base their practice on contingency fees, under which they get a portion of the recovery but receive nothing if they are not successful. Few if any lawyers would agree to a smaller and uncertain fee as Allstate suggested, particularly before they have a chance to investigate the case. The result is that the claimant will end up without a lawyer and Allstate will have the advantage in settlement.

Appearing empathetic and building trust can deceive someone injured in an accident into thinking that the defendant's insurance company really has their interests at heart. Priscilla Young was eighty-four years old at the time she was rear-ended in Hilo, Hawaii, by a car operated by Daryl Fujimoto, who admitted he had fallen asleep and caused the crash.[1] Young's car was demolished and she suffered injuries to her neck, ribs, knee, and spine. Allstate's adjuster contacted her the same day and promised to provide "quality service" and treat her fairly so she would not need an attorney. A letter from Allstate followed reaffirming the quality service pledge and, in addition to reminding Young that "You're in Good Hands with Allstate," explicitly promising "If you qualify, *we will* make an appropriate offer of compensation for any injuries you may have suffered." (The italics were in the original letter.)

Allstate didn't live up to its promises. Young had over $6,000 in medical expenses alone, but Allstate only offered her $5,000, then $5,300, to settle her claim. When she finally sued and the case went to arbitration, the arbitrator recommended she be awarded $7,689 in medical expenses and $37,000 in additional damages for the pain, depression, and loss of normal activities she suffered, but Allstate still refused to raise its offer.

Young offered to settle for $25,000, but Allstate refused again. A jury agreed with Young that "appropriate" compensation was more than Allstate had offered and awarded her $198,971 on her claim.

In Janet Jones's case, Allstate's "quality service" went further, with the Allstate adjuster acting as a claimant's lawyer and doing a bad job of it.[2] Jeremy France, an Allstate policyholder, ran a stop sign and broadsided Jones's Plymouth Voyager minivan. Jones suffered severe injuries to her face, head, and right eye, requiring multiple surgeries to insert plates into her face and head and causing medical expenses of $75,000. Part of the injuries may have resulted from Jones being thrown out of her seat; apparently her seat belt would not lock into the floor mount, and the release button was pulled up by force and would not reset.

Christy Klein, an Allstate claims adjuster, sent Jones a letter stating Allstate's Quality Service Pledge, which promised "quality service to anyone who has been involved in an accident with one of our policyholders." Over the next few months Klein spoke often to Janet Jones and her husband Terry, and Klein helped Jones obtain payment from Farmers, her own insurance company. Three months after the accident, Klein sent Jones a letter, a check for $25,000, and a release form; if Jones and her husband signed the release, they would be giving up all claims they had, including claims against France and claims that they might have against Chrysler for a defective seat belt. The Washington Supreme Court held that in advising Jones to sign the release, Klein was in effect acting as their lawyer. Moreover, she "intentionally developed a trusting relationship with the Joneses . . . Klein led the Joneses to believe that she had their best interests in mind." The court knew that was not true because of Allstate's program to reduce attorney representation as part of its claims process redesign. The trial court had reviewed the documents revealing McKinsey's plan to redesign Allstate's claims practices, although, consistent with Allstate's years-long attempt to conceal the plan, the documents were then sealed from public view. Part of the program revealed in the documents was "a goal of reducing attorney involvement to achieve a higher rate of return on settlement claims."

Janet Jones and Priscilla Young were not Allstate policyholders; they were trying to get money for their injuries from Allstate and its policyholders, Jeremy France and Daryl Fujimoto. At first glance, maybe it's not so bad that Allstate was tough with them, because the insurance company was representing both itself and the policyholder in resisting the claim. If cases like these go to court, the victim will sue the policyholder and the insurance company will defend. Therefore, it seems, the insurance company should owe nothing to the victim and should be entitled to resist the claim mightily. The problem with Allstate's Quality Service Pledge in cases like those of Jones and Young, under this view, was not that Allstate didn't have their interests at heart but that it deceived them into thinking that it did.

In fact, both the law and accepted claims practices require that insurance companies act fairly and responsibly when dealing with accident victims who are third-party claimants (the policyholder and the company are the first and second party). The logic is simple. The policyholder has a lot to lose if the company takes an unreasonable stance in denying a claim. In Young's case, Daryl Fujimoto, the driver who injured her, had a policy with Allstate that would pay up to $25,000 if he caused an accident. Even though she could (and would) get more at trial, Young offered to settle the case for the $25,000 policy limit. The lawyer Allstate hired to defend Fujimoto even recommended that Allstate take the deal, but the company refused. Eventually Young won $198,971 at trial. At that point, if there was no requirement that Allstate act fairly in trying to settle the case, Allstate could pay its $25,000 and walk away, leaving its policyholder Fujimoto on the hook for the additional $173,971. Under the terms of the insurance policy, the company provides the lawyer and controls the defense in the suit against its policyholder, and if it is free to deny and defend it gets to gamble with the policyholder's money.

Moreover, the policyholder and the company are not the only ones interested in resolving a claim brought by a third party. The injured victim has something at stake, obviously, and so does society at large, especially in auto cases. In a nation with 255 million registered cars and trucks and 205 million licensed drivers, there will be lots of crashes and lots of injuries; more than one quarter of the deaths from injuries each year are attributable to traffic accidents. As a society, we want to make sure that accident victims have at least a minimum degree of security that they will be compensated for their injuries. For traffic accidents, we use the system of private insurance to provide that security. Forty-seven of the fifty states require drivers to carry liability insurance so that they can compensate the injured victims of accidents that they cause. (The other states at least require that drivers be able to demonstrate they are financially responsible if they are in an accident.) But requiring insurance is not enough. Insurance also has to work, and that is up to the insurance company, not the insured driver.

The law and claims handling standards require companies to act fairly toward claimants in two ways. First, some rules speak directly about a company's obligation to third parties. The National Association of Insurance Commissioners' model statute on claims handling, for example, prohibits behavior that hurts third parties even if it does not affect the policyholder. For example, companies are prohibited from misrepresenting facts or information about insurance coverage and from "not attempting in good faith to effectuate prompt, fair and equitable settlement of claims submitted in which liability has become reasonably clear."

Second, the company has a duty toward its policyholder that requires it to act responsibly in attempting to settle a case, and that duty indirectly benefits the third-party claimant. Under the terms of the insurance policy the company controls the settlement negotiations with the claimant. If the company fails to attempt to settle in good faith, it is liable for the losses the policyholder suffers even if they are in excess of the limits of the policy, and sometimes for punitive damages as well. This obviously benefits the claimant in the many cases in which the policyholder will be unable to satisfy a judgment against him except from the insurance policy. The result is that when the company fails to meet its obligations there is a second lawsuit after the initial claim is resolved, in which the policyholder sues the company. As a practical matter, this suit is often prosecuted in cooperation with the third-party claimant, who is the one most interested in getting the insurance company to pay the full amount of the judgment against its policyholder.

Numerous cases show the different ways that companies violate their obligation to policyholders and accident victims in third-party cases. In Priscilla Young's case, it was simple stonewalling. Allstate knew that its policyholder was at fault in causing the accident (he admitted falling asleep at the wheel) and the claimant, Young, was an eighty-four-year-old woman with serious injuries and substantial medical bills. Nevertheless, it refused to even offer to compensate her for her medical bills, rejected an arbitrator's recommendation, and forced the case to trial, where it and its policyholder predictably lost. At the other end of the strategic spectrum from stonewalling is hardball litigation. In a Tennessee case, Allstate was alleged to have originally hired a "highly competent and effective Memphis attorney" to defend an auto accident claim against its policyholder and then, after discovery in the case was substantially complete, to have fired this attorney and hired another firm instead.[3] The new firm started discovery all over, as the plaintiff alleged, to "weaken [her] resolve to pursue the suit to the extent that she [would] abandon it." The tactics included requiring the plaintiff and her attorney to answer 237 written interrogatories, even though most of the information asked for had already been disclosed, subjecting her to an eight-hour deposition asking about matters both trivial (every illness she had ever had) and personal (whether she had been sleeping with the defendant), and submitting more than seventy subpoenas to her doctors, employer, auto repair shop, former insurance companies, and every hospital in the Memphis area.

One of the largest and surely the most controversial segment of auto claims in which denial and aggressive defense are the keys to increasing profits is MIST claims. While some accidents cause catastrophic injuries like those suffered by Janet Jones, there are many more crashes at low speeds, in which the damage to the vehicle is small and the victim's injuries involve something other than broken bones, large lacerations, or similarly obvious harm.

MIST injuries or connective tissue injuries or musculoligamentous injuries or whiplash injuries—there is no neutral term—have a long and colorful history, both as a medical disorder and as an insurance issue.[4] Their ancestor was "railway spine," a syndrome first diagnosed in the 1860s. Charles Dickens reported his own, typical experience following a train crash in Kent, England. Immediately after the crash he was "shaken" and his hand "unsteady," but days later his ailment grew worse, not better. "I am curiously weak . . . I begin to feel it more in my head. I sleep and eat well, but I write half a dozen notes, and turn faint and sick." Doctors, lawyers, and railroad executives debated whether railway spine was a physical disorder, a psychosomatic response, or simply "legalized depredations on the treasuries of railway corporations, and . . . a nice harvest to shyster lawyers and conscienceless physicians."

Whiplash was identified and first named in the 1920s to describe injuries to airplane pilots and then to victims of traffic accidents. For decades there was a lack of scientific agreement on how the injuries occurred; did an impact cause the head to snap back then forward, or forward then back? (Today the National Institute of Neurological Disorders and Stroke of the National Institutes of Health reflects the consensus that it is the former.) The injury is an odd one and often difficult to diagnose; the National Institute's summary of the disorder echoes Dickens's description of his experience, noting that symptoms may occur immediately or may be delayed for several days after the accident. The symptoms are diffuse and variable, potentially including a dizzying array of "neck stiffness, injuries to the muscles and ligaments (myofascial injuries), headache, dizziness, abnormal sensations such as burning or prickling (paresthesias), shoulder or back pain . . . memory loss, concentration impairment, nervousness/irritability, sleep disturbances, fatigue, or depression."[5] And whiplash, focused on the neck and back, is only one of the different kinds of soft tissue injuries that can result from an accident; injuries to extremities and joints are common, too. Even naming the disorder is controversial, and not only the use of "whiplash" as a term of disapprobation suggesting fakery. Social scientists have found that "soft tissue" injury, the term adopted by the insurance industry, resonates with the public as much less severe than the more medical-sounding "connective tissue" injury, which sounds less serious (or perhaps less understandable) than the generic "neck injury."[6]

Claims involving soft tissue injuries have long been a target of the insurance industry. The Defense Research Institute (DRI), the self-described "voice of the defense bar," mounted the attack in its 1960 publication of *The Revolt Against "Whiplash,"* a collection of scientific articles discounting the likelihood or significance of such injuries and condemnatory articles by defense lawyers and insurance executives. DRI distributed the volume to more than 11,000 judges, public officials, and lawyers, and followed up four years later with a successor volume, *The Continuing Revolt Against "Whiplash."* In the defense view, whiplash was not a physical response to crashes but either a psychological response as a result of the publicity about such injuries—"accident victim syndrome" was one name—or was outright fraud: "compensationitis," which, as was said, was a pain in the neck that lasted until litigation had ended. Either way, part of the remedy was to drive the term out of the language or make its association purely negative; DRI leaders suggested that the word "whiplash" should never be used without scare quotes, and defense lawyers were advised to file pretrial motions to prevent victims' lawyers from using the term in trials.

The attack on soft tissue claims was longstanding, but it became systematic with the redesign of claims processing in the 1990s. MIST claims were recognized as a fruitful segment in which new company strategies could produce large profits. The injuries can be serious but not catastrophic, so the amount at stake in any individual claim is relatively small. But there are many such claims, and precisely because the amounts are relatively small, changing the game can have a significant effect on claimants' behavior. The approach is a clear violation of the company's obligation; a Pennsylvania court explained that "a claim must be evaluated on its merits alone," and the court specifically condemned using an individual claim to "send a message" to other claimants.[7]

McKinsey & Company's study of Allstate's claims handling practices identified MIST claims as an area of particular "opportunity." Aggressive defense of MIST claims would be the new watchword. There would be "a willingness to try all cases where settlement cannot be reached," and the "emphasis of the defense would be that an injury is unlikely to have occurred." The Allstate Claims Manual also stated the basic principle of aggressive defense of MIST claims: "A compromise settlement is not desired." The results would be significant: There would be "an increase in the number of CWPs" (claims Closed Without Payment) and "improvements in CWA severity," or a decrease in the average cost of claims Closed With an Amount paid.

Allstate was not alone in the new approach to MIST claims. Grace Hess, a former senior claims adjuster for State Farm, acknowledged that a similar MIST policy permeated the State Farm claim process. She was specifically told by her supervisors, she stated, "that the company was going to start forcing soft tissue cases through arbitration and trial for the purpose of sending a message to claimants, their attorneys, and the public in general, that it is simply not profitable to pursue a soft tissue case when State Farm is the insurer. This policy was applicable both to third-party BI [bodily injury] claims, and claims made by State Farm's insureds."[8]

As its name indicates, the typical MIST claim has two elements: a minor impact accident and a soft-tissue injury. Each is essential to the operation of the MIST strategy. A minor impact accident, at low speed and involving only modest damage to the vehicle, enables the insurance company to argue that such a minor crash could not cause serious injury to the claimant. And soft-tissue injury, not easily demonstrable on X-rays or other diagnostic instruments, permits the company to contest how much harm the claimant has suffered. This combination means that the money damages a claimant can expect at trial are relatively small, which becomes the key to the strategy.

Where the victim is not represented by an attorney, has suffered a soft-tissue injury, and has had only a few visits to the doctor, an offer is often made to settle the case—for a nominal amount, perhaps less than a few hundred dollars. The victim is tempted to take the offer, either believing the insurance company's statement that the offer reflects all the claimant is entitled to or discouraged by the difficulty of finding a lawyer to litigate a claim that size.

Where the victim is represented by an attorney, the case is slated for more aggressive treatment. The essence of the MIST strategy for a represented claim is to take a small case and, metaphorically speaking, make a federal case out of it. The longer the company can drag it out, requiring the claimant to provide more and more information, to submit to onerous depositions, or simply to wait, the more likely it is that the claimant will give up and take a very small offer, or just go away. Moreover, the MIST strategy, as McKinsey often said, allows the company to "exploit the economics of the practice of law." In MIST cases medical expenses, lost income, and noneconomic losses are, as litigated personal injury cases go, relatively modest, usually in the thousands of dollars, but not in the tens or hundreds of thousands of dollars that justify major lawsuits. And that is exactly the point. By treating a minor case as if it is a major one the company makes it difficult or impossible for the victim to find an attorney willing to take the case. The attorney has to advance all the costs, including expert witness fees, the cost of court reporters for depositions, and more, as well as his own time. The lawyer gets paid out of the recovery, if any, and then only an agreed-upon and statutorily limited portion of it. No matter how much he has invested in the case, his fee is limited by the size of the recovery; the higher the costs of litigating a small case, the less likely it is that an attorney will be able to take it.

Adjusters are trained in detail how to handle MIST claims. The first step in the investigation, according to Allstate's training manual, is to "identify and transfer fraud files to SIU [special investigations unit]." One of an adjuster's responsibilities is to assume that a certain percentage of claims are fraudulent and to send those to the SIU. There they will be subject to a more searching investigation, the claimants treated and often reported as potential criminals, and the pressure to give up the claim will be greater.

For those remaining, the adjuster is to "discuss CWP [closing the claim without payment] or nominal amount with client attorney." She makes either a lowball offer for a nominal amount, or no offer at all, on a take-it-or-leave-it basis. When she meets with the victim's attorney, the purpose is "to send a message to attorneys of our proactive defense stance on MIST cases. . . . It forces the claimant and attorney to think about the obstacles they must overcome to recover a significant settlement or the benefits of a smaller 'walkaway' settlement." This has both a short- and a long-term benefit for the company. In the short term it persuades the attorney that the only reasonable thing to do is to walk away with what the company offers, however inadequate. In the long term it deters the lawyer from taking similar cases in the future.

If the offer is rejected, the full-court press begins. First the adjuster secures the "complete medical/employment records" of the victim. Then, in most cases, a "vigorous investigation" is pursued; they can "use vendor database; hire biomechanical expert; consider accident reconstruction; surveillance; drivers license history; paper review of medical reports for likelihood of serious injury [discussed in Chapter 7]; IME [Independent Medical Examination of the claimant by an insurance company doctor, also discussed in Chapter 7]; WC [Workers Compensation benefits] check via Medical Index Bureau."

This list is exhaustive and, for the claimant and her lawyer, exhausting. For example, the use of a biomechanical expert is designed to prove that a low-speed crash could not have caused the victim's injuries. A minor industry of experts has grown up on both sides of the controversy. Plaintiffs' lawyer Karen Koehler reports that one specific biomechanical engineer has been retained by insurance companies in four hundred cases,[9] and Koehler's own treatise on MIST claims reprints thirty-seven technical articles on the subject. The effect of the extensive use of experts by the insurance company is to make it uneconomical for a victim's lawyer to pursue the case; it is not unusual for expert and attorneys' fees to go into the tens of thousand of dollars on a case in which the damages are a fraction of that.

Vigorous investigation typically includes using medical-bill review systems (MBRS), databases and software programs that filter medical records and bills and recalculate their value. Various programs by different vendors are supposedly designed to check the accuracy, appropriateness, and integrity of medical bills submitted with insurance claims. Checking, that is, to see if the bills can be reduced; MBRS are usually advertised to insurance companies as "cost-containment systems."[10] They measure bills against what the program considers to be "reasonable" amounts for the service in the region and reduce any "unreasonable" amount. They match a procedure against a diagnosis, cutting the reimbursement for it if it exceeds the system's determination of appropriateness. They flag for more review procedures that are questionable according to the system's determination, including some surgical procedures and pain control techniques. As a result, in a MIST case with relatively modest bills, MBRS can make them even more modest.

After MBRS reduces the medical expenses, other software is used to set a value for the general damages (noneconomic loss such as pain and suffering). Colossus, explored further in Chapter 7, is the most widely used program of this type. It takes information on the claimant's injuries, symptoms, and treatments and, by using rules built into the program and financial parameters set by the insurance company, produces a dollar figure for the general damages. Ostensibly an information tool to aid the adjuster's judgment in valuing the claim, it is widely used to fix the amount the insurance company will offer. In MIST claims, because of the parameters of the program and the way insurance companies "tune" it to produce limited dollar values, that amount is almost certain to be low.

After all this, final negotiations focus on using the company's willingness to spend far more than the value of the case to litigate and the inability of the claimant's attorney to litigate a case on a basis that makes economic sense for both the lawyer and her client. This includes: "Apply understanding of attorney economics: Present historical verdicts to opponents; discourage disposition by trial based on likely costs." If settlement for little or nothing is not forthcoming, the scorched-earth litigation that has been threatened comes next; where deny fails, defend follows.

The MIST strategy works in reducing the amount paid in individual claims, decreasing payments overall, and deterring some victims from even pursuing their claims. In one study conducted by McKinsey, Allstate's average paid on MIST claims through the use of the new strategy declined 38 percent, from $4,500 to $2,783. The cumulative effect on a company's bottom line is dramatic. McKinsey projected that Allstate's increased profits over time from the new approach to MIST claims would be $100 million to $150 million.

Insurance companies argue that this is simply good business, and they have persuaded some courts to agree. Sabrina Young, an Allstate policyholder in Arizona, was rear-ended while stopped at a traffic light. In the two and a half months following the accident, she received treatment from three doctors and two physical therapists. Her medical bills were $4,407 and her lost wages were $276; Allstate offered her a sum equal to the total of those two numbers, $4,683. Young refused, and the claim went to arbitration, where she was awarded $9,500 for her economic and noneconomic losses, which Allstate paid her. Young then sued Allstate for violating fair claims practices in not fully investigating her claim, making a lowball offer, and delaying payment. The court held that those issues needed to go to trial. However, it did find that Young had failed to prove that Allstate's MIST strategy was "anything other than sound business and claim-handling practices." (Nor had she proven that if it was an improper strategy, the elements of the MIST scheme actually had been used in handling her claim.) The law, the court said, has not "reached the point where it is wrong for an insurance company to make a profit, much less [to] follow good business practices."[11]

But a later case, also from Arizona, looked at more evidence and reached a strikingly different conclusion. In *Crackel v. Allstate Insurance Company* the court found Allstate's conduct so egregious in abusively defending MIST claims that it fashioned a new legal rule to provide a remedy for victims.[12] Tammi Drannan and her infant son were passengers in Erika Guenther's car. While the car was stopped at a traffic light, Harvey Hamilton drove his car into the rear of their car, causing abdominal pain for Drannan, who was six months pregnant, and neck and back pain for Guenther. Both women were examined in a hospital emergency room and released; Drannan's medical bills were $890 and Guenther's were $720, which they sought from Allstate, Hamilton's insurance company, along with general damages.

For Allstate, these were MIST claims, and they became the responsibility of adjuster Shirlee Kopin. Kopin admitted that Hamilton was 100 percent at fault but still told Blaine Gaub, the attorney Allstate hired to defend the claim, to offer Drannan and Guenther only a total of $101 in settlement. The low offer was based on Allstate's position that any MIST injury was "suspect." When the victims refused the lowball offer, Allstate spent over $4,500 defending the claims. Kopin hired a biomechanical expert and, even though nineteen months had passed since the accident and Drannan and Guenther were no longer in treatment, she required them to submit to medical examinations by a doctor Allstate selected; the doctor in those exams found that Guenther and Drannan had acted appropriately in going to the emergency room after the accident. More than two years after the accident, Kopin told Gaub to offer Guenther $801 and Drannan $1,001 to settle the claims. They rejected the offers because, as Guenther said, by this time the settlement offered would not have "fairly compensated" her lawyer for his work, which of course was Allstate's point—to exploit the economics of the practice of law.

After Allstate's offer was rejected the case went to an arbitration panel. The arbitrator asked Gaub what value Allstate placed on the case. He replied that it was worth "zero" and that Guenther and Drannan deserved "nothing," not so much because of the merits of the individual cases but because Allstate "draw[s] a line in the sand in these cases" under its MIST strategy. The arbitrator awarded Guenther $2,300 and Drannan $3,400. Kopin directed Gaub to appeal the arbitration by taking the case to trial. The trial judge, Judge O'Neil, conducted a mandatory settlement conference, at which Gaub violated a local court rule requiring him to distribute pretrial memoranda in advance, misrepresented the conclusions of Allstate's expert at the medical examinations it had compelled, and told the judge that nothing he said would affect Allstate's negotiating position. Judge O'Neil found that Hamilton and Gaub had not participated in the settlement conference in good faith, so he refused to allow Allstate to defend the case on liability and allowed it to proceed only on the issue of how much Allstate should pay. Allstate then finally paid Guenther and Drannan the amounts originally awarded them in arbitration.

Because of Allstate's violation of the standards of fair claims handling, that was not the end of the story. Guenther and Drannan then sued Allstate for "abuse of process," a tort designed to punish misuse of a legal procedure. Usually the tort is brought against someone who initiates litigation; this case was unique because the court felt it necessary to fashion a remedy for Allstate's abusive actions in defense of a suit. The court found that Allstate's misconduct at the settlement conference was so egregious that it did not even need to consider Allstate's other misdeeds. The ulterior purpose for the misconduct was Allstate's MIST scheme to use "the prospect of sustained and expensive litigation as a 'club' in an attempt to coerce them, and other similarly situated claimants, to surrender those causes of action that sought only modest damages." The trial judge concluded that "[Allstate's] own manual regarding Claims Core

Process Redesign (CCPR) and Minor Injury Soft Tissue (MIST) claims seems to support this argument." The jury awarded Guenther and Drannan $7,500 each in damages, and the trial judge and the Arizona Court of Appeals upheld the verdicts. What happened to Guenther and Drannan was just one example of Allstate's strategy in all MIST cases, and the court appropriately condemned it.

7

"Insurance Company Rules" for Auto Claims

A VIDEO PRODUCED by Health Care for America Now, an advocacy group for health insurance reform, portrays an unusual approach to games: A golfer tackles another player who is about to swing; a tennis player aims Ninja throwing stars at his opponent across the net; and when one poker player shows four aces, another shouts, "I've got nunchuks!" The justification for the unorthodox behavior? "Insurance company rules." The video explains: "There's two ways to go through life. You can play by the rules. Or you can follow insurance company rules, where you can do whatever the hell you want."[1]

Property/casualty insurance isn't that bad. (Health insurance isn't quite that bad, either.) But insurance companies sometimes seem to make their own rules in order to pay less to people injured in auto accidents than they really owe. The stated rules are simple. The basic principle is, as everywhere else, pay what you owe. The company owes the victim of an auto accident, or a policyholder filing a claim covered by uninsured/underinsured motorist insurance, damages of two kinds. "General damages" are the specific monetary losses suffered, such as medical costs and lost wages. "Special damages" are less tangible but no less real, such as the pain and suffering that results from the injury and the loss of the ability to enjoy activities due to a resulting disability. The policyholder also can have his medical expenses reimbursed under the medical payments coverage of the standard automobile insurance policy. In each case the company is obligated to pay for the damages caused by the accident. Period.

Insurance company rules come into play when the company denies payment of what it owes and backs up the denial with defense of litigation. Because an insurance company, unlike a nunchuk-wielding poker player, has to appear to be following the rules, the company attempts to justify the denial by proclaiming that whatever injuries the claimant suffered weren't caused by the accident; if they were, the injuries aren't as bad as he says; and the injuries don't justify as much payment for general damages as he wants.

Insurance companies commonly use two devices to determine whether the claimant's injuries were caused by the accident and how severe they really are: a review of the claimant's medical records and a physical examination by a doctor other than her own physician. From the company's point of view, both of these have a laudable objective: to make sure that only valid claims are paid, and then only in the proper amount. Claimants, the companies say, exaggerate their injuries, malinger, or commit outright fraud. The appropriate check is to scrutinize claims carefully. Claimants who really are injured as a result of insured risks should not object, because the scrutiny is not done by the insurance company but by an independent expert who has no financial interest in the outcome of the claim.

Dozens of medical review companies provide these services for insurance companies through their own employees and networks of individual physicians and other experts. The hard part is ensuring that the third party really is expert and really is independent. If the insurance company benefits by denying some claims and paying less on others, then it is likely to choose a reviewer who tends to provide the right answers, and reviewers who want to be chosen over and over may be inclined to give those answers; the right answers, of course, are that the injuries either do not exist, are exaggerated, or were not caused by the accident.

The first device is a review of a claimant's medical records. This is known as a "utilization review" or a "quality review," or more commonly, a "paper review," because the reviewer does not examine the patient but makes a decision solely by reviewing the claimant's paper (or electronic) medical records. The insurance company provides the reviewing company information that may include the details of the accident, the claimant's statements, and some of their medical records, and the company examines those documents to make its judgment.

The ostensible purpose of a paper review is to make sure the medical expenses are appropriate, but inherently the process is to reduce payments, not to increase them. A paper review never reveals that more care or more service is needed, issues that should be brought to the attention of the insured. And the purpose is explicit. One major provider of such reviews, National Healthcare Resources, proclaims that the company's purpose is "to provide cost containment services to the auto insurance industry."[2]

The most notable case that illustrates how paper reviews can be used and abused is *Robinson v. State Farm*, from Idaho.[3] Cindy Robinson was driving her Chevrolet Monte Carlo when suddenly the left rear wheel came off, causing the car to drop with a jolt. Robinson consulted Dr. Michael O'Brien, a neurologist, for pain and soreness in her head, back, and neck. Dr. O'Brien referred her to a physical therapist for treatment, but the treatment did not alleviate her pain. She returned to Dr. O'Brien, whose tests concluded that Robinson had a herniated disk in her back. About a month after the accident Dr. Floyd Johnson operated on Robinson to repair the disk. Although the operation was partially successful, the residual pain became extreme, and two years later Robinson underwent a second surgery.

Robinson was insured by State Farm and filed a claim for her injuries. State Farm's adjuster, Scott Bengoechea, sent the file to Medical Claims Review Service (MCRS), a medical review company often used by State Farm. MCRS's report, signed by Dr. Alfred Taricco, concluded that "the documentation does not support a causal relationship" between the accident and Robinson's herniated disk and the subsequent surgeries. Over the next several months Robinson's lawyer contested the adoption by State Farm of MCRS's conclusion, submitting a letter from Dr. Johnson and other material. State Farm had MCRS review the new material, but the company did not budge from its position. State Farm then sought a paper review from another local physician, Dr. Richard Wilson, who initially agreed with MCRS after reviewing the records; but then, after examining Robinson, he concluded that the herniated disk "would not be incompatible" with an injury caused by the accident.

State Farm proposed settling for about half of Robinson's medical bills, but she refused. More than two years after the accident, Robinson sued. State Farm then sought the opinion of another orthopedic surgeon, who concluded that "it would be extremely difficult to attribute her disk herniation . . . to anything but the accident." State Farm finally paid the remainder of the policy limits on Robinson's policy, but she pursued an additional action against State Farm for its bad faith in denying her claim and delaying payment. At trial the jury awarded her compensatory damages of $102,520 and $9.5 million for punitive damages. The Idaho Supreme Court initially affirmed the decision, but State Farm asked the court to reconsider, perhaps not coincidentally after a justice who had voted with the majority was defeated for reelection. A new majority of the court held that the trial judge had instructed the jury incorrectly on the burden of proof and sent the case back for a new trial. Robinson and State Farm settled before the retrial, with the final terms held confidential.

Although the trial court's decision was vacated on procedural grounds, the findings of the trial judge, D. Duff McKee, still speak to State Farm's abuse of paper reviews. First, he concluded that the evidence was "overwhelming" that MCRS was

> a completely bogus operation. The company did not objectively review medical records, but rather prepared "cookie cutter" reports of stock phrases, assembled on a computer, supporting the denial of claims by insurance companies. The insured's medical records were not examined and reports were not prepared by doctors, or even reviewed by doctors.

Next, Judge McKee observed that State Farm was complicit in the wrongdoing.

> The machinery was set up within State Farm for the utilization of this paper review organization with the knowledge that the reports were not objective, but slanted to favor the denial or reduction of claims, that State Farm management knew of the fact that the reports from the review agency utilized in this case were false, that they were not signed by physicians as represented, and that, nevertheless, State Farm permitted and directed the use of such agencies anyway.

Rather than observing the basic principle that the company should pay what it owed, State Farm was following "insurance company rules": State Farm's adjuster sent the claim to MCRS, according to Judge McKee, without

> any intent of obtaining an independent, objective review of the plaintiff's medical circumstance. Rather, he did so with the expectation that the reports issued would support his denial of the claim. The evidence was further clear that the procedures which enabled the claims examiner to utilize these slanted and biased reviews and examinations were set up by State Farm management, included in the training given to claims examiners, and encouraged by management as a cost-cutting device.

The *Robinson* case generated a storm of publicity about paper reviews. Following a fifteen-month investigation, NBC's *Dateline* broadcast a report that featured Robinson's story and other examples, such as the case of Lecreca Duffy, who incurred $10,000 in medical bills in an accident of which a paper review found only $780 to be justified. It questioned MCRS's practice of issuing reports that had not been approved by a physician. It also reported on another paper review company, Comprehensive Medical Review (CMR) of San Diego, the firm involved in Duffy's case, which used a paralegal, a nurse, and a news writer with no medical training—not a physician—to prepare reports for State Farm. The firm used computer programs with standard paragraphs favoring the insurance company to insert in reports. Doctors would ostensibly review and sign the reports, but would spend as little as a minute or two on each, approving thirty to fifty reports in an hour.

State Farm vigorously contested the *Robinson* case, defending the actions of its adjusters and the legitimacy of its paper review process. Jack North, State Farm's senior vice president, pointed out that when the company learned about the problems at CMR it stopped doing business with the firm and argued, "[T]hat just isn't the way we do business." In fact, State Farm had stopped using CMR but didn't reexamine the claims it had denied using CMR reports until three years later, after public attention was drawn to the issue. State Farm chief operating officer Vincent Trosino stated that "State Farm's goal is to pay what we owe. Medical utilization review is used in only a small percentage of cases." Small, perhaps, because in cases involving very small claims the cost of the review is greater than the cost of paying the claim, and in cases involving large claims, the adversarial nature of the claim makes it of little use. "We always aim to assure the objectivity of third-party reviewers to obtain a fair evaluation of claims. But we know that, like *Dateline*, we're not perfect. . . . We have established new, more stringent guidelines for firms that conduct our utilization reviews."

The *Robinson* litigation and *Dateline*'s investigation caught the attention of state regulators. Spurred to action by the television program, the insurance commissioners of Alaska, Arizona, Colorado, Florida, Illinois, Indiana, Kansas, Kentucky, Maryland, Missouri, Oregon, and Vermont joined forces to study State Farm's use of paper reviews. Minnesota separately investigated State Farm, and Washington insurance commissioner Deborah Senn cooperated with the other states but also launched her own, broader study of the practices of Allstate, Safeco, Farmers, and other carriers as well as State Farm.

The multistate report concluded that "State Farm failed to appropriately or sufficiently monitor its medical review activities" and "State Farm did not verify that all Utilization Review Vendors were using properly qualified medical providers for Utilization Review, including reporting recommendations relative to medical services." State Farm then began its own audit of some of the medical review services it used; at the time of the states' report, when State Farm's audit was still ongoing, it had found 1,313 claims in which it had underpaid over $3.1 million. Later, individual states examined more recent claims with mixed results. Many of the states' subsequent examination found that State Farm had appropriate documentation for its medical reviews and that there were no violations of the claim practices statutes. In other states, the extent to which paper reviews were still used to deny full payment on claims was less clear. Several states found that a significant proportion of claims submitted for review were recommended for denial or reduced payment: ten of nineteen in Oregon; eighteen of twenty-eight in Alaska; and seventeen of eighteen in Illinois. In Maryland, the average amounts by which the reviews recommended the claims be reduced were 54 percent.

Paper reviews are typically used for smaller claims and claims by policyholders. In contested claims, insurance companies more commonly use Independent Medical Examinations (IMEs) to contest the cause of the claimant's injuries and how serious they really are. An IME is a physical examination of the claimant by a physician purportedly independent of the insurance company, to give an objective assessment of the injuries and their possible relationship to the accident. But trial lawyer Karen Koehler quotes Confucius: "If an urn lacks the characteristics of an urn, how can we call it an urn?"[4] Insurance critics deride the IME as an "insurance medical exam" rather than an independent medical examination, or a "defense medical exam" whose purpose is not to give an objective assessment but to provide fodder for denial or defense of a claim, and one conducted by a physician who is not actually independent of the insurance company's interests. Among themselves, insurance company representatives may share the sentiment. Everett J. Truttman, a State Farm actuary, commented in an internal memorandum on the provision in its policy allowing the company to seek an IME: "Dale Nowell has suggested a minor change in the wording of the provision which would give us the right to review medical bills. His concern is that the use of the words 'independent review' in the original language infers a free of influence relationship which does not always exist."[5] Or, as put more pithily by Judge Thomas P. Smith of Prince George's County, Maryland, "Of all the oxymorons in the world, an Independent Medical Examination occupies first place by thousands of leagues. There is nothing Independent about the process; it is hardly undertaken for Medical purposes and all too often resembles an inquisition rather than an Examination."[6]

Bias, incentives, and selection are enough to make IMEs not truly independent even if there is no actual collusion. Because the insurance company profits from keeping claims costs down, there is a natural tendency to select a physician or network of physicians that will be more conservative in its evaluation and more likely to find no injury, a lesser degree of injury, or malingering. On the other side of the deal, a physician or company that sells its services only occasionally or on an equal basis to insurance companies and plaintiffs' lawyers alike has an incentive to provide accurate reports. But a physician or company that does many IMEs, the bulk of which are ordered by insurance companies, has an incentive to provide reports that will be favorable to its repeat clients; he who pays the piper calls the tune. As insurance expert Frank Caliri testified in a case in which an IME was used to rebut a claim of disability, when an insurance company uses the same IME examiners continually, the examiners become "biased" and "lose their independence." The IME physician in that case had rejected claims of total disability in every one of the thirteen cases in which he had been an expert. Caliri's own experience provided a counterpoint to the potential bias inherent in an IME; he has been employed by defense firms 35 percent to 40 percent of the times he has served as an expert, including by the firm that challenged his qualifications in the case in which he testified.[7]

For some physicians, performing IMEs can be a substantial part of their practice and therefore their income. In one Kentucky case, Dr. Daniel Primm was the company's independent medical expert. IMEs constituted between 10 percent and 25 percent of his practice, amounting to an annual income of as much as $832,500. The Kentucky Supreme Court noted that the fact that an expert earns a significant portion of his income from IMEs and testimony does not mean that his testimony is not "honest, accurate, and credible." However, the court commented, "it is undeniable that an expert's tendency to slant his testimony may be affected not just by how much he is being compensated on one particular occasion, but also by how much of his annual income is derived from similar testimony."[8]

Bias can show itself in a number of ways. The conduct of the examination can be designed to elicit statements from the insured, or other information, that has the potential to discredit the claims, information that is not necessarily a typical part of what should be a focused physical examination. Koehler reports several examples of such behavior, including: devoting one hour to rehashing a plaintiff's history but seven minutes to the physical exam; dictating the report while referring to the summary of the medical records prepared by the defense attorney or claims adjuster instead of the actual medical records; spending more time examining non-injured portions of plaintiff's body than the areas at issue; and declining to look at the actual X-rays and imaging studies brought to the exam.[9] The examination may also be incomplete. The physician may reach conclusions without having the results of the full battery of tests available to a treating physician. In a Michigan case, a Dr. Taylor's IME reported no injury to Archie Clack's right knee, but that assessment was made without seeing the MRI that had been done; when presented with the MRI at the trial, he admitted that it did show an "internal derangement" of the knee.[10]

In rare cases plaintiffs' attorneys are able to do more than raise the possibility of bias and actually discover direct evidence that the examination had been slanted to benefit the insurance company. In a 2003 case in Putnam County, New York, an insurance company contracted for an IME with Juris Solutions, which advertises that it has a network comprised of over three thousand board-certified physicians in all fifty states. The form sent by the company ordering the IME directed the physician: "Please provide specific answers to the questions asked and make no recommendations unless so requested. Your report should address the following." It then listed a series of topics, of which the most important was item number six, concerning the "causal relationship" between the accident in which the claimant was injured and the claimed injuries. The physician was instructed to address whether the accident caused the injury "Only if in negative." That is, the insurance company was only looking for an opinion that the accident had not caused the injury; any other conclusion was not welcome. To make sure that the board-certified, supposedly independent physician got the point, "only if in negative" was double-underlined on the form.

For insurance companies relying on IMEs to delay or deny claims, ambiguity is often as good as outright disagreement. Virginia Villegas's two treating physicians concluded that she suffered back injuries in a car accident, injuries for which she eventually had surgery. Allstate's independent examiner concluded that some of her injuries were related to the automobile accident, and some might not have been, an ambiguity that was good enough for Allstate to deny her claim.[11] Similarly, Fouad Hannawi's doctor diagnosed his condition as a herniated disk, using an MRI among other diagnostic tools; when his insurance company's expert did not find a herniated disk but could not rule out the possibility, the company refused to pay.[12]

When an insurance company does pay for damages to a policyholder under uninsured/underinsured motorist coverage, or to a victim of an accident caused by a policyholder, the claimant is entitled to compensation for general damages, including physical pain, emotional distress, and the loss of enjoyment of normal activities. The more serious the injury, the larger the general damages, and they can be substantial. According to the Insurance Information Institute, for every nine dollars paid out in medical expenses, five dollars is paid for general damages. Therefore, reducing general damages can have a dramatic impact on an insurance company's costs.

General damages paid in settlement of a claim are a prediction of how a jury would value the case. Traditionally the amount the insurance company would offer in settlement was set by the adjuster, based on his evaluation of the details of the case and his experience with other cases. Today the amount is more likely to be produced by a computer-based expert system; the most famous of these is Colossus.[13]

Colossus, sold by Computer Sciences Corporation (CSC), is aptly named, at least as to its dominance in claim evaluation. CSC reports that Colossus is used in the United States by thirty-four insurers that represent 60 percent of premiums paid for personal auto insurance, and it is used by many more companies in the United Kingdom, Europe, and elsewhere around the world. Reportedly its users include Hartford, Allstate, Farmers, St. Paul, Travelers, MetLife, and Westfield.

The program is an ideal component of the redesigned claim process established by insurance companies, because it is easy for front-line adjusters to use with minimal training, and therefore obviates the need for experienced adjusters, and it produces consistent results. As insurance executive Jason Chinn, former chair of the Colossus Users' Group, boasted, "In two-and-a-half days I can get people from having no knowledge to an acceptable level of personal injury evaluation."[14] Training in Colossus at Allstate, for example, consisted of workshops lasting between one and three days, with the emphasis on properly putting data into Colossus and letting the program do its work. According to its developers at CSC, it is "designed to simulate the adjuster's decision-making process [and] to implement and reinforce a 'Best Practices' approach to claim evaluation." But it has its limitations. CSC emphasizes: "It is *not* a replacement for the adjuster's judgment and experience" or "capable of assessing all factors pertinent to a claim."

Here is a paradox: Colossus fits into the systematic approach to claim handling because it is easy to use and simulates the adjuster's decision-making process, but it is not capable of assessing all pertinent factors and does not replace the adjuster's judgment. This paradox has given rise to three controversies about insurance companies' widespread use of it to fix claims payments and their ability to play by insurance company rules. First, GIGO—garbage in, garbage out. The information about a claim that goes into Colossus is not necessarily garbage, but it is limited by the records available to the adjuster and the limitations of the program. Without complete and accurate information, Colossus cannot possibly yield a complete and accurate evaluation. Second, Colossus as designed by CSC produces a "severity point" total for a claim, not a dollar figure; the severity points get converted into dollars only when the program is "tuned" by each individual company. In tuning Colossus, companies can direct the program to produce numbers that are artificially low, and those numbers then become the ostensibly objective basis on which the companies are willing to settle claims. Third, CSC markets Colossus as a tool adjusters can use, not a substitute for the judgment of an experienced adjuster, but companies can make the figures derived using Colossus, with their limitations from GIGO and tuning, binding amounts rather than just benchmarks.

The controversial elements of Colossus naturally have led to litigation. For example, a class action was brought in Oklahoma against Farmers and settled in February 2005. The plaintiffs, representing 41,791 claimants who had been paid general damages totaling $150,897,498 in uninsured/underinsured motorist settlements, alleged that Farmers used Colossus in bodily injury claims in a way that systematically led to underpayments. As usual, Farmers denied any wrongdoing but still settled. It agreed to pay the plaintiffs an additional 7.5 percent to 12.5 percent of the general damages they had received, or to have their cases reviewed by new adjusters, who could order additional payments of up to 25 percent of the original amounts, at a total estimated cost of $30 million to $40 million, plus attorneys' fees.

Colossus can process only the facts the adjuster gives it, and the adjuster can give it only the kinds of facts it can process. The adjuster begins by inputting facts about the claimant's injury, treatment, period of care, complications, and "impairments to lifestyle," choosing from a limited list of entries for each type. Injury types include, for example, fracture, fracture at or near a dislocated joint, displaced bones at a joint, laceration or penetration injury requiring sutures, and superficial cuts and abrasions. For each injury Colossus asks the adjuster a range of questions about symptoms related to the injury, such as spasms, range of motion, and radiating pain. Only symptoms that are documented appropriately in the medical treatment records can be entered into the system. Treatment entries include the dates and numbers of treatments, the treating physician's specialty, and the patient's prognosis. Soft tissue neck and back injuries are analyzed separately from other injuries, probably because of insurance companies' reluctance to pay for them. Entries for loss of enjoyment of life includes loss of enjoyment of work (including loss of status or promotional prospects), domestic and household duties, hobbies, and sports.

In all, Colossus contains categories for approximately six hundred injuries and ten thousand factors, which would seem to make it remarkably comprehensive. It has long been a maxim of insurance claims that if it's not in the claim file it didn't happen, but the importance of documentation is exaggerated with Colossus. Injuries, complaints (including loss of enjoyment of life), and treatments have no value to Colossus unless they are both reflected in the medical records and fit within the categories allowed by Colossus. Injuries have to be specified with precision in the medical records, and by the adjuster, or else they are discounted; a neck injury that radiates pain to the back is worth less than the same one recorded separately as a neck injury and a back injury. Injuries, particularly those to the neck and back, need to have caused what Colossus considers to be objective symptoms, such as muscle spasms. Even if the medical records are precise, Colossus may not allow that to be reflected in its system; lawyer/physician Aaron DeShaw, the leading expert on Colossus outside the industry, points out that Colossus cannot differentiate between types of leg fractures that have different likelihoods of permanency.[15] And some treatments are worth more than others to Colossus; in particular, treatments by medical doctors are valued more highly than treatments by chiropractors, and the longer the chiropractic treatment the less highly it is valued.

Moreover, even a fuller set of inputs would not give Colossus an accurate basis for setting the value of an insured's or tort victim's general damages compared to the amount that a jury might award if the case went to trial. As federal judge Robert Jones explained in his ruling on litigation brought by Farmers' agents, "Colossus is incapable of considering external factors such as the character and credibility of witnesses, injuries or complications to pre-existing conditions not programmed into the system, the reputation and caliber of counsel, the availability and potential for exemplary damages, possible aggravated liability, and a multitude of other external factors."[16]

Once the information from the claim file and medical records are put into Colossus, the system uses decision rules programmed into it to assign "severity points" as a means of arriving at a value for the claim. The program itself as designed by CSC does not convert the severity point total into a dollar value; each insurance company assigns its own conversion factors—so many points equal so many dollars—in the tuning process. As CSC promotes the product, "You decide how to tune Colossus in a manner appropriate for your business. With tuning customized for each insurer and for each region, consumers can obtain a fair and accurate settlement."

Perhaps. But the ability to tune Colossus presents a tremendous opportunity for insurance companies to reduce claim payments.

Colossus is designed to predict general damages, the amount that a jury might award if the case went to trial. By excluding all trial verdicts, any trial verdicts, or the highest trial verdicts from the Colossus tuning process, insurance companies can scale down the program's ability to assess the reasonable value of the case. Companies do not volunteer precisely how they tune Colossus; Allstate claims it uses "a fair sampling" of closed cases, both settlements and jury verdicts. But insurance company whistle-blowers and litigation have revealed that companies exclude important data. Linda Brown, formerly an Allstate claims manager, admitted that when she first helped tune it for Allstate in Kentucky, her supervisors told her to omit jury verdicts and settlements of more than fifty thousand dollars, and that high settlements were subsequently excluded as well. Maureen Reed, staff counsel at Allstate when Colossus was rolled out in the early 1990s, was told by David Silverman, Allstate vice president:

> They were going to change the value of claims by instituting a nationwide program to set the values by a computer program called Colossus. We were told by Mr. Silverman that Allstate could set the values as whatever level they wanted and those values would be enforced by Allstate through the CCPR programs. By setting claim values at lower levels through the Colossus program, we were told that profits would go up. We were also told by Mr. Silverman, among others, that high level corporate executives had committed to reducing amounts paid on claims by lowering the Colossus values, which would result in significant bonuses to those executives.[17]

Robert Dietz told a similar story about tuning Colossus at Farmers Insurance:

> I was asked to assist in the initial "tuning" session of a software program called Colossus. . . . Present were claims employees (perhaps 30–40) who were selected because of their experience at accurately

> evaluating injury claims. . . . Each group reviewed and evaluated about ten or twelve injury claims, discussed issues and differences amongst themselves, and reported the values to the facilitator . . .
>
> We were told that the values we supplied would be reduced to 80% of what we proposed as claim value, and along with results from closed file reviews, would be incorporated into establishing a benchmark for values on claims that would be evaluated by Colossus. Management would then thereafter tune or modify Colossus, at their discretion, based on whatever results they were seeking.[18]

In short, experienced Farmers adjusters evaluated a limited set of claims, using their judgment to come up with reasonable values for them. The company then cut off 20 percent of what the experts believed the cases were worth so Colossus would produce results that were consistently 20 percent below the fair values of claims.

Tuning by exclusion continues today. In a 2008 California case, insurance expert and former State Farm and USAA adjuster Thomas Corridan testified that AMCO Insurance tuned Colossus only by using their prelitigation settlements and those of its parent company, excluding broader relevant information such as arbitration awards, jury verdicts, or postlitigation settlements. Moreover, the Colossus calculations were done by a separate unit of the company, and front-line adjusters were not told of the limits of the reliability of Colossus numbers.[19]

The tuned version of Colossus produces a report that takes the data the adjuster has put into the system, processes it through its thousands of decision rules, arrives at severity points, converts the severity points into dollar amounts, produces its assessment of general damages, and adds that number to the information on special damages already processed through separate software that sifts through the medical bills. The bottom line result is Colossus's "Evaluated Amount" (EA)—the dollar value it determines the claim is worth, and a range within which the adjuster should settle the case, which is from 85 percent to 100 percent of the EA. (As usual, less but not more; the range is 85 percent to 100 percent of the supposedly fair value of the case, not 85 percent to 115 percent of that value.) CSC and insurance companies suggest that the EA and the range are simply guidelines to promote consistency among adjusters and fairness to claimants, but reports are widespread that the EA—the product of Colossus's limitations and the insurer's tuning—binds the adjuster in settlement negotiations. (Widespread but not universal; the judge in a Pennsylvania case concluded that an adjuster for Allstate did not rely on the Colossus EA in setting the amount offered on a claim.)[20]

Adjusters at Farmers Insurance were required to have supervisor approval to settle a claim above the Colossus range.[21] After its first few months in use at Allstate an adjuster needed permission from a claims manager to override the EA and offer a higher amount, and 95 percent of the time the approval would not be given. Jeffrey Mangone, an AMCO adjuster, testified that he had no authority to settle a claim outside the Colossus EA range.

The restrictions on adjusters' authority to exceed the EA amount can be reinforced by monitoring, reporting, and incentive programs. Shannon Brady Kmatz, formerly an Allstate adjuster in New Mexico, revealed the extent to which settlements relative to the EA were tracked by individual adjuster, specialized unit, and office, and "good" results were praised and rewarded; adjusters were trained that the EA "was etched in stone." Maureen Reed confirmed the practice elsewhere at Allstate: "The reason the adjusters were so reluctant to run a second Colossus evaluation when there was new information was because adjusters' performance evaluations would go down and their chances for raises and advancement would suffer." Farmers was the subject of a class action suit concerning its improper use of Colossus, and of government investigations for tying employee incentives to claim reductions. It ostensibly stopped using adherence to the EA in individual performance reviews, but the message did not always make it down the management chain to claim managers. Farmers' management in California revised its personnel forms to state: "Because our overall goal in Claims handling is to pay what we owe—no more, no less, [Farmers] employees should not establish an individual goal in support of Overall Company Goal # 1." ("Overall Goal # 1" was profitable growth for the company.) The form specified a key performance indicator with a qualifier: "Proper Colossus usage. Expectation is to properly utilize Colossus for 3rd party BI [bodily injury] claims [and] effectively negotiate settlements. Settlements outside the Colossus range need to be well supported with valid external factors." Four of the fifteen California claims offices had widespread problems creating incentives for individual adjusters to adhere to Colossus results, and senior management had to discipline the claim managers to get the message through.[22]

Even when claims are referred to lawyers because the claimant refuses to settle the claim for the amount the adjuster offers, the lawyers are subject to the constraints imposed by the company's use of Colossus. McKinsey recommended to Allstate that the fees paid to outside attorneys should depend on their ability to obtain settlements or verdicts that tracked the Colossus EA. The measure for compensating them became: "Deviation from evaluated amount plus expenses," and the action that resulted from that measure would include: "Base fee raised or lowered"; "Gain or loss of cases"; or "Bonus at end of year."

The use of Colossus produced immediate results in reducing claim payouts. Even in the early stages of McKinsey's development of Allstate's CCPR program, it could report positive, striking results: "The use of evaluation decision support tools and a second look have resulted in lower settlement values. The Colossus sites have been extremely successful in reducing severities, with reductions in the range of 20% for Colossus-evaluated claims."

8

The Risk of "All Risks" Homeowners Insurance

LONG BEFORE THE advent of Starbucks, the coffee craze in London in the late seventeenth century matched in fervor the coffee craze in the United States at the turn of the twenty-first century. London's coffeehouses served tasty if less exotic forms of coffee and provided convivial gathering places for the like-minded. Edward Lloyd's coffeehouse became particularly popular among ship owners and merchants who transacted in risk because Lloyd, anticipating Starbucks's provision of free Wi-Fi by more than two centuries, made available paper, pens, and shipping news to his customers. A ship owner or merchant desiring financial protection for a ship or the cargo it carried would prepare a paper describing the ship and its journey, its cargo, and their value. Individuals willing to accept part of the risk would write their names and how much of the value they would guarantee against loss under the description; that is, they would "underwrite" the risk. In 1769 what the present-day Lloyd's describes as the "more reputable customers" organized a society that became a separate business rather than a coffeehouse gathering. Shortly after, the society drafted a standard form for marine insurance—the "Lloyd's policy"—that continued in use largely unchanged for two hundred years. Although it is a group of individual and corporate "members" rather than a single insurance company, the modern Lloyd's is still the best-known insurer in the world, not only for its ability to back extreme commercial risks but also in the popular imagination for reportedly insuring Betty Grable's legs and Bruce Springsteen's voice.

From Lloyd's underwriting voyages at sea, property insurance spread inland, first to goods in transit to the ships, and then to ordinary property. New companies formed, such as the Philadelphia Contributionship for the Insurance of Houses from Loss by Fire, America's oldest existing insurance company, which, as its name suggests, protected homes against fire losses only. Over time the perils covered by a policy expanded, but for many decades insurance against property loss was still written by one type of company, and casualty insurance, or insurance against liability for harm caused to others, was written by another. It was not until the late 1940s that state regulators permitted a company to offer both types of policy, which gave rise a decade later to the modern homeowners insurance policy; they now cover the risk of loss of the dwelling and its contents as well as the risk of liability for harm to others caused inside and outside the home.

Today, 96 percent of homeowners carry insurance, paying a total of $55 billion in premiums each year. The average cost of homeowners insurance is $804 per year, with much less variation in the average cost among the states than for auto insurance. On average, six or seven of every hundred homeowners file insurance claims each year, with fire the largest cause, and the average amount paid on a claim is $7,567. Of every dollar paid to insurance companies in premiums for homeowners insurance, $.56 is paid out in property damage losses and $.03 in liability claims.

Homeowners insurance is complicated. The policy most commonly purchased by homeowners, the HO-3 produced by the Insurance Services Office (ISO), contains: three pages of declarations (the name of the policyholder, the location of the property, the policy limits, and a list of the forms and endorsements that comprise the policy); two pages of general definitions (not counting definitions stated elsewhere); six pages describing what property is covered; three pages stating what risks are covered; two pages describing what risks are excluded (not counting exclusions stated elsewhere); three pages of conditions on the property coverage; and seven pages describing the liability coverage (including more statements of risk, exclusions, and conditions). And that is only the basic policy; attachments might include limited earthquake coverage, workers' compensation for employees working at a residence, oil tank coverage, and other special provisions.[1]

The policy is complicated not only because it is long but because it is, simply put, complicated. Consider the description of what risks are insured against. Once most property damage policies sold were for fire insurance. By convention, however, "fire" includes lightning, and fire policies also nearly always include Extended Coverage, which, depending on the policy, includes such risks as windstorms, hail, smoke, and explosions. Today most homeowners have "Special Form" policies, which cover different risks for different types of property. Under the HO-3 policy the dwelling has "all risks" coverage under which the insurance company's basic promise is: "We insure against risks of direct physical loss." (Incidentally, the definition of dwelling includes such subtleties as an attached garage but not a detached garage.) All risks does not mean all risks, however. After the basic promise there follow fifteen paragraphs (with multiple subparagraphs and sub-subparagraphs) of exclusions to the all-risk provision, including, for example, damage during construction and loss caused by ice or snow, mold, or pollutants. Then there are exceptions to the exclusions, such as "any ensuing loss to property described in Coverages A and B not precluded by any other provision of this policy not excluded is covered." Personal property (things other than the buildings), on the other hand, is insured on a "named peril" basis; that is, it is protected only against risks specified in another sixteen paragraphs of the policy. Not all personal property, however. The policy has dollar limits on the coverage of some property, such as fifteen hundred dollars for loss by theft of jewelry, and excludes others, such as "animals, birds or fish." (Presumably, the policy drafters knew of birds or fish that are not animals.)

Even with this level of detail, the policy is not complete. It is further complicated because its terms require interpretation, an interpretation set against a background of centuries of judicial interpretation and insurance company practice. Professor Tom Baker's insurance law textbook poses problems for students to ponder.[2] A kitchen fire causes a heating oil tank outside the house to explode. The insurer agrees to pay for the damage caused by the fire but not for the cost of cleaning up oil-soaked soil in the backyard, arguing that the cost was excluded by the provision in the policy that excludes loss caused by "discharge, dispersal, seepage, migration, release or escape of pollutants," with pollutants defined as "any solid, liquid, gaseous or thermal irritant or contaminant." If oil is a pollutant, the harm is not covered. But the policy does cover discharge of pollutants "caused by a peril insured against under Coverage C of this policy" (even with respect to damage to the dwelling, which is Coverage A), and coverage C includes fire. So the loss may be covered. But the policy also excludes coverage for "any loss that results from a peril excluded or limited by this policy, even if a covered peril is a concurrent cause of loss." So the loss may not be covered. And, Baker asks, suppose the kitchen fire had been caused by nail polish remover that was mistakenly spilled on the stove? Is nail polish remover a pollutant and is a spill a "discharge," triggering a series of events that excludes coverage? Or is the fire then an "ensuing loss"?

Finally, homeowners policies are complicated because they apply to complex and widely varying sets of facts. Imagine the kitchen fire in Baker's hypothetical. Soot from the fire seeps into the suspended ceiling; can the ceiling be cleaned or must the ceiling tiles be replaced? Water used to extinguish the fire wets drywall in an adjoining wall. Can the drywall be sanded and painted? Is spraying with a mold preventative sufficient or must it be replaced? If replaced, can only the new portion be painted, or will the whole wall have to be repainted to match? The whole room? One of the benefits of the policy is "any necessary increase in living expenses incurred by you so that your household can maintain its normal standard of living" when the residence premises are "uninhabitable." If the kitchen is out of commission but the rest of the house is undamaged, is the house uninhabitable so that the residents can move out temporarily?

Particularly because the homeowners policy is complicated, the policyholder depends on the insurance company to honor its promise to indemnify them and to follow the rules of the road in handling a claim. But the company is also able to use the policy's complexity to profit at the homeowner's expense.

McKinsey & Company identified this ability in the early stages of its engagement with Allstate. With McKinsey's help, Allstate's homeowners insurance business could become the "Premier Claims Management Services Group" by achieving "sustained, demonstrable, positive impact on both homeowners claim severity and customer satisfaction." Customer satisfaction was all to the good, but when tied to severity it was chimerical. Severity means the average amount paid on claims. Having a sustained, demonstrable, and positive impact on severity could mean only one thing: paying policyholders less. Having a positive impact on customer satisfactions and on severity meant paying them less and having them like it; among con artists, the technique is known as "cooling out the mark," or making the target—the mark—believe that he hasn't been swindled.

Every loss under a homeowners insurance policy is likely to involve complicated interpretations of its terms and a unique set of facts. As Deborah Moroy and Dennis Martin, adjustment experts and commentators on the industry, put it, "Tom Hanks' line in the movie *Forrest Gump* may well be the insurance adjuster's mantra: 'Adjusting claims is like a box of chocolates. You never know what you're gunna get.'"[3] Accordingly, the path laid out by McKinsey directly violates the basic principles of fair claim practices. As *The Claims Environment*, a basic text for training adjusters published by the American Institute for Chartered Property Casualty Underwriters and the Insurance Institute of America, states, the first objective of claim management is "fulfill the insurer's promise to the insured."[4]

For a homeowner to receive what she is owed under the policy, she must know what is owed. The complexity of the policy and its unfamiliarity to the homeowner means that in many cases the homeowner will only know what the company tells her, especially about some of the more esoteric coverages and interpretations. This is the first responsibility of the adjuster, required by law in many states: to disclose all benefits, coverages, and time limits that may apply to the claim and to assist the policyholder with the claim.

Adjusters do not always live up to this responsibility, and no one outside insurance companies knows how much this failure is due to a lack of training, carelessness, or a McKinsey-like determination to delay and deny claims. Some examples:

A homeowner telephones the insurance company's claims call center and reports that his chimney has collapsed. The claims representative on the other end of the phone may simply respond correctly that collapse is not covered, the homeowner accepts the explanation, and that is the end of the story. In fact, "collapse" is excluded but that does not mean the damage to the chimney was. If the chimney was struck by lightning or a falling tree branch, if wind loosened bricks, or if some other external force had caused the collapse, then the damage would be covered. If the claims representative fails to fulfill the company's responsibility to advise its policyholder of these coverages, the homeowner would not know and the insurance company would escape payment.

When a home outside San Antonio was damaged by hail, causing water damage, a claims-handling expert found that Farmers Insurance failed to advise the homeowner of the provisions in the policy requiring Farmers to pay for additional living expenses and for repairs to protect the house against further damage. An additional living expense provision requires the company to pay for "any necessary increase in living expenses incurred by you so that your household can maintain its normal standard of living." Some homeowners will not move out while repairs are made, subjecting themselves at least to inconvenience and possibly to health hazards. Others will not have the means to rent fully comparable accommodations and will have their standard of living reduced. The provision only reimburses for expenses the homeowner actually incurs, so if the homeowner is not told about it and does not know it exists, she is denied the benefit she has purchased and the company has violated its promise.

If a claim appears to be covered, the necessary next step in good claims handling is good investigation. Good investigation of the cause of the loss can fail to occur because of inattention, carelessness, or worse. In a 2007 California case, for example, Mary Ann Jordan discovered that a window had fallen out of the wall of her living room, and floorboards in a corner of the room were "giving way." She hired DeLaCruz Wood Preservation Services to investigate, and the firm's conclusion was that the damage was caused by a fungus. Experts hired by Allstate, her insurance company, agreed, so Allstate denied Jordan's claim because her policy excluded damage from "wet or dry rot." When Jordan sued, the court concluded that Allstate's interpretation that fungus is a form of rot, while perhaps not correct, was at least reasonable. What was not reasonable, however, was Allstate's failure to investigate whether Jordan was entitled to be paid under another provision of the policy that paid for losses in the event of collapse. DeLaCruz and Allstate's own expert had warned that the house was in "imminent danger of collapse" and had recommended inspections by a structural engineer. Jordan wrote to Allstate, warning that "damage is now spreading at an alarming pace," and Allstate's adjusters and claims supervisor recognized the possibility of coverage for collapse but never investigated. Instead, Jordan alleged, the company left the evaluation entirely in the hands of adjuster Tina Bulmer, who had no credentials or background in structural engineering.

Sometimes the investigation appears to be deliberately inadequate. Ioan and Liana Nicolau noticed cracks in the walls of their Corpus Christi, Texas, home.[5] Over a five-year period they hired a foundation contractor, a civil engineer, and a structural engineer to diagnose and correct the problem. Ultimately those experts determined that leaks in the sewer line of the plumbing system were causing the soil at the back of the house to swell, putting pressure on the structure and producing the cracks. With that report the Nicolauses realized that the damage would be covered by their State Farm homeowners policy; settlement cracks would not have been covered, but damage caused by discharge from the plumbing system was. After seeing the Nicolauses' engineering report, State Farm authorized the adjuster to retain Haag Engineering to do another investigation. Without looking at the leaking pipe or taking soil samples, Haag concluded that the sewer line leak did not affect the foundation, and State Farm used Haag's report to deny coverage for the foundation damage. The Nicolauses obtained another expert report, this time from a licensed professional engineer with a master's degree in geotechnical engineering and a specialty in soils analysis, who concluded that the plumbing leak had traveled throughout the soil layer, confirming the earlier opinion that the leak had caused the damage. Nevertheless, Haag reaffirmed its opinion, and State Farm again rejected the claim.

During the trial of the case, the Nicolauses offered proof as to why State Farm hired Haag and why the Haag report came out the way it did. David Teasdale, the Haag engineer, admitted that 80 percent to 90 percent of his work consisted of investigations for insurance companies, and that he knew the companies would have to pay for damages caused by leaking plumbing. Haag had a "general opinion" that a leak beneath a house could not cause foundation damage, and Ralph Cooper, State Farm's claims superintendent, admitted that he knew of that opinion. The evidence of bias was bolstered by a review by the Nicolauses's foundation contractor of more than eighty reports by Haag in the area. In only two incidents had Haag found that a leak contributed to foundation movement, and the Haag engineers who worked on those cases never worked on another slab foundation case again.

Haag and State Farm had a notorious relationship in other cases. As discussed in Chapter 9, the jury in an Oklahoma case found that State Farm had hired Haag knowing that it would produce favorable reports on the cause and extent of damage to a house destroyed by a tornado. State Farm also stopped using Haag in Hurricane Katrina investigations as a result of similar charges of collusion.

The Nicolauses were not the only victims of insurance company denial based on dubious expert reports. State Farm also denied Terry and Johnnie Hamilton's claim for foundation problems.[6] When the Hamiltons first reported leaks and foundation and other structural problems, State Farm hired Barker Brothers Plumbing to conduct tests. Barker discovered severely deteriorated cast-iron pipe and a foot and a half of water underneath the living room. State Farm then turned to an engineering firm, George Perdue & Associates, to determine whether the leak caused the structural problems. Perdue concluded it did not, and State Farm could not have been surprised by the conclusion; it had hired Perdue 1,440 times in the previous four years and paid it more than $3 million, more than half of Perdue's business, and Perdue had never testified against State Farm. (Policyholder attorney William F. Merlin, Jr., likens the Hamiltons' chances with Perdue to an American trying to get a fair trial in Iran.) On top of the obvious opportunity for bias, Perdue's report failed to explain the effect of water it found in soil samples, showed no investigation of how much water had leaked from the broken pipe under the living room, and relied on old evidence about moisture in the soil but ignored the effect of the water from the broken pipe. As a result of State Farm's violation of its promise, Terry suffered depression and anxiety; having recently received a heart transplant, he had a suppressed immune system and worried that living in the house was unsafe. Johnnie expressed emotions common to those let down by their insurance companies: "I felt violated. I felt hurt. I felt betrayed." Both had to deal with the two-foot hole in their living room, which State Farm wanted to cover with dirt without repairing the leak. A jury found that State Farm violated the law by failing to make a prompt and fair settlement of the claim and awarded $72,800 for the cost of repairs and an additional sum for emotional distress caused by State Farm's denial.

After investigating the cause the adjuster next has to determine the extent of the loss and the cost of repairs. There are two steps in assessing the value of the loss. First, the adjuster "scopes" the damage, determining what has been damaged, to what extent, and what must be done to repair it. Second, the adjuster estimates the cost of repairs based on the scope of the damage. The result is called an estimate "for a reason." James Markham's basic text, *Property Loss Adjusting,* notes that "estimating is not an exact science, and legitimate differences are common."[7] But legitimate differences are not always what happen.

Property Loss Adjusting recommends that after an adjuster is assigned to a claim, he should meet the policyholder at the property "either on the same day or within the next few days."[8] Often this does not happen, scoping is delayed, and an inaccurate assessment of the damage results. A loss occurs and the policyholder calls her agent or the company call center. The information is relayed to the claims department, then to an individual adjuster, or perhaps outside the company to an independent adjusting firm, and then to that company's adjuster. By the time he begins work, several days may have passed, time during which the damage continues, emergency steps have already been taken, and the policyholder is going through the process alone. Disaster recovery services, which are often first on the scene after a fire or water damage report, for example, that adjusters seldom appear on weekends.

Insurance consumer advocates United Policyholders (UP) gives other common examples of the ways in which an adjuster might fail to properly scope the loss. Windows need to be replaced, but the adjuster fails to separately specify the need to replace wood trim on the inside of the windows. The measurements of the room are taken inaccurately or rounded down; since the drywall, paint, baseboard, and floor coverings, and the electrical, heating, and air-conditioning costs will be based on room dimensions, underestimating here will result in an unreasonably low estimate. Measurements may be taken accurately but may not account for waste, particularly where more material is needed to match complex color combinations or borders in carpeting, vinyl flooring, or wood flooring.[9] Adjusters may calculate the dimensions of a wall and then deduct the area of cutouts for doors and windows even though those cutouts may increase, not decrease, the cost of repair; the drywall removed for a window opening cannot be used elsewhere, and it takes more time to paint around an opening than to paint a solid wall.

Problems in scoping the extent of a loss sometimes result from industry trends. Trade publications, training courses, and word of mouth spread "common wisdom" among adjusters from different companies, and policyholder advocates report seeing many companies adopt the same unfair scoping tactics at the same time. The concept of an "abandoned floor" is one recent example. A homeowner suffers a plumbing leak that is included in the policy. Water from the leak inundates a room in which wall-to-wall carpeting covers a hardwood floor. Many insurance companies have taken the position that the hardwood floor is abandoned because its sole value is to provide a base for the carpeting; therefore, paying for the water damage requires only replacing the carpeting and providing a cheap underlayment of particleboard rather than also replacing the hardwood floor. Of course, if the homeowner someday would prefer to have hardwood floors rather than wall-to-wall carpeting, he will have to pay for the installation of a new floor; at that point, the homeowner realizes that the insurance company has not honored its promise to fairly adjust the claim and indemnify the homeowner for his loss. The difference can be substantial. One Pennsylvania homeowner was offered four thousand dollars by his insurance company to adjust a water loss in precisely these circumstances; after pursuing the claim with the aid of a public adjuster he ultimately received $15,000 as the full measure of his loss. (A public adjuster is an independent adjuster not employed by an insurance company who is hired by a policyholder to help with a claim.)

The abandoned floor problem illustrates several problems with the process of scoping property losses. The homeowner files a claim for the damaged floor, and the adjuster responds that the value of the hardwood floor is not covered under the obscure, legal-sounding concept of an "abandoned floor." The homeowner may question the decision, and the adjuster responds that this is an accepted interpretation and "all the companies do it" (which may well be true, at least when they can get away with it). At this point the homeowner suffers from two disadvantages. The adjuster is, or at least appears to be, the expert, and without expertise it is difficult to contest his argument. Nor is it necessarily easy to get a real expert to contest the decision. The difference in the Pennsylvania claim was $11,000, enough to justify hiring a lawyer or public adjuster. But on many claims the difference will be smaller. If the difference is a few hundred or even a few thousand dollars, it will not be worth it to hire professional help, so the adjuster's improper determination of the loss will go unchallenged. The homeowner has not received what the insurance company promised, but it's only a few hundred or a few thousand dollars. The insurance company has benefited by those relatively few dollars, but a few dollars on a lot of claims add up to a lot of dollars.

Part of the problem with scoping a loss is the degree and range of expertise involved. Houses are complex things, and tracking down the cause and nature of damage can be even more complex. The experts that the Nicolauses hired spent five years figuring out what was causing their cracks. Adjusters lack the expertise to do all of this, so good ones look to experts for help. But not all experts are expert enough, and experts on an insurance company's list of approved experts, through inadvertence or bias, sometimes produce findings about the scope of loss that are unduly favorable to the company. A Philadelphia town house was damaged by an explosion in the gas line of the house next door, including damage to the wall shared by the two homes. The insurance adjuster properly recognized the limits of his expertise and brought in an engineer to assess the damage to the wall. The engineer concluded that the top foot and a half of the wall needed to be replaced, but it was otherwise structurally sound. The homeowner's public adjuster brought in a better qualified engineer who found that the entire wall had to be replaced and, after a four-hour meeting at the site, persuaded the insurance company's engineer that that was the correct position. That change, and other corrections to the insurance company's scope of the damage and estimate of the needed repairs, were the difference between the company's original offer of $250,000 and its final payment of nearly $600,000.

Once the extent of the damage is scoped, the adjuster has to estimate the cost of repairs. Today many companies automate the process with software estimating programs that appear to remove discretion and to substitute for the adjuster's lack of experience. Although there are many such programs, the industry leader is Xactimate, sold by Xactware Solutions, a division of ISO, the industry's central source for policy forms, information on policyholders, and other products.

The concept of estimating software like Xactimate is, as described by Dan Kerr, owner of the adjuster training company AdjusterPro, that "Xactimate knows more so the adjuster may know less."[10] The adjuster described by the *Property Loss Adjusting* textbook who has "a vast knowledge of property values, costs, and methods of repair and at least a working knowledge of accounting and construction methods and materials" has been supplanted by, as the phrase goes about Hurricane Katrina adjusters, "a guy with a ladder and a laptop."[11] The adjuster takes the scope of the work, such as the replacement of a twelve-foot-by-eight-foot wall made of drywall and containing one window of specified dimensions and two electrical outlets, types it into Xactimate, and the program produces a cost estimate for the job, including material and labor costs.

The costs are drawn from one of 467 regional pricing databases covering the United States and Canada; they are updated monthly. As Kerr notes, "Xactimate takes the guesswork out, and not surprisingly, the days of handwritten claims are essentially over."

The days of handwritten claims may be over, but all the guesswork or, more important, error, is not out of the process. Xactimate is a tool and, like any other tool, it is neither perfect nor impervious to misuse. It first depends on an accurate scope of the work and, as with any program, garbage in, garbage out applies. Any errors in scope will produce an inaccurate estimate. Although its categories of items are vast, they are not infinite. As United Policyholders points out, Xactimate is "generic software" that is better suited to address "cookie-cutter" homes. The Philadelphia town house damaged by the explosion next door contained custom woodwork that needed to be replaced by an especially experienced carpenter, and the adjuster is hard-pressed to use Xactimate to allow for that additional expense. The costs built into the database are, like the results of any survey, somewhat generic and may not account for particular market conditions or the higher quality work done by some contractors. Studies by DataLath Inspection Services have demonstrated that for high-end homes, estimating software produces error rates of 20 percent or more half the time; the estimate for rebuilding a $800,000 home therefore would be off by $160,000.[12] And the figures built into the software can be unknown and hard to challenge. The California insurance commissioner investigated State Farm's use of Xactimate and concluded that the program "specifies depreciation dollar amounts but does not document how these figures were determined, resulting in low and unsupported settlement offers."[13]

Xactimate works off choices made by the adjuster, and because it needs to cover many different situations, the program is designed to give him a wide range of choices. Each of these choices affects the repair estimate. When drywall is replaced, the new drywall needs to be painted; the adjuster must choose the appropriate application—seal/prime, seal then paint, paint one coat, or paint two coats—each of which will produce a different cost estimate. If a large area of drywall needs to be replaced, the adjuster may or may not decide the furniture and other contents need to be removed to allow for work space and to protect the contents; that cost can be accounted for as labor and contents manipulation, with the adjuster adding a variable for the time needed or the size of the room as small, medium, or large.

Consider the consequences for choices like these on three comparable jobs for water damage to buildings in the Philadelphia area. All involved the same national insurance company, and two were estimated by the same adjuster. First there were issues of scope. On the first job the adjuster first saw the property three days after the loss, at which time much of the initial cleanup work had been done. As a result, he estimated the cost of cleanup at six thousand dollars, when the company performing the work had workers on the job for three days and billed a total of fifteen thousand dollars for the time of workers and the materials used. Nor did his determination of scope accurately take account of all of the work that needed to be done. He scoped one room's damages as the need to tear out two hundred square feet of wet drywall, bag it, and remove it from the premises. Not included in that estimate was any assessment of the details of the work. If the contractor needed to carry bags of waste some distance away to be disposed of, that would take more time; if they needed to carry them through undamaged portions of the property, the floor would need to be covered to prevent dirtying it and damage, and that cost accounted for.

The decisions of the adjuster also controlled the eventual cost of the estimate. On the first job the rate estimated for a technician was $39 per hour (on a time-and-a-half basis for overtime), with no estimate for a supervisor, while the repair company's cost was $57. On the second job the same adjuster entered a rate of $42 for a technician and added $51 for a supervisor. On the third job a different adjuster for the same company used a rate of $29 per hour for a technician and $41 for a supervisor.

What Xactimate produces is an estimate of repair costs. An estimate is not the same thing as a price. Many homeowners have found that reputable local contractors are unwilling to do the repairs for an Xactimate price. One step to avoid this controversy is the use of preferred contractors by the insurance companies. State Farm has its Premier Service Program, and Allstate and others have similar ones, under which a contractor chosen by the insurance company will do the estimating and perform the work for the estimated price, receiving payment from the insurance company and offering a limited guarantee on the work. Often these programs operate through national cleanup and restoration services franchises. The fact that a preferred contractor will do a job at a low price that an established local builder would find insufficient does not mean that the work is of lower standard, but of course it does not prevent that result either.

Even when the insurance company and the homeowner settle on an amount of loss and cost of repair, the insured may not get everything that she expected from the company's promise of indemnity. Homeowners policies are not what they seem. Another way insurance companies reduce payments is to reduce coverage. Instead of denying claims that are covered by the policy, increasingly companies deny claims because they are *not* covered by the policy. The denials often violate the reasonable expectations about coverage held by ordinary homeowners who are ill equipped and little inclined to engage in painstaking examination of their policies.

Homeowners can purchase two kinds of policies: one that pays for the "actual cash value" of the loss, and one that pays for "replacement cost." Actual cash value is essentially the lower value of used property compared to new; kitchen cabinets that are ten years old are worth less than new kitchen cabinets, so their actual cash value is less than the cost of new cabinets. Many homeowners, in order to be fully protected in case of loss, purchase replacement cost insurance, which, as its name suggests, is designed to pay the full cost of repairing or replacing an item, even if that cost is greater than the item's current value. Under a replacement cost policy the homeowner would get new kitchen cabinets rather than having to make up the difference between the actual cash value of the old cabinets and the price of new ones.

Or maybe not. Once insurance companies sold "guaranteed replacement cost" coverage, which, as the term suggests, guaranteed that the company would pay the cost of replacing the damaged or destroyed house, even if that cost exceeded the policy limits. A string of natural disasters in the 1990s, beginning with the Oakland, California, wildfires, imposed catastrophic losses on many companies, and in response they reduced their risks by limiting coverage. As a result, today replacement cost does not really mean the cost to replace, and, as former Texas insurance commissioner J. Robert Hunter notes, "It puts people in a rather fragile situation."[14]

The widely used HO-3 policy, which provides the most extensive coverage generally available, is part of the problem. If the home is damaged, the loss will be measured "at replacement cost without deduction for depreciation, subject to the following." "The following" takes away much of what the preceding gives. First, anything resembling replacement cost is only available "if at the time of loss the amount of insurance in this policy on the damaged building is 80% or more of the full replacement cost of the building prior to the loss." If the house would cost $300,000 to rebuild, the homeowner has to purchase a policy with a limit of at least $240,000 or the replacement cost coverage becomes actual cash value coverage. Most homeowners neither know about this limitation nor have a good idea what it would cost to replace their house. A house's value is set by the real estate market; a house's replacement cost is set by the construction market. Even if a homeowner has an idea what the house is worth, they are unlikely to know what a builder would charge to rebuild it. More than two thirds of homes across the country are insured for less than replacement cost, and insurance consumer advocates United Policyholders reports that 75 percent of California homeowners affected by the 2007 wildfires in San Bernardino and Riverside counties were underinsured by an average of $240,000.[15]

It would seem to be in insurance companies' interest to make sure that homes are insured at their full replacement costs, because higher policy limits yield higher premiums. Not necessarily: The additional premiums may not be worth the additional risk, particularly if price competition among companies keeps premiums artificially low. Moreover, as the marketing of insurance moves from local agents to corporate call centers, the ability to arrive at an accurate estimate diminishes. Insurance companies draw on vast databases in assessing the value of homes, but whether a house contains hardwood floors or custom cabinetry and the current costs in the local construction market are impossible to determine from a distance.

The problem of underinsurance is not only one of ensuring the replacement cost. In the HO-3 policy, even if the house is insured for more than 80 percent of its replacement costs, the insurer's payment is limited to "the least of the following amounts," the first of which is "the limit of liability under this policy." So replacement cost means replacement cost up to the policy limits. If the house costing $300,000 to rebuild is insured for $275,000, the homeowner will be out $25,000 if she has to rebuild.

Even if the house is insured to its full value, the insurance company may still try not to pay. A second limitation on replacement cost in many versions of the HO-3 caps the homeowner's claim at the replacement cost "for equivalent construction." Equivalent to what? Insurance companies routinely argue that means equivalent to the house that was damaged or destroyed. Moreover, most policies contain an exclusion for "loss resulting directly or indirectly from ordinance or law." If the policyholder reads the policy, she might think this means that if the house is condemned because it is in disrepair, that loss is due to the enforcement of a law and is therefore outside the coverage. The insurance company, however, interprets the clause more broadly to cover situations in which "indirectly" means whenever the law affects the extent of the loss as well as its occurrence.

Suppose the house was fifty years old. The repairs or rebuilding cannot be to a fifty-year-old standard using fifty-year-old construction methods. The new house has to be built to modern standards, which are set by the building code, using modern construction methods, all of which are likely to exceed the cost of repairing or rebuilding to the fifty-year-old standard. Faith Dupre's ninety-one-year-old house in Mesa County, Colorado, was severely damaged by fire.[16] Allstate's adjuster hired a builder who estimated the cost of repairing the house to the condition it was in before the fire at $60,680. When an inspector from the county building department walked through it with Allstate's builder, however, he pointed out a number of respects in which the house would have to be improved to bring it up to the current construction code. These included expanding the staircase, providing sufficiently sized exits from the bedrooms, replacing one-by-fours with two-by-fours in the walls, and bringing the burned portions of the roof and the electrical wiring up to modern standards. Allstate argued that improvements required by the code would be excluded from the policy, either because they made the new building not substantially equivalent to the old or because they were a loss caused by the law and not the fire. The court rejected both contentions, pointing to the definition of replacement cost used by the American Institute of Real Estate Appraisers, which focused on providing the policyholder "a building with utility equivalent to the building being appraised" not an exact duplicate of the original, which would be worthless, because it would be legally uninhabitable.

Even if the home is fully insured to value, the homeowner is entitled to replacement cost, and the work only involves the construction of a replacement house identical to the original the homeowner will find that the insurance company will not pay the full cost when it initially settles the claim. The company's policy form allows it to delay payment of the full replacement costs "until actual repair or replacement is complete." Until then, the homeowner is entitled only to the actual cash value of the loss, which is the depreciated value. The effect is to turn a *replacement cost* policy into a *replacement* policy. Meanwhile, the company keeps the difference and earns investment profits on it. Indeed, the company may keep the homeowner's money forever. If the homeowner does not rebuild, the company never makes the final payment. The insurance company will pay only if asked, of course. Some homeowners, receiving an initial check for actual cash value from the company, do not know about their right to get the rest. Others may read the policy and, as in some policies, find a provision that the additional payment will only be made for repairs completed within 180 days; if repairs take longer, they may not understand that a court will refuse to enforce the 180-day limit if there are good reasons not to do so. In either event, the homeowner may not claim the additional amount, leaving the company with a profit at the policyholder's expense.

Not satisfied with this provision in the policy allowing them to hold back part of what is owed, insurance companies have attempted to reduce the amount that they owe as actual cash value pending the completion of repairs. Brian Salesin suffered water damage to his home from a leaking washing machine and made a claim to State Farm, the insurer from which he had bought a homeowner's "extra" policy that provided replacement cost coverage.[17] After investigating, State Farm sent Salesin a check for $20,778.75, with this explanation: "As we agreed, the total repair cost including the ceramic tile floor in the kitchen came to $27,908.98. From the above figure was subtracted $1,048.44 in betterment and $5,581.79 in profit and overhead for a total amount withheld of $6,630.23." ("Betterment" here meant the difference between the replacement cost and actual cash value, consistent with a policy term like that described above.)

The controversial deduction was the $5,581.79 in profit and overhead. This was the insurance company's technique of deducting from the actual cash value an additional amount often described in the insurance trade as "10 and 10." If the job was done by a general contractor, the contractor would incur overhead above the costs of labor, materials, and payments to subcontractors specific to this job, such as the expense of running an office, and also would be entitled to earn a reasonable profit; by convention in the trade, the usual figures are 10 percent overhead and 10 percent profit. State Farm's in-house operation guide (which the court pointed out was not part of the contract between State Farm and Salesin) justified holding back this 20 percent: "General contractor overhead and profit is not a component of actual cash value since the cost is not actually and necessarily incurred unless the property is repaired or restored by means of a general contractor." Therefore, State Farm argued, it was entitled to hold on to not just the difference between the replacement cost value and the actual cash value, but also an additional 20 percent of the replacement value. Hold on to that difference, that is, and profit from the float of investing it until it was eventually paid, or, if Salesin did not make the repairs, did not use a general contractor, or simply forgot to reclaim it, hold on to it forever.

The Michigan court rejected State Farm's argument that because Salesin had not incurred the cost of the contractor's overhead and profit, it was not yet due to Salesin. Prior to the repairs Salesin had not incurred any costs, including for labor and materials, but he was still entitled to the estimated actual cash value of the loss. The court relied on a Pennsylvania case in which State Farm had made the same arguments and lost. In that case the court discovered that State Farm always deducted the 10 and 10. (State Farm was not alone in this; Farmers Insurance, among others, also is reported to have engaged in the practice.) It rejected State Farm's illogical argument that it should not have to pay for some of the costs not yet incurred, and it made a more important point about the company's promise: "The issue is what State Farm agreed to pay to its insureds prior to actual repair or replacement. It agreed to pay 'actual cash value,' which means 'repair or replacement cost less depreciation.'"[18]

Allstate tried a variation on the tactic in an Arizona case in which its preferred contractor program went awry. When Jules Tritschler's home was damaged by rain, he contacted Allstate, his insurance company, which sent out Better Way Services to perform emergency repairs.[19] Because Better Way was a Quality Vendor for Allstate, the insurer and Tritschler agreed that Better Way would complete the repairs and be paid directly by Allstate. Tritschler became dissatisfied with Better Way's work, however, ordered the company off the job, complained to Allstate, and told Allstate he would finish the job himself. When he did, he submitted a claim to Allstate for $36,377, the cost of the job on top of what the company already had paid, including $7,967 for general contractor's overhead and profit. Allstate refused to pay the overhead and profit, rehearsing the arguments State Farm made in the earlier cases and adding a new one: Because Tritschler had acted as his own general contractor, he had not actually incurred these costs, so he was not entitled to them. The court disagreed. The actual cash value payment included the 10 and 10, even if Tritschler had done the work himself rather than incurring the expense in cash.

State Farm and Allstate have not been alone in withholding payment for overhead and profit. Nationwide Insurance settled a class action in 2009 that provided for additional payments to homeowners who filed claims over a thirteen-year period. Without admitting that it did anything wrong, Nationwide agreed to pay 20 percent more for general contractor's overhead and profit to homeowners whose estimated repairs involved three or more trades (such as electricians and drywall installers) even if the repairs weren't actually made.

Any single violation of standard claim practices in failing to investigate, improperly assessing damage, or relying on obscure terms of the policy is bad enough, but sometimes they coalesce in an amalgamation of delay, deny, defend all at once.

Thomas Anderson, a homeowner insured by Allstate, encountered that problem when he filed a claim for water damage to his house.[20] Neighbors discovered water running down the side of Anderson's house and called the local water company to have the water shut off. When he discovered the damage, he reported it to Allstate. Allstate sent its emergency service contractor, ServiceMaster, to the home. It pulled up carpeting and applied an antimicrobial substance to remove mold from the floor, and walls; it also suspected that there might be asbestos in the walls and ceilings, a suspicion that was confirmed by an environmental management company that recommended that all soft goods be removed as hazardous materials and all hard goods be decontaminated.

Glen Plumlee, Allstate's adjuster, inspected the home and documented that a pipe in the attic had ruptured, soaking carpets, cabinets, walls, and ceilings. He noticed that there was little furniture in the house, though he was told that that could be explained because Anderson's son was in the process of renovating the house. Concerned about inconsistencies in the claim, Plumlee referred the case to Allstate's SIU, where Brenda Burg, an SIU claims agent, took charge.

As the court noted, the claim process "became contentious." Anderson complained that Allstate was "jerking [him] around," while Allstate argued that Anderson was being "evasive" and had "overstated" claims for damages to the contents of the house. Burg suspected that the house had been unoccupied and the heat off, which had led to freezing of the pipe that burst, which would give the company a basis for denying the claim. But Allstate never fully investigated, never considered evidence offered by Anderson, and never made a decision on the matter. After a year and a half, during which the house was uninhabitable due to mold, Anderson sued Allstate. The result, after five years of litigation, was a jury award against Allstate of $484,853 for breach of its duty to act in good faith and

$18 million in punitive damages. On appeal, the U.S. Court of Appeals upheld the breach of good faith award but found that, although Allstate's conduct violated fair claims practices, it was not so "despicable" that it should be punished with punitive damages.

The court identified several factors that supported the jury's determination that Allstate had failed to act in good faith. First, "[o]ne of the most critical factors in determining the unreasonableness of an insurer's conduct," it wrote, "is the adequacy of its investigation of the claim." Here Allstate particularly failed to honor its obligation to act fairly and reasonably and not favor its own financial interest over that of its policyholder. "Allstate's pattern of investigation on Anderson's claim suggests that it was looking for reasons to deny Anderson's claim rather than to find coverage."

Second, Allstate took what the court described as an "inflexible position" in failing to decide on the claim and failing to consider Anderson's evidence. For example, it consistently refused to approve the replacement of sagging, moldy drywall. It even threatened to take the drywall issue to appraisal, a process under which the company and the policyholder each select an appraiser, and the two appraisers select a third, neutral appraiser, to determine the extent of the loss. Appraisal is not inexpensive; Anderson would have to pay about a thousand dollars for a simple appraisal, and the cost of a more formal appraisal could go "into never, never land," according to Allstate's own expert. Yet the threat was particularly offensive here, because appraisal would not resolve the issue; appraisal would determine the value of the loss and the cost of the repairs, but Allstate still had not admitted that the drywall was covered under the policy at all.

Third, Allstate was aware of the dangers of mold but failed to take adequate steps to remedy the situation and protect Anderson. The company had proposed spraying an antimold solution on the affected drywall and then sealing it, but it was established in the industry that that was an inadequate treatment. In fact, during the claim process Plumlee suggested spraying bleach on the mold, a method that even he admitted at trial would be ineffective.

As the court summed up the matter: "If Allstate had attempted to resolve the coverage issue instead of leaving it hanging over Anderson's head, it would have investigated and made decisions on whether the house was unoccupied and whether Anderson had failed to keep the house heated. Particularly with regard to the heat, Allstate did nothing." Nothing, that is, except delay, deny, defend.

9

Hurricane Katrina and Other Insurance Catastrophes

INSURANCE COMPANIES DEAL with hundreds of thousands of claims each year, usually through a steady flow of auto accidents, home fires, and other events that can be catastrophic for those involved but are, individually and in the aggregate, routine for the companies. But every now and then there are real catastrophes, events usually of natural origin that generate huge numbers of claims all at once. The Insurance Services Office (ISO) defines a catastrophe as an event that causes $25 million or more in insured property losses and affects a significant number of policyholders and insurance companies.[1] By that measure even a winter storm affecting a few northeastern states or a Texas-size windstorm is a catastrophe, and in the last decade no year has seen fewer than twenty. Major catastrophes are exponentially larger. The three largest natural disasters in U.S. history, measured by privately insured property losses, were: Hurricane Katrina in 2005, with losses of $41.1 billion; Hurricane Andrew in 1992, $15.5 billion; and the Northridge, California, earthquake in 1994, $12.5 billion. (The terrorist attack on the World Trade Center and Pentagon of September 11, 2001, caused insured losses of $18.8 billion.)

A catastrophe happens to many people at once, and the scale of the loss for individuals and regions is such that emotions run hot, charges and countercharges fly, and massive efforts are devoted to shifting loss and assigning blame. Lawsuits following Hurricane Katrina numbered in the thousands, and not only for individual claims; other litigation included: class actions on behalf of tens of thousands of policyholders; an antitrust action by the Mississippi attorney general; another class action by the Mississippi attorney general that led to a settlement with State Farm, and then to another suit alleging that the company breached the prior settlement; and a suit on behalf of residents by the Louisiana attorney general. State Farm tried to move Katrina lawsuits out of southern Mississippi, presenting as evidence a survey showing that 49 percent of the people in southern Mississippi "believe that insurance executives are on the same level as child molesters."[2] Insurance companies were successful in shifting many cases from state to federal courts, where they hoped to find more congenial judges, and where the flood of suits would delay trials for years, putting more pressure on homeowners to settle. Competing False Claims Act suits are still pending, in which insurance company whistleblowers assert that companies routinely and wrongfully shifted losses from their policies to the federal government's flood insurance program, which they were paid to administer. The most bizarre episode surely was the Shakespearean fall of Mississippi's legendary class action lawyer, Richard "Dickie" Scruggs. Scruggs had become famous first in asbestos suits and then for engineering the $246 billion settlement of health care claims by forty-eight states against the tobacco industry, for which his fee was a reported $800 million. He aimed the same three-barreled strategy—public relations, political pressure, and litigation—at the insurance companies. Scruggs formed a consortium of law firms (the Scruggs Katrina Group) that brought litigation in parallel with Mississippi attorney general Jim Hood. He represented the Rigsby sisters, Cori and Kerry, in their whistle-blower suit against State Farm (after the sisters had spent an industrious first weekend in June 2006 downloading and copying documents that they alleged proved fraud by their employer) and then hired them as "consultants" at an annual salary of $150,000 each. He also represented his brother-in-law, then U.S.

senator Trent Lott, whose home in Pascagoula had been damaged by the storm. Scruggs agreed to a settlement in a class action against State Farm of $80 million, plus $26.5 million in attorneys' fees, and then withdrew from the settlement. Finally, in a case brought by another lawyer in the Scruggs Katrina Group, he conspired to bribe a judge to have the case sent to arbitration, a crime to which he pleaded guilty and was sentenced to up to five years in prison.[3]

One basic question emerges from all the complexities of human tragedy and legal wrangling that followed Katrina: What do policyholders expect from their insurers when disaster strikes, and what do they get? The Katrina story is a different version of the same story told elsewhere in this book, that insurance companies have economic incentives, from the boardroom down to the individual claim adjuster, to break the promise of indemnity and security made to the policyholder by delaying payment, denying valid claims, and defending litigation brought to enforce those promises. The Katrina story actually began with an added twist: The companies' ability to deny claims was plotted in advance by painstakingly drafting terms in the insurance policies that allowed them to argue, when disaster struck, that they were well within their rights to delay, deny, defend.

Hurricane Katrina first struck southern Florida on August 25, 2005, strengthened in the Gulf of Mexico, made landfall in southeast Louisiana on August 29, and swept across the Louisiana/Mississippi border with sustained winds in excess of 120 miles per hour. It caused massive damage from Florida to Texas, with its most dramatic effects in New Orleans, where the levees protecting the city failed, causing 80 percent of the city to flood and the residents ordered to evacuate. Its destruction was staggering. Over 1,800 deaths were attributed to the hurricane and 275,000 homes were destroyed, with many more damaged. It struck the high and lowly alike; along with the devastation visited on New Orleans's Lower Ninth Ward, it destroyed the homes of then senator Trent Lott and Congressman Gene Taylor.

The insurance effects of Katrina were equally dramatic. The Mississippi insurance department reported that over 380,000 insurance claims were filed as a result of Katrina, and the Insurance Information Institute estimates 1.75 million claims were filed across the region. In addition to the $41.1 billion paid by private insurance companies, the National Flood Insurance Program (NFIP), the federal insurance system designed to fill the gap left by insurance companies' refusal to offer flood coverage, received 209,404 claims on which it paid $15.8 billion. Yet despite the enormity of these numbers, Katrina was a failure of the insurance system. Estimates of the total damage inflicted by the hurricane vary widely, from a low of $81 billion to a high of $135 billion, but any of those numbers leaves a huge share of the loss uninsured. Dissatisfied policyholders complained to the Louisiana Department of Insurance at the rate of 20,000 a month for the six months after the storm; 4,700 additional complaints were filed as late as 2007. Thousands of policyholders went further and sued their insurance companies; more than 6,600 suits were filed in federal court in New Orleans alone, and in the last week claims could be filed, at the end of August 2007, 2,489 suits were filed in civil court in New Orleans.

Hurricane Katrina provided the ultimate test of the New Orleans levees, a test they failed, as the city was inundated when protection was most needed. It set the ultimate test to the Federal Emergency Management Agency (FEMA), which also failed to rescue, transport, house, and care for New Orleans residents when they were most in need. So too it tested the property insurance system and the processing of policyholders' claims and found the system wanting.

The insurance industry trumpets its massive response to catastrophes such as Katrina as great successes that show the strength of insurance and the effectiveness of their claim processing. The companies pour enormous resources into the affected areas; fifteen thousand adjusters were brought in from across the country to respond to Katrina claims, some employed by the insurance companies, some by independent adjusting firms to which the companies outsourced their claim processing, and some trained on the spot. As best as can be done under the press of extreme circumstances, policyholders are dealt with promptly and fairly, and nearly all claims are resolved according to policy terms. Companies also need to be vigilant for the large number of fraudulent claims that often follows disasters. Problems arise, of course, they acknowledge; as in any massive effort, mistakes are made, and those mistakes are corrected when brought to the companies' attention. Litigation inevitably ensues, but that has two unfortunate sources: policyholders who don't understand the limits of their policies and lawyers who spin spurious claims out of public concern and resentment. After Katrina, many homeowners who had not purchased federal flood insurance tried to recover under their homeowners insurance policies for flood claims that were specifically excluded.

Consider State Farm's account of its response to Katrina, widely considered to be the largest deployment of resources. State Farm assigned more than 5,600 employees and contract adjusters to the Gulf Coast after the hurricane, and its call centers logged 1.1 million calls from customers. It processed more than 295,000 property claims and 99,000 auto claims, for which it paid $3.6 billion. Although its conclusions were contested by policyholder advocates, a study of State Farm's response by the Mississippi Department of Insurance found that the company "did make errors," but it found no violations of the unfair claim practices laws. As insurance commissioner Mike Chaney said in releasing the report, "Although there were questionable decisions and irregularities by State Farm in handling claims, no scheme or plan to systematically mistreat policyholders was found."[4]

Policyholders, their attorneys, and consumer advocates tell a different story. At the extreme, insurance companies engaged in what bloggers at slabbed, a Web site devoted to Katrina claims, calls "The Scheme." Insurance companies and their agents deceive policyholders into thinking they are covered for hurricane claims, but when the hurricane comes the companies rely on arcane language, dubious interpretations of insurance policies, and outright fraud to limit or deny their responsibility to pay for losses. The companies manipulate the software that evaluates claims, generate inadequate or biased inspections of damaged property and fraudulent or doctored engineering reports, and otherwise distort the claims-handling process as part of a large-scale, industrywide system of underpaying claims. James W. Greer, president of the Association of Property and Casualty Claims Professionals, lamented, "It was as if some small group of high-level financial magnates decided that the only way to save the industry's financial fate from this megadisaster was to take a total hands-off approach and hide beneath the waves and the flood exclusion."[5] And they can largely get away with it because of massive public relations, campaign contributions producing industry-friendly judges, and lobbying efforts to influence legislators and regulators. The vast majority of claims are settled, but that does not mean they have been settled fairly, for the proper amounts due. Insurance companies have inherent authority to which their policyholders often acquiesce, so that the overwhelming proportion of claimants take what the insurance company offers, lowball or not, and even those who complain do not necessarily sue. Particularly after a traumatic event such as Katrina, policyholders are in great need, financial and emotional, and are even more inclined to accept an insurance company's payment and try to rebuild their lives. Ordinary biases may be at work too. After Hurricane Andrew in Florida, Hispanic policyholders were only 50 percent to 60 percent as likely to receive prompt payment from their companies as other homeowners, probably because adjusters' prejudices led them to treat them as hard to communicate with or untrustworthy.[6]

At the institutional level, the story is an example of what J. Robert Hunter, the former Texas insurance commissioner and federal insurance administrator, calls "privatizing profit, socializing risk." In order to maximize profits, insurance companies take fewer and fewer risks, shifting some to the public fisc through programs like the National Flood Insurance Program and state catastrophe funds and some to homeowners who find less coverage available. As a result, the federal and state governments pay a large part of the losses from Katrina, most of the losses are borne by homeowners themselves, and insurance company profits rise; in 2005, the year of Hurricane Katrina, property/casualty companies amassed recorded profits of $48.8 billion, a record exceeded the next year when profits rose to $68.1 billion.[7]

To sort out these conflicting accounts, begin with a typical homeowner along the Gulf Coast in 2005. As is common throughout the United States, the homeowner's insurance policy would be an all-risk policy, which would suggest to the homeowner that it covers the insured property against damage caused by all risks, including fire, falling trees, and lightning. (All-risk policies are different than "named peril" policies that cover property against specific types of harm—perils—named in the policy.)

The policy also is likely to have a "hurricane deductible." Ordinarily a deductible is stated as a dollar amount of loss ($100, $500, or $1,000 are typical) that the policyholder must cover before the insurance company pays anything. A hurricane deductible dictates a special deductible amount, typically larger than the overall deductible and stated as a percentage of the insured value; a homeowner with a 5 percent deductible and a $100,000 policy would have to pay the first $5,000 of loss.

The homeowner also may have known about federal flood insurance but, depending on the location of the property, is unlikely to have purchased it; only about 30 percent of property owners affected by Katrina maintained flood insurance. Or the homeowner may not have known about the federal program, or, as was often the case, may have been advised by his insurance agent that he didn't need it.

When Hurricane Katrina struck and damaged or destroyed this homeowner's house, he might reasonably have expected to be insured. He was covered for all risks, including presumably hurricane damage above the amount of the hurricane deductible. But not so fast. In the insurance business, all risks does not mean all risks, the presence of a hurricane deductible does not mean that damage caused by a hurricane above the deductible amount is covered, and even if damage is caused by a risk covered by the policy, it may not be covered.

Under an all-risk policy an insurance company does not cover damage from any source. In its underwriting, the company determines that risks of a certain kind are too great to be covered under the standard premium, or perhaps to be covered at all, so it excludes them from coverage with special provisions. A standard policy (the ISO's HO-3, the widely used homeowner's policy) has nine classes of overall exclusions, including damage caused by earth movement, power failure, war, and nuclear hazard, and an additional thirteen exclusions applicable to damage to the structure itself, including loss caused by freezing of a plumbing system, settling, smog, birds, vermin, rodents, or insects, and a final ten or so exclusions applicable to damage to personal property.

It may seem odd to have a policy called "all risks" that excludes several dozen kinds of risk, and particularly at odds with the policyholder's expectation that coverage for all risks means all risks. But the courts have upheld this insurance company practice, with one limitation. What the insurance company gives it can only take away if it does so specifically and unambiguously in the policy. This is an application of the ancient maxim of interpretation known in lawyer's Latin as *contra proferentem*, interpreting a document "against the one who proffers" it: Because the drafter of a document is in the best position to write it in a way that says what it means, he should suffer the consequences if it is not clear. Thus "all risks" includes all risks except to the extent that certain risks have been specifically excluded.

Insurance companies and their lawyers are nothing if not good at drafting detailed policy language, and to a large extent they exclude the risks as they please. Floods are one of the early and now nearly universal exclusions. Flood insurance was widely offered by insurance companies through the mid-1920s, but the Mississippi River flood of 1927 that inundated portions of ten states, and floods from New Hampshire to California the following year, led companies to stop offering coverage for flood damage.[8] As those calamities taught, there is a particular problem with correlated risks, or risks that cause loss to a large number of insureds at the same time, and insurance companies strive mightily to reduce or avoid those risks. A typical homeowners policy today will carry a broad flood exclusion:

> We do not cover loss resulting directly or indirectly from . . . water damage, meaning (a) flood, surface water, waves, wave wash, tidal water, overflow of a body of water, or spray from any of these, whether or not a result of precipitation or driven by wind; (b) water (1) which backs up through sewers and drains; (2) which overflows from a sump; or (c) water below the surface of the ground, including water: (1) which exerts pressure on, or seeps or leaks through a building, driveway, roadway, walkway, pavement, foundation, spa, hot tub, swimming pool or other structure; (2) which causes earth movement.

The presence of flood exclusions is one reason that the insurance industry geared up its public relations campaign after Katrina struck to rename the tragedy from a "hurricane" to a "flood." Risk Management Solutions, the industry leader for assessing and managing losses from catastrophes, coined the term "The Great New Orleans Flood," emphasizing water damage and diminishing the effect of hours-long, hurricane-strength winds. The phrase was quickly picked up by the news media, at least until *BusinessWeek* exposed the strategy.[9]

Therefore, a homeowner whose house was damaged or destroyed by Hurricane Katrina would face the insurance company's assertion that the policy specifically excludes coverage for water damage, whether that damage came from torrential rain, the storm surge of wind-driven water, or the deluge caused by the failure of the levees in New Orleans. If the policy had a hurricane deductible, amounts above the deductible are still not covered if they come within the exceedingly broad language of the flood exclusion.

This is only the beginning of the journey for the policyholder. A hurricane, according to the *New Oxford American Dictionary*, is "a storm with a violent wind." Wind damage is obviously not excluded as water damage is, nor is it excluded elsewhere under the all-risks policy. (Although in areas prone to wind damage, particularly along the coasts or in the central plains, insurance companies have increasingly reduced their risks by excluding damage caused by wind.) Some of the damage in Hurricane Katrina was caused by water, including rain, storm surge, and flooding, and that damage is excluded. Some of the damage was caused by wind, and that damage is covered. What happens when damage is caused by multiple sources, such as a house damaged by both high winds and flooding?

Courts generally solve this conundrum by employing a doctrine known as "efficient proximate cause." In a case in which more than one event contributes to damage—covered wind damage and excluded water damage, for example—the court's task is to determine the predominant cause of the loss.[10] Efficient proximate cause is not a factual inquiry about the cause of harm but a legal judgment, considering issues of policy and fairness, as to which cause the harm should be assigned. Prior to Katrina the doctrine was well established in the Gulf states. As the Mississippi Supreme Court had stated, "[I]f the cause designated by the policy is the dominant and efficient cause of the loss, the right of the insured to recover will not be defeated by the fact that there were contributing causes."[11]

Efficient proximate cause, though well established in many states, is not a doctrine that insurance companies find attractive. The point of writing detailed exclusions into policies is to limit the companies' liability in the event of loss. Efficient proximate cause, as a flexible doctrine that allows the court to determine to which of several factual causes to assign responsibility, raises the fear that companies will not get the benefit of their assiduous drafting of exclusions.

After its potential to expand coverage became clear, insurance companies returned to the challenge by drafting new policy provisions. In the early 1980s the companies and their surrogate ISO promulgated a policy provision to deal with the problem, known as "the anti-concurrent causation clause" or, as it was called by Representative Gene Taylor, a "concurrent fraud" clause.[12] Here is a version that was at issue in one of the leading Katrina cases:

> We do not insure under any coverage for any loss which would not have occurred in the absence of one or more of the following excluded events. We do not insure for such loss regardless of: (a) the cause of the excluded event; or (b) other causes of the loss; or (c) whether other causes acted concurrently or in any sequence with the excluded event to produce the loss; or (d) whether the event occurs suddenly or gradually, involves isolated or widespread damage, arises from natural or external forces, or occurs as a result of any combination of these: [listed excluded perils including water damage].[13]

Thus, the all-risks policy grants broad coverage, the exclusions take away some of that coverage, and the anti-concurrent causation takes away much of what is left. The policy covers the home for all risks except for damage by water (and another couple dozen or so causes). It still covers damage caused by wind. Under the anti-concurrent causation clause, however, it does not cover for damage by wind if the damage "would not have occurred in the absence of" damage by water "regardless of" how the causes interact to produce the loss.

After Katrina, the effect of the anti–concurrent causation clause was much litigated. Could an insurance company take away with one hand what it gave with the other, and then take away a little more?

In several cases Judge L. T. Senter, Jr., of the federal court in Mississippi, who was the trial judge in much of the Katrina litigation, ruled that the anti-concurrent causation clause was ambiguous and therefore unenforceable.[14] The U.S. Court of Appeals for the Fifth Circuit disagreed and overruled Senter's approach, concluding that "the clause unambiguously excludes coverage for water damage even if another peril contributed concurrently or in any sequence to cause the loss."[15] In addition, the appellate court found a more fundamental error in Judge Senter's analysis.

> The fatal flaw in the district court's rationale is its failure to recognize the three discrete categories of damage at issue in this litigation: (1) damage caused exclusively by wind; (2) damage caused exclusively by water; and (3) damage caused by wind "concurrently or in any sequence" with water. . . . The only species of damage covered under the policy is damage caused exclusively by wind. But if wind and water synergistically caused the same damage, such damage is excluded.[16]

What the Fifth Circuit saw as the "fatal flaw" in Judge Senter's rationale was a poorly understood element of the problem, and much disputed when it was understood. Under the court's analysis, the ordinary policyholder should know that water damage was excluded (assuming that she read the policy, and assuming that she was not misled by the presence of the hurricane deductible, which did not extend coverage to hurricane damage). She might have believed that the policy covered wind damage; it was an all-risks policy that did not list wind among the excluded perils. Under the court's reading of the anti–concurrent causation clause, however, much wind damage during a hurricane would not be covered, because the wind damage would occur "concurrently or in any sequence" with water damage.

In any event, even the Fifth Circuit judges conceded that damage caused exclusively by wind was covered. Covered, that is, if it could be established which damage was caused by wind and which by water. Clearly wind caused extensive damage to many homes in many places. Before the storm surge hit, coastal areas endured winds over 100 miles per hour for hours. At a U.S. House of Representatives committee hearing on the insurance industry's response to Katrina, Mississippi attorney general Jim Hood testified, "My home in Jackson, Mississippi, at that capital is about 180 miles north of the coast, and it blew the shingles off of my roof. . . . People on the coast got hit with 140 miles-per-hour winds; you know it knocked shingles off their houses, at least, when it did 180 miles north at 100 miles-per-hour winds." But how to determine what damage was caused by wind, not by water or wind and water together, each of which would be excluded? Often there were no witnesses to the damage, since many residents had followed the government's advice and evacuated. Either there would be a total lack of evidence, or the chain of events would have to be reconstructed from meteorological data or evidence of damage in the surrounding neighborhood. Even more problematic were the "slab cases," instances in which nothing remained of a building but the concrete slab that had served as a foundation. Slab cases were the most hotly disputed, even giving their name to the blog called slabbed, which expresses the frustration of Gulf residents by defining "slabbed" as "blown down, knocked down, or just down."[17] Slab cases were numerous; State Farm insured nine thousand homes hit by storm surges in Mississippi, of which twelve hundred were left with nothing but slabs.[18] And denials in slab cases were numerous too. Congressman Taylor of Mississippi summarized the problem: "Insurance companies paid Katrina wind claims in every county in Mississippi, every parish in Louisiana, most of Alabama, Northwest Florida, and even into Tennessee and Georgia. Yet, on the Mississippi Gulf Coast where winds were strongest, thousands of homeowners were left with uncovered losses because these companies denied their claims for wind damage."[19]

Because of the enormity of destruction and the lack of evidence, particularly in slab cases, insurance personnel sometimes took the position that it was difficult or impossible to determine how much damage was caused by wind and then reached exactly the wrong conclusion: The failure of proof meant a failure of coverage. Lansing Vargo, a State Farm manager of catastrophe services, asserted that "with a home in which there was no structure left, there would be no way [for] that claim representative . . . to be able to determine what was wind vs. water." If that is true, the long-established result under an all-risks policy with a water exclusion is that the insurance company pays. The logic is simple. Under an all-risks policy the insurance company makes a promise to "insure against risks of direct physical loss" or something similarly general. The flood exclusion and the anti-concurrent causation clauses are exceptions to this general promise. Once the homeowner proves that there has been a direct physical loss, the burden shifts to the insurance company to try to prove that the loss was from an excluded cause, such as flood, or the concurrence of an included and excluded cause; if the company can't meet that burden, the loss is covered.

A week after Katrina Mississippi insurance commissioner George Dale issued a bulletin reminding insurance companies of this rule:

> In some situations, there is either very little or nothing left of the insured structure and it will be a fact issue whether the loss was caused by wind or water. In these situations, the insurance company must be able to clearly demonstrate the cause of the loss. I expect and believe that where there is any doubt, that doubt will be resolved in favor of finding coverage on behalf of the insured.[20]

In litigation, the courts consistently reaffirmed the principle. Norman and Genevieve Broussard's Biloxi, Mississippi, home was reduced to a slab by Katrina. State Farm's adjuster concluded, "Evidence suggests [the] home was more damaged by flood than wind," so State Farm denied their claim. The Broussards had $120,698 of all-risk coverage (called "open peril" in Mississippi) on the building and $90,524 of named-peril coverage for personal property. Without proof of what damage was caused by wind and what by water, the Broussards could not recover for the loss of their personal property, because they could not establish that it was destroyed by one of the named perils in the policy. The destruction of the building was different. Once the Broussards established that their house had been destroyed in a hurricane—State Farm could hardly deny it—they met their burden of proving that they had been harmed by an accidental direct loss. Then State Farm had the burden of proving that the loss fell within the policy exclusion for water damage, and if it could not, it had to pay.[21]

The law was clear, but litigation like the Broussards' was necessary, because insurance companies took different and often inconsistent positions on the question of proof. The most controversial interpretation was State Farm's "wind-water protocol."[22] Stephan Hinkle, a thirty-year veteran at State Farm and one of its experts on bad faith, had worked on State Farm's response to the Northridge earthquake in 1994 and was working in its southeast region when Katrina hit. Hinkle's survey of the damage in Biloxi and Gulfport spurred him to separate the types of damage: "I went down there, and I actually saw what we had and that made it—that gave me the clarity in my mind that—to separate the damages here." In response he drafted the wind-water protocol, which was vetted by other State Farm executives and distributed to managers throughout the Gulf Coast. Some managers gave it to adjusters to control their decisions while others used it only as a training tool. The Mississippi insurance department delicately concluded that given the differing uses it was impossible to clearly determine its effect, but "the evidence is conclusive that at least some amount of confusion occurred which may have had a detrimental effect on the Company's policyholders."

The protocol is revealing for its approach to the causation issue as well as for its statement of standards for the investigation of claims. It begins with an obvious if platitudinous principle: "Each claim should be handled on its merits." Then it describes the steps to be taken in investigating a claim: First, collect "any available information . . . which will include, but is not limited to, an on-site examination of physical evidence such as water lines and debris, evidence gathered at neighboring locations, reports of damage by eyewitnesses and others, and expert reports." Then the protocol advises what to do in cases in which the damage is established due to wind (including a reminder to apply a hurricane deductible) and then states the key sentence about the uncertain cases: "When the investigation indicates that the damage was caused by excluded water and the claim investigation does not reveal independent windstorm damage to separate portions of the property, there is no coverage available under the homeowners policy."

State Farm defended the protocol. Terry Blalock, a senior manager in Mississippi, called it "a restatement of the way that we have always handled claims."[23] Hinkle would later testify "in a situation where a roof is blown off factually and water from rain inundates the structure making it a total constructive loss and then afterwards flood washes everything away, that under State Farm's wind/water protocol would not be a covered loss."[24] When insurance commissioner Dale pointed out the error of this interpretation, State Farm reiterated that it would pay for wind damage that it could prove occurred prior to flooding, but that simply retained the incorrect shifting of the burden of proof to the insured. As a State Farm manager said, "If you can't see the damage, we don't pay for it."[25] The company has maintained this position over the years since Katrina, its Web site stating, "When credible proof exists that a covered loss—like wind—damaged a home, that portion of the loss will be paid, regardless of whether flood later destroyed the home. However, we must be able to determine that a covered loss occurred, and the amount of damage, in order to pay."[26] The Mississippi insurance department emphasized that this was the wrong approach, reaffirming that "it is incumbent on the company to separately calculate the separate damage attributable to each peril"—incumbent on the company, not on the insured.

Applying the approach of the wind-water protocol, State Farm adjusters denied claim after claim because the policyholder (through the adjuster's investigation or otherwise) could not prove how much damage had been caused by wind. In a sample of 101 homeowner claims reviewed by the Mississippi insurance department, State Farm had denied 64 of the claims despite evidence of wind damage.

In slab cases, State Farm denied coverage where the storm surge washed away evidence of the damage done by wind. Victor Cimino owned a home on Hillcrest Street in Waveland, Mississippi. On October 17, 2005, a State Farm adjuster visited the site and noted in the claim file, "The only thing remaining is the slab. In this area a reported 35' tidal surge came on shore. The physical evidence point to flood and tidal surge doing the damage to the home." If all that remained was the slab, there was no physical evidence, and the adjuster was unable to determine the damage caused by wind. Because he could not, under the protocol Cimino would get nothing, a position State Farm took when it denied his claim three days later.

The misleading direction from company policies such as the State Farm wind-water protocol presented even greater problems, because many adjusters were simply not up to the task of properly assessing damages. Because of the tremendous need, companies supplemented their own employees with independent adjusting firms and persons who flocked to the Gulf Coast to become adjusters despite their lack of education and experience. Training was conducted on the fly; some adjusters were given two days of training at locations as unusual as a Burger King and then issued "a laptop and a ladder," the former loaded with software for evaluating damage and estimating claims, the latter representative of their limited means of conducting extensive investigations. Homeowners' claims would be investigated by a single adjuster, commercial claims by teams of adjusters, but poor training rendered the size of the team irrelevant; as one policyholder's lawyer noted, stupid plus stupid does not equal intelligent. One adjuster for State Farm had been a towboat pilot with no prior experience in insurance adjusting prior to the one-week course that purportedly prepared him to investigate Katrina claims. Little wonder that he denied a claim by the residents of one side of a duplex because of the flood exclusion in their renter's insurance, though another State Farm adjuster had approved a claim based on wind damage for the owners of the duplex under their homeowner's insurance.[27]

Even in slab cases, however, it was possible to try to determine the extent of loss by wind and water, and the protocol's direction to adjusters to conduct an investigation was nothing more than a restatement of the legal requirement and industry standard of a full and fair investigation of each individual claim. One means of investigation was the use of experts, engineers or others who could assess signs of damage to a structure, debris, meteorological conditions, and other factors that would shed light on the nature and timing of the damage. Like almost everything else in the Katrina claim process, this became controversial too.

One controversy concerns the number of cases in which experts were used: enough or too few? State Farm used experts in 1,100 of the 84,700 property damage claims it processed in Mississippi. Stephan Hinkle stated that "there was a point in time that we felt the need to retain further engineering reports was not there."[28] And State Farm manager Lansing Vargo concurred: "At the time of our on-site inspection, that there was no direct physical wind damage that we could find to the structure, the home's proximity to the water, the debris that was in the trees, the overall condition of the neighborhood in that all homes surrounding this home were destroyed, I was comfortable in maintaining a denial of coverage based on those facts"[29] Another State Farm employee described the practice more generally: "More information was out there on the internet, the newspapers, our weather data information was coming in, our physical inspection of locations and seeing the actual physical damage throughout the Gulf Coast, just more and more of that type of information was coming in so that we could more easily determine what had caused the damage to certain homes in certain locations."[30] When adjusters wanted to use engineering experts, the request typically had to be approved at the management level.[31]

By State Farm's own admission, it ended up paying claims in 60 percent of the cases in which it used expert engineers, for a total of $26.5 million. That, according to policyholder advocates, is the problem. By failing to use experts in many cases, companies failed to make the full investigation they owed their policyholders. In case after case, when policyholders' attorneys brought in experts they proved damage that insurance company adjusters had missed. One New Orleans private school was initially offered several hundred thousand dollars and was tempted to take the offer to get the school back in operation as quickly as possible. Their lawyer retained experts who described additional elements of damage. For example, wind had caused apparently minor damage to a brick wall, but the damage allowed rain to penetrate; the experts demonstrated that the resulting damage required all of the brick to be repointed and the drywall underneath to be replaced. As a result of that and other additions to the claim, the insurer agreed to pay almost $5 million, more than five times the original offer.

Sometimes when experts were used, they were used improperly. The charges and examples in which insurance companies cooked the engineering reports to find water rather than wind damage are as numerous as the denials and rebuttals are vigorous. Forensic Analysis & Engineering Corp. CEO Robert Kochan e-mailed Randy Downs, the firm's vice president of engineering services, on the need to "redo" reports on State Farm cases, and noted that State Farm avoided local engineers because they were "working very hard to find justifications to call it wind damage when the facts only show water induced damage." State Farm countered that it had complained about the quality of the work by one of Forensic's engineers, not his conclusions. Congressman Gene Taylor offered more than a dozen examples of changes by various engineering companies, at the behest of insurance companies, between the draft and final reports.[32] In practically every case the companies involved claimed misinterpretation or misstatement and denied wrongdoing. A typical example: On a claim by homeowner Smith, the on-site damage assessment by engineer James Overstreet of Rimkus Consulting Group concluded that the home was destroyed by the combination of "wind gusts, tornadoes, and wind-driven storm surge." Overstreet also reported eyewitness accounts and "snapped and uprooted trees" to support the possibility of a tornado. After revision by Rimkus staff who never visited the site, the report was changed to conclude that "the storm surge associated with Hurricane Katrina destroyed the portion of the residence above the concrete foundation slab." Overstreet's name was signed to the revised report without his knowledge.

Considerable credibility was given to the policyholders' claims by what turned out to be an unfortunate coincidence for State Farm. On May 25, 2006, nine months after Katrina struck and as disputes about insurance claims were intensifying, a jury in Grady County, Oklahoma, awarded Donald and Bridget Watkins $3 million in actual damages and

$10 million in punitive damages in a suit against State Farm that raised many of the same issues as the Katrina disputes. The Watkinses' home was damaged in one of a series of tornados that swept through Oklahoma on May 3, 1999, killing thirty-six people and causing a billion dollars in damage; they were among seventy families that sued State Farm in a class action for improperly denying their claims, and the jury found by "clear and convincing evidence"—a higher standard than the normal legal burden of proof—that State Farm intentionally breached its duty to deal fairly with its policyholders. A core allegation was that State Farm had hired an engineering firm, Haag Engineering, knowing that the firm would produce reports favorable to the insurer about the cause and extent of the damage, giving State Farm an excuse to deny or reduce payments. State Farm and Haag denied the allegations, but the jury concluded that the insurer had intentionally used the firm as a vehicle for breaching its duty to act fairly toward its policyholders.

The claims were bolstered by an earlier Texas case (discussed in Chapter 8) in which a jury had found that State Farm used Haag in a similar scheme to avoid payment for damage to the foundations of the home of Ioan and Liana Nicolau due to a leaking drainage system.[33] Haag did 80 percent to 90 percent of its work for insurance companies and routinely reported in such cases that leaks did not cause foundation damage; State Farm knew of Haag's proclivity and hired it for that reason. Even though State Farm found some of Haag's conclusions about the source of the water and the condition of the soil unreasonable, it still used their report as the basis for the denial of the Nicolauses' claim.

The parallel between the improper use of experts in the Oklahoma tornado cases and the Gulf Coast Katrina cases was uncomfortably close. Shortly after the verdict State Farm CEO Edward B. Rust, Jr., admitted that State Farm had placed a moratorium on its use of Haag.[34] While disputes remained about the use of engineering reports in Katrina cases, in April 2007, State Farm and the Oklahoma homeowners settled the tornado class action.

Evaluating insurance companies' responses to natural disasters such as Katrina is difficult. There are many individual stories of insurance companies lowballing property owners, deliberately or through carelessness.

One New Orleans law firm that represented a number of residential and commercial property owners after hurricanes Katrina and Rita reports that, on average, its clients received payments under insurance policies that were three times the companies' original offers, not even counting the cases in which calculating the multiple is arithmetically impossible because an initial outright denial was changed to a payment of, for example, $350,000.

Government agencies also have investigated the problem. The California insurance commissioner performed a market conduct examination of State Farm's response to the 1994 Northridge earthquake. It reviewed 746 claim files in which the company had resolved the claim without litigation and found 971 violations of claim-handling standards, an average of more than 1 per claim. It also reviewed 79 claims that policyholders had been forced to litigate to seek payment and found 418 violations, an average of 5 per claim. The most common violations included: failing to explain the coverage available to the policyholder, such as for rebuilding to legally mandated standards and for the rental of temporary living quarters; improperly reducing payments because of depreciation; reducing the amount of a settlement to the insured without explaining why; and failing to properly investigate claims. As to the last, the report concluded that there was a pattern of failing to investigate thoroughly. The report concluded with a dramatic implication: "The findings of this examination indicate that State Farm's practices affect all first party property losses and are not necessarily exclusive to earthquake claims."

The Department of Homeland Security's FEMA studied companies' responses to wind and water claims following Hurricane Katrina as part of the National Flood Insurance Program (NFIP). One of the oddities of the NFIP is that it is a federal program whose administration is contracted out to private insurance companies, called Write Your Own (WYO) companies. The companies sell the policies, receive commissions on the sale, and process claims, determining which are eligible for payment. But these same companies insure the properties for wind damage or mixed damage. They therefore have an incentive to find that damage is caused by water, which is compensable by the government, rather than by wind, which comes out of their own pockets, a situation that the

Government Accountability Office (GAO) correctly characterized as "an inherent conflict of interest."

Based on examinations of a sample of claim files, DHS concluded, "There is also a perception that adjusters, especially those working for the same WYO company on both flood and wind claims, are not objective and tend to attribute more damage to flooding than to wind thereby benefiting the WYO company at NFIP's expense. We did not find any evidence of such attribution of damages in our review."

This was not a surprising conclusion. There was no evidence of bias because there is no requirement that adjusters document the relative effect of wind and water in the claim file. A later report by the GAO pointed out that "NFIP does not systematically collect and analyze both wind and flood damage claims data, limiting FEMA's ability to assess the accuracy of flood payments on hurricane-damaged properties. The claims data collected by NFIP through the WYO insurers—including those that sell and service both wind and flood policies on a property—do not include information on whether wind contributed to total damages or the extent of wind damage as determined by the WYO insurer."

Even more importantly, after Katrina the insurance companies and DHS officials agreed on an expedited claims-handling process that minimized investigation and made determination of the effect of wind practically impossible. David Maurstad, the federal insurance administrator, first conferred with executives from the largest insurance companies and then, at a meeting on September 7, 2005, at the Atlanta Airport Marriott, told insurance industry representatives, state insurance commissioners, and insurance agents that the expedited process would be "up and rolling pretty soon." Within two weeks—just before the onset of Hurricane Katrina's follow-up, Hurricane Rita—the process was in place, reducing the documentation that had to be included in claim files, minimizing adjuster training requirements, and permitting them to settle flood claims without a site visit if the home was in an area of storm surge. As the GAO stated, "Such expedited procedures facilitated the prompt processing of flood claims payments to policyholders, but once these flood claims—and others—were processed, NFIP did not systematically collect corresponding wind damage claims data on an after-the-fact basis." And remarkably, as GAO pointed out, the WYO insurers do not provide the information they do have on wind damage claims to the federal government, a shortcoming that GAO recommended be changed by statute.

Even more curious was the discrepancy between estimates of damage produced by insurance companies when they were acting as administrators of the NFIP versus when they were writers of wind insurance. As reported in the *New Orleans Times-Picayune*, public adjusters found that Allstate estimated the costs for flood damage, borne by the taxpayers, at much higher rates than the same repairs caused by wind damage, which it would have to pay for. In one house, Allstate estimated the cost of removing and replacing drywall at $.76 per square foot when the cost was charged to its homeowners policy and $3.31 per square foot when charged to the NFIP. And on: homeowners insurance–covered carpet, $23.48 per square foot, and identical NFIP-covered carpet, $28.43; texturizing and repainting walls under the homeowners policy, $.80 per square foot, and under the NFIP, $1.15. Public adjusters reported similar discrepancies throughout Louisiana and Mississippi; Allstate denied the charges, saying costs were the same for wind and flood, and any discrepancy had to be due to differences in the actual cost of repair.[35]

Mississippi insurance commissioner George Dale and his successor, Mike Chaney, also pursued an examination of State Farm's conduct in processing Katrina claims that provides an appropriately strange coda to the Katrina insurance story. The process of examination was difficult. The company produced some documents, but other times its responses to requests were untimely, unresponsive, and insufficient, in the department's opinion. Some witnesses were "less than forthright" and even failed to acknowledge obvious contradictions in their claim files. And the results of the examination were controversial and curious. The department studied a sample of the 43,000 claims that were filed with the company. It found "when wind and water were an issue in a claim, the Company initially failed to completely fulfill its policy obligation to some policyholders." Completely, indeed. The report found that hundreds of claims in the sample failed to show a thorough investigation; the company disregarded engineers' reports that indicated wind damage; 64 of 101 homeowners claims that were closed without payment showed wind damage to the insured's house, neighboring houses, or the general area; and State Farm employees were confused about the proper interpretation of the anti-concurrent causation provision. Nevertheless, "while the Company did make errors, [the department] found no violations" of the claim practices standards. Gulfport trial attorney Joe Sam Owens summed up the opinion of many policyholder advocates: "If I didn't know he was the Commissioner of Insurance, I would have thought he worked for State Farm."

10

Insurance Fraud and Other Frauds

PARENTS EMBARRASS THEIR teenage children in many ways—it's almost part of the job description—but a television commercial produced by the Pennsylvania Insurance Fraud Prevention Authority portrayed a new one. A despondent father is driving his silent, seething teenage daughter to school, where she faces humiliation by her classmates. The cause for her distress? Her father has been arrested for insurance fraud. The commercial is part of a vigorous campaign to convince the public and lawmakers that the real problem in insurance is not unjustified delay, denial, and defense of claims by insurance companies—it's unjustified claims for payment by fraudsters.

The insurance industry has developed a vocabulary for the types of fraud in insurance claims. "Hard fraud" involves faking a loss, such as staging an auto accident or setting fire to one's own house in order to collect insurance money. "Soft fraud" involves fudging an insurance claim by exaggerating injuries or the value of property destroyed or stolen. The colorful lexicon of types of fraud also includes: "fibbers" and "padders" who exaggerate claims; the "swoop and squat" (the vehicle you are in back of is suddenly passed by another that swoops in front of it, causing the vehicle in front of you to stop abruptly, or squat, so that you can't avoid colliding with it); and the "drive down" (one driver waves on another, indicating that it's okay to proceed, and then intentionally hits the passing car).

The umbrella group Coalition Against Insurance Fraud (CAIF) defines insurance fraud as "when someone intentionally deceives another about an insurance matter to receive money or other benefits not rightfully theirs."[1] This definition is broad enough to include fraud by insurance companies that delay, deny, defend, but that is not the target of this campaign. At the urging of the insurance lobby, many states have enacted statutes that require companies to report whenever they have "reason to believe that a fraudulent insurance act" has been committed. The statutes have been carefully drafted to apply only to false statements made by applicants for insurance, policyholders or victims who present claims to companies, or the doctors who treat them and the lawyers who represent them; they do not apply to insurance companies that defraud their customers.[2] It hardly could be otherwise; a prosecutor for the Insurance Fraud Bureau of the Massachusetts attorney general's office reportedly said that investigating fraud by companies would present a conflict of interest with the division's primary role in helping the companies pursue fraud by their customers.[3]

The campaign against insurance fraud is an example of social marketing, the use of the techniques of marketing, advertising, and public relations to sell an idea or a behavior rather than a product. From campaigns to stop smoking or littering, to promote the use of condoms or seat belts, and to prevent forest fires or AIDS, social marketing campaigns have become increasingly sophisticated, and the insurance fraud campaign is one of the best. Like others, it employs a multipronged strategy, including advertising to shape public sentiment and rewrite laws. Unlike some of the others, the insurance fraud campaign produces direct benefits for its sponsors in the industry; Smokey the Bear has no pecuniary interest in stopping forest fires, and increased use of condoms is aimed at preventing the spread of sexually transmitted diseases, not at increasing the profits of condom manufacturers.

The insurance fraud campaign merges two stories, named by Professor Tom Baker as "the immoral insured and the depravity of those who threaten the public interest."[4] Quoting insurance adjusters, Baker tells the story of the immoral insured: "The normally decent, law-abiding American, . . . if left to his own devices, has a little larceny in his soul. . . . And really, people can't see it as anybody's money. The insurance company and the federal government—people like that—they are fair game where the public is concerned." This threatens the public interest, at least as defined by insurance companies, because it takes away money that rightfully belongs to the policyholders and justified claimants. "We have an obligation to the public and to our policyholders to detect fraud and resist fraudulent claims," say adjusters.

The immorality of insureds is alleged to increase in times of stress. Talking about Hurricane Andrew, one adjuster said, "I don't want to sound too cynical, but most people, when they see money laying on the ground, will pick it up."[5] After the attacks on the World Trade Center on September 11, 2001, insurance companies were as concerned about fraud as about paying claims. The trade journal *Claims* reported that

> officials are gearing for a possible wave of insurance fraud that will inflate the event's financial cost, according to the Coalition Against Insurance Fraud. "Disasters inevitably attract scam artists who try to exploit emergency conditions for profit," said Dennis Jay, the coalition's executive director. "The only question is how much insurance fraud will occur, and how much it will cost policyholders."[6]

And in response to the subprime mortgage crisis of 2008, as if the nation was not facing enough problems, CAIF warned of "a spike in home arsons by desperate homeowners looking for insurance fraud to bail them out of foreclosure."[7]

The first step in any successful social marketing campaign is to convince the public of the enormity of the problem, and that has been a principal focus of the insurance fraud campaign. The claims are dramatic: If all insurance fraud was conducted by a single corporation, it would rank in the top 25 of the Fortune 500. The total amount lost to fraud every year is $4.8 billion to $6.8 billion in auto insurance and $30 billion overall. Fraud is the second most costly white-collar crime, trailing only tax evasion. Between $.11 and $.30, or more, of every claim dollar is lost to soft fraud ("small time cheating by normally honest people," as CAIF describes it). More than one third of people hurt in auto accidents exaggerate their injuries. Some 10 percent or more of the insurance industry's claims payments and expenses annually are attributable to fraud. Arson and suspected arson account for nearly half a million fires a year, or one of every four fires in the United States.[8]

Like the claims for sugarless gum ("four out of five dentists recommend . . .") or headache medicines ("the number one pain reliever"), these claims are promulgated by those with something to sell. The figures are generated by the insurance companies themselves, who have an interest in creating an environment that gives more credibility to companies' aggressive investigation and frequent denial of claims and that makes victims more reluctant to file claims lest they be accused of fraud. Within the companies, the figures come from employees who have an interest in alleging fraud. Adjusters are expected to identify questionable or difficult claims as fraud and to refer them to the company's Special Investigations Unit. The questionable claim becomes evidence of criminality, particularly as the suspicious claims are reported to the industry-supported National Insurance Crime Bureau (NICB), even if the claim is eventually paid and no evidence of fraud is ever proven. Indeed, the more aggressive the pursuit of fraud, the more likely that it will produce behavior that can be labeled as fraud. An aggressive investigation may frustrate and delay the claimant who needs the money to pay for medical bills or repairs to a house, so she may give up and settle, or even abandon her claim; that behavior then becomes evidence of the fraud that was initially alleged.

There is no doubt that insurance fraud occurs, that it is wrong, and that it should be prevented, investigated, and punished. But the social marketing of insurance fraud likely has exaggerated the problem and therefore has been used to justify an excessive response. For example, it was the Insurance Research Council that came up with those figures of $4.8 billion to $6.8 billion in excess payments, and that fraud is found in 10 percent or more of claims. But a more reliable study tells a different story.[9] The Massachusetts Insurance Fraud Bureau is a quasi-governmental agency with investigative authority that is controlled by the insurance industry and receives referrals of fraud from the companies. Over a ten-year period, 17,274 cases of fraud were reported by insurers to the bureau. Then the winnowing began. Only 6,684 referrals were accepted by the bureau, yielding 3,349 cases to be investigated. Of those, only 552 were referred to law enforcement authorities for possible prosecution. Combining completed prosecutions and cases still pending at the conclusion of the study, 368 of the original 17,274 referrals actually involved criminal fraud. Therefore, Richard Derrig, author of the ten-year study and the bureau's vice president for research, concludes, "It demonstrates that the ratio of suspected fraud (not abuse) by industry personnel and the public to provable fraud is on the order of 25 to 1. Even if the unsupported suspected fraud estimate of 10 percent were accurate, the true level of criminal fraud would be less than one-half of 1 percent."

The extent to which insurance fraud is believed to be a major problem because it has been marketed as a major problem is apparent when it is compared to another form of nonviolent theft with significant social consequences: shoplifting. The National Association for Shoplifting Prevention, an advocacy group like the CAIF, labels shoplifting "our nation's 'silent crime.' Parents don't want to believe it, schools don't address it, retailers don't want to talk about it, police don't want to respond to it, courts don't want to deal with it, and the people who do the shoplifting either rationalize it as 'no big deal' or are too ashamed or too afraid to admit it."[10] That group claims that shoplifting happens 550,000 times each day, resulting in $13 billion worth of goods stolen each year. Like the insurance fraud numbers, these statistics are hard to verify and may be exaggerated. According to the FBI, law enforcement agencies reported 978,978 incidents of shoplifting in 2007, only two days' worth of the association's figures; even if the incidence of unreported crime is much higher, it is hard to imagine that it is more than two hundred times higher. Whether shoplifting is more of a social problem than insurance fraud or less, it is a silent crime because it has been less effectively marketed; there are few television commercials about shoplifting and no legislatively mandated enforcement mechanisms that lead to high-visibility criminal prosecutions as there are with insurance fraud.

Insurance fraud, whatever its scale, is not new, nor is the campaign against it. What may be the first American insurance fraud predated the founding of the nation itself. John Lancey, a young sea captain, unwisely succumbed to the persuasion of his father-in-law to scuttle an old sailing vessel on its way to the American colonies; when the scheme was revealed by a crew member, Lancey was hanged on June 7, 1754.[11] Lancey and other ship scuttlers were followed by a colorful succession of "professional litigants, 'fakirs,' false witnesses, shyster lawyers, tricky doctors, ambulance-chasers, and runners."[12] "Firebug gangs" burned properties for the insurance proceeds, ghoulish schemers produced charred body parts to claim that insured relatives and friends had been killed in fires, and "floppers" looked for cracks in sidewalks on which to conveniently trip.

The targets of insurance fraud organized against the practice from early days. Accident insurers and streetcar companies formed the Alliance Against Accident Fraud in 1905; it created a rogues gallery of fifty thousand alleged swindlers, lobbied Congress, and urged bar and medical associations to discipline and prosecute "the ambulance chaser and the shyster lawyer." (Efforts to cleanse the bar of lawyers who, lacking "character," were likely to participate in fraudulent personal injury cases often had an ethnic tinge; while the Philadelphia bar was conducting a study of ambulance chasing, the study's leader, lion of the bar and ethics expert Henry Drinker, castigated the "Russian Jew boys" who practiced law "merely following the methods their fathers had been using in selling shoe-strings and other merchandise.")[13] When its sponsors concluded that the alliance was insufficiently effective, the National Bureau of Casualty and Surety Underwriters formed a Claims Bureau that put former FBI agents in secret offices around the country to "checkmate the lone wolves" and "to smoke out the ambulance chasers and fake claim syndicates." In 1971 insurance companies formed what was essentially their own national police force to investigate fraud, the Insurance Crime Prevention Institute.

The modern campaign against insurance fraud took shape in the early 1990s. In 1992 the National Insurance Crime Bureau (NICB) was formed by the merger of the National Automobile Theft Bureau and the Insurance

Crime Prevention Institute. The NICB would grow to include more than a thousand insurance companies, rental car companies, parking services providers, other transportation-related firms, and utility companies. The next year the Coalition Against Insurance Fraud was founded with many of the same players, including the NICB as a charter member and insurance companies, the NAIC, enforcement groups such as the National District Attorneys Association, and, somewhat oddly, some consumer organizations, including the Consumer Federation of America.

The campaign against insurance fraud was being reorganized at the same time McKinsey was redesigning the claim process at Allstate and other companies. An increased effort to label, identify, and punish fraud was a significant part of McKinsey's strategy. (Strangely enough, in the early stages of its work for Allstate, in addition to studying closed claim files it conducted interviews at several other insurance companies to "gain insight" about how they approached potentially fraudulent claims; strangely because the other companies were of course Allstate's competitors rather than its collaborators.) Its general conclusions were: "Fraud was investigated less frequently than it should have been," "The 'discovery' rate for fraud is very low," and "Proactive fraud detection and handling of suspected claims should reduce fraudulent activity and positively impact claim costs."[14] That is, investigating more fraud would lead to paying out less in claims. As a result, McKinsey recommended changes in the processing of auto bodily injury and homeowners property damage claims to encourage adjusters to treat more of them as possibly fraudulent and refer them to the Special Investigations Unit for more aggressive handling. For example, the new first step in investigation of a minor impact, soft tissue auto claim would be to "identify and transfer fraud files to SIU."

Arnold Schlossberg, Jr., a retired army major general and the Defense Department's drug czar under President George H. W. Bush, took the helm of the NICB and bemoaned the previous lack of a unified approach: "What we need now is a team approach involving our industry, law enforcement agencies, and other sectors to begin dealing with this problem in a coordinated and systematic way." The team approach would focus on enforcement and social marketing. As Sean Mooney, senior vice president of the Insurance Information Institute, put it, enforcement can shape public perceptions,

> particularly if the arrest is done right—leading the suspect away on the evening news. . . . The insurance industry can acquire some of the fearful respect presently enjoyed by the Internal Revenue Service. . . . There's no way we want to drag little old ladies in North Dakota off to jail. We just want to put the fear into them that we could.[15]

That fearful respect was to be gained through a three-part campaign. The first was largely internal to insurance companies. In a modern version of the Alliance Against Accident Fraud's rogues gallery, companies would create national databanks of insurance fraud claims in order to compile statistics and share information on individual claimants. The second was the public campaign, marketing insurance fraud as a crisis. CAIF was unabashed about the strategy and its role in it. Media reports on insurance fraud doubled in the five years after the coalition's creation: "The media didn't make that happen by itself. Sources first had to convince them insurance fraud was a story worth covering, then supply the information for the story." The techniques are sophisticated. "It also helps to increase the comfort level if the press office compiles what Dan Johnston, president of the Insurance Fraud Bureau of Massachusetts, refers to as a "'one-stop shopping' packet for the media, which allows for greater control of the story and the message. The goal is create a package so complete that the reporter or producer never has to leave his or her desk."[16] The third part was to partner with legislatures and law enforcement agencies to create new laws that could be used to pursue ostensibly fraudulent claims and to aggressively pursue the claimants.

Coordinating enforcement efforts and public relations requires a close working relationship between the enforcers and the marketers. CAIF touts Allstate as a master of the technique.

> When the company identifies a case with media potential, they bring in the lawyers as early as possible to work with the special

> investigation unit and determine how they're going to conduct the investigation. When it gets to a point where everybody is satisfied that the evidence is as good as it's going to get, Ed [Moran, a former prosecutor now working for Allstate] asks the lawyers to analyze the facts, exactly what they have seen and the law itself. He encourages them to take calculated risks, possibly into new legal areas, while also looking for cases that give the most bang for the buck.... At that point, Allstate's corporate communications people are brought in on the case, get an explanation of the case and asked for advice on getting the best media play.

And the bottom line: "Allstate also measures the effects of filing of these actions and has seen claim counts go down."[17]

A peculiar instance of the insurance industry's marketing of insurance fraud as a great social problem is its involvement in raising the profile of arson as a matter of public and law enforcement concern. Arson is clearly a serious problem; the FBI Uniform Crime Reports counted 57,224 incidents of arson in 2007, of which 10,995 involved single-family homes and 15,105 involved motor vehicles. How arson became a matter of federal concern and why the FBI collects these figures, however, is part of the insurance fraud story.

In the 1970s the insurance industry began a campaign to raise public consciousness of arson.[18] State Farm, the largest property insurer, was a leader in the campaign to make it a matter of public concern. Insurance critics questioned State Farm's interest in the subject. As a highly regarded insurer with many top-level customers insuring single-family homes, it may have had less of a problem with arson than other companies; State Farm's benefit from a campaign against arson would be more indirect, in a broader consciousness about insurance fraud and more skepticism of insurance claims. Nevertheless, from 1970 to 1990 it engaged in a two-pronged program, having its own adjusters focus more on suspicious fires and increasing the awareness of the public and the efforts of law enforcement officials about arson. As a company report proudly noted, "State Farm people helped draw up a blueprint for a coordinated nationwide attack on arson that has produced action on many fronts." Some of the efforts were modest but of great publicity value, such as providing arson-sniffing dogs to local fire investigators. But as part of the industry's broader program, those efforts helped shape the law and perception of arson.

At the time there was no consensus among federal law enforcement officials that arson was a serious national problem, nor that federal prosecution of arson-related crimes was warranted. The FBI did not consider arson to belong in the most serious class of crimes that were included in its Uniform Crime Reports. Even though arson might be a lucrative source of income for some criminals, the Internal Revenue Service did not monitor the situation, and the postal service, which investigated mail fraud, of which insurance fraud through arson could be a part, did not regard it as a crime of great magnitude.

Nevertheless, the industry pressed the issue. Even after congressional hearings on the matter the FBI refused to categorize arson as a Class I crime, so in 1982 Congress enacted a statute ordering it to do so. Other legislative action followed. At the federal level, the Violent Crime Control and Law Enforcement Act of 1994 made insurance fraud affecting interstate commerce a federal crime. The Bureau of Alcohol, Tobacco and Firearms joined the campaign by creating arson task forces with federal and local officials in twenty-three cities. That move ultimately may have saved the bureau's existence; when the Reagan administration subsequently attempted to dismantle the bureau, insurance groups and fire prevention associations testified on its behalf.

The close cooperation between insurance companies and the federal government is illustrated in a 2006 case from Indiana, in which a private investigator from the National Insurance Crime Bureau was as much a member of the investigative and prosecution team as the FBI agents involved.[19] Joseph Jaskolski, the NICB investigator, was the primary moving force behind the investigation and prosecution, assisted the FBI agent assigned to the case in conducting it, had access to secret grand jury information, accompanied the FBI agent on interviews of witnesses and inspections, assisted in reviewing documents, escorted witnesses at the grand jury proceeding, and worked with the U. S. attorney at trial.

The insurance industry's campaign also resulted in antifraud legislation in every state.[20] Although the details vary, most follow some or all elements of CAIF's Model Insurance Fraud Act. All states now make insurance fraud a crime, with two thirds of the states treating it as a felony. About the same number require that the state establish some form of insurance fraud bureau, as if Walmart and Macy's had successfully lobbied for legislation requiring the state attorney general to set up a special shoplifting division. In nearly every state these statutes have created a mixed regime of private and public attacks on insurance fraud. Three fourths of the states have a specialized antifraud agency within the insurance department or the attorney general's office, and a few rely on less formal relationships between insurance companies and prosecutors, even to the point of having the companies pay private investigators to work with public officials.

Massachusetts is unique in having a statutorily created Insurance Fraud Bureau, a quasi-governmental agency that is controlled by private insurance companies. The Massachusetts IFB is not unique, however, in touting its results in terms of savings for the companies. In a 2006 report, publicly demonstrating the link between the insurance fraud campaign and insurance company profits, it announced, "Good News! . . . For the second year, available statistics show a major reduction of total claim dollars and the number of injury claims reported."

Many states, such as New York, require insurance companies to set up full-time special investigations units staffed by investigators with law enforcement or other experience to cooperate with state enforcement agencies, in order to make sure that all insurance companies participate in the campaign. Companies are also required to report suspected fraud to state law enforcement authorities. Suspected fraud is defined broadly to include any claim in which there is "reason to believe" that a claim may be fraudulent; to make it easier for companies to report, they are given special immunity from criminal prosecution and lawsuits by policyholders who are falsely accused of fraud.[21] The breadth of the mandate results in insurance companies reporting many claims as fraudulent that obviously are not. In 2008, insurance companies referred 23,054 cases of suspected fraud to the state's fraud bureau. During the same year 1,367 cases were deemed worth an investigation and prosecutors obtained convictions in 402 cases, some begun in previous years.[22] The winnowing of spurious allegations to cases of real fraud is not cheap; nationwide, each conviction for insurance fraud costs an average of $60,907 for the fraud bureau, on top of the ordinary expenses of the criminal process.

The attack on insurance fraud also becomes an attack on lawyers who represent accident victims seeking compensation from insurance companies. Philadelphia district attorney Lynne Abraham warned victims' attorneys that her office was interested in "deterring attorneys from considering taking any case which has that faint, but unmistakable, odor of fraud, which gets stronger and stronger the closer one digs."[23]

Even more ominous was the Florida prosecution of attorneys Marvin Marks and his son and law partner Gary for representing their clients in settlement negotiations against insurance companies.[24] On March 10, 1989, Florida insurance commissioner Tom Gallagher and his agents raided the Markses' law firm's North Miami offices, seizing 253 confidential client files. Within the week the Florida Supreme Court suspended the Markses from the practice of law, and the state attorney general initiated proceedings for the forfeiture of all of the firm's assets under the Florida Racketeer-Influenced Corrupt Organizations Act. Eventually the attorney general's office and the insurance department indicted the firm, three of its lawyers, and two doctors who had examined their clients. The key allegation of the indictment was that the firm had been a tough bargainer by not revealing all relevant medical information when representing its clients. Under that theory, failing to report all available medical information was fraudulent under the insurance fraud statute. All available information: even the failure to reveal the report of one doctor who had found a client's disability to be minor when four other doctors had certified her as 45 percent disabled. But the duty to disclose was a one-way street because insurance companies could conceal all the information they wanted; in one of the cases for which the lawyers were charged, the defendant's insurance company withheld a statement that confirmed that its insured was negligent.

Ultimately the Florida Supreme Court upheld the dismissal of all of the charges against the lawyers, relying on the obligation of a lawyer to represent his client, which in negotiation requires that sometimes the attorney not tell all he knows. Thirteen years after the dramatic raid on the Markses' law firm offices, the case ended with a final decision of the Florida Supreme Court. But the message had been sent to victims' lawyers: The firm and its lawyers had spent millions of dollars in their defense, and the firm was unable to reopen.

Whatever its effects on the incidence of actual fraud, the social marketing of it as a major problem has been very successful. The Insurance Research Council periodically surveys public attitudes toward insurance fraud, and the most recent survey reported that while one in three adults believe it is acceptable to exaggerate an insurance claim in at least some circumstances, the rate has been declining steadily. Perhaps more important, 78 percent stated that they were very or somewhat concerned about insurance fraud, and 92 percent had been persuaded by the industry's campaign both that "insurance fraud leads to higher rates for everyone" and that "persons who commit insurance fraud should be prosecuted to the fullest extent of the law."[25] In another poll, more than half of the respondents believed it was more likely that an individual would commit insurance fraud than that an insurance company would deny a valid claim, and only one-fourth thought the opposite.[26] But in a perverse twist, the campaign against insurance fraud may breed fraud and cause it to infiltrate the claim process. As risk management consultant Thomas Laffey notes, "The claims- and loss-settlement process has become a battleground for many policyholders. It breeds an environment that, not surprisingly, encourages fraudulent activity. I am convinced that if the insurance industry treats its policyholders in an honorable manner, fraudulent claims activity will be significantly reduced." Forty percent of those surveyed in one study believed that fraudulent acts were in response to not being treated with respect by the industry.[27]

Laffey is correct; the insurance fraud story has become integral to the claims process. Attention to the potential for fraud involves three steps. The claims adjuster is on the front line and uses a variety of tools to identify potential fraud. When potential cases are found the results are sometimes used in the adjusting process, and sometimes the cases are referred to the company's special investigations unit for more careful scrutiny.

Claims in which litigation is threatened or brought, particularly those alleging a bad faith denial, then involve the use of even more sophisticated experts who specialize in proving fraud and refuting claims of bad faith.

The attention to fraud throughout the claim process turns the adjuster's role on its head. In a perversion of the insurance adjuster's proper role as keeper of the promise of indemnity and security made by the company to its policyholder, the adjuster becomes their adversary, acting more like a cop than a good neighbor and treating victims as suspects. An Allstate Best Practices Manual accurately represents the conflict in its statement of basic principles. On the one hand, it directs adjusters, "When in doubt, you should honor a questionable claim rather than refuse payment of a possibly legitimate one. . . . Reducing fraud does not eliminate your responsibility for good faith and fair dealing." On the other hand, it also informs them, "To maximize your success in identifying, investigating and handling fraudulent claims, you should incorporate fraud control techniques into your regular claim handling procedures."[28]

The first step for adjusters in detecting fraud, however, is not to treat claimants as if they were guilty, at least not directly. Presenting an attitude of service, not suspicion, is the best tactic: "Interrogation with a smile."[29] Adjusters are initially trained to be empathetic about the claimant's loss, to engage in open-ended discussion, and only after a rapport has been established to get into more detailed questioning. Often much of the information that will later be used to justify an allegation of fraud is gleaned from the initial call, when the adjuster oozes support while looking for fraud.

Insurance companies and trade groups have developed lists of red flags that allegedly indicate the potential for fraud. Adjusters are instructed to be alert for their presence in a claim and to send the claim to the SIU if there are too many. Red flags are often weighted with points, and accumulating a certain number requires that the claim be treated as fraud. This is a logical system if the red flags actually are indicators of fraud, but the systems are set up so that many legitimate claims are flagged as well. State Farm, for example, had a system in which indicators had a point value of one to ten. Scoring a five or above was a reason for further inquiry into possible fraud, and scoring ten mandated a full investigation.[30] An insured who was unemployed rated a four; an insured who was hard to reach (perhaps because he works long hours?) also rated a four. If the car involved in an accident had been involved in a previous collision, the car scored a seven; if it had mechanical problems, four. A rear-end accident rated a five; if the victim of an accident was "overly pushy for settlement"—say, by demanding what is owed to him under the insurance policy—the behavior rated a three. Allstate's SIU's "segment training," prepared as part of its Claims Core Process Redesign, used a scale in which one hundred points required referral to the SIU.[31] Consistent with its attack on MIST victims, a minor impact accident immediately scored twenty points. If the claimant had a bodily injury claim requiring more than emergency room treatment in the past three years, forty points. In a bit of a catch-22, unrelated claimants who have the same doctor and the same attorney, fifty points; the same doctor but not the same attorney, twenty-five points; and the same attorney but not the same doctor, twenty-five points. The NICB list of red flags includes three or more occupants in the claimant's vehicle, subjective injuries such as headaches and muscle spasms, the claimants' submitting medical bills from the same doctor or medical facility, and an older vehicle.

The red flag systems also have flexibility—a category for "other reasons" with an open point value. If an adjuster is busy and wants to move the case to the SIU, or if the adjuster or office has a goal of the number of claims to be sent to the SIU and is just short, other reasons might appear in the investigation to push the claim over the top.

Professor Aviva Abramovsky explains how these red flags turn everyday events into evidence of criminality and are used to deter accident victims from pursuing the compensation that is owed them.[32] Imagine a family of five involved in an accident in the old reliable family car. After the accident they all seek treatment from their family doctor and are diagnosed with neck and back injuries. This entirely typical story contains multiple red flags of fraud—multiple occupants, older car, neck and back injuries, same doctor—so an adjuster would be likely to refer it for potential criminal investigation. For this family and all future injury victims, Professor Abramovsky writes, "Awareness of these criteria, or even awareness of frequent insurance fraud prosecutions, forces the family to include the potential for criminal investigation alongside the denial of claim benefits when determining whether to go forward on a contested claim. Under such circumstances, they might well decide not to file a claim at all, thus relieving the insurance company of its promise to pay made in exchange for collected premiums."

The red flag systems are valuable to companies, but improvements in computer technology and the increasing sophistication of databases have enhanced their ability to label claims as potential frauds.[33] Rules-based analysis, data mining, and predictive modeling are among the techniques the use of which is spreading. MetLife Auto & Home, for example, decided to increase the number of claims referred for fraud, so it partnered with Computer Sciences Corporation (the producer of Colossus) to create an automated system. Its Fraud Evaluator scores the potential for fraud beginning at the first notice of loss. The company can set parameters for what it considers to be fraud, giving it considerable flexibility in deciding which and how many cases will be referred to the SIU. The program's search engine compares the elements of a claim against external databases, looking for, among other things, doctors whose treatments are suspect. Then it analyzes all the information to see how closely the elements of a claim match others believed to be frauds and creates a score; all scores above a certain point are sent to the SIU. The system produced the desired results, a doubling of claims sent for investigation for fraud.

In 2003 Erie Insurance of Pennsylvania also implemented a data mining and predictive modeling system, and even created graphical representations of links among the data to give adjusters a picture of potential fraud, drawing on years of claims data to model potentially fraudulent claims. The results were an increased number of claims identified as potentially fraudulent. Human identification of red flags is still used, though, in a mix of computerized and human efforts to label the largest number of claims as frauds. Erie's vice president, Dave Rioux, commented that computer systems "will never capture all of the questionable claims, because the vast majority can only be captured by real human intelligence and gut feelings that something is not right about the claim."

Many of these systems draw on databases of ISO. ISO ClaimSearch collects data from many insurance companies and other organizations into a single database that insurers can use to investigate claims. It contains information on more than 600 million claims, with more than 210,000 new reports submitted daily. When an insurer submits a claim—the system is used by companies with over 90 percent of the property/casualty business—ClaimSearch searches for matches by name or similar name, address, Social Security number, vehicle identification number, driver's license number, tax identification number, and other parties to the loss, and reports on other claims filed by the same individuals or businesses. ISO also has its own claim scoring system, on a thousand-point scale, to model for suspected fraud.[34]

These vast databases and sophisticated systems give the appearance of certainty. Despite this seeming precision, insurance experts admit that they are inexact, and inexact in favor of the insurance companies. Erie Insurance's Rioux criticizes rules-based systems as less sophisticated than more modern predictive modeling systems and particularly prone to false positives—cases in which the system found evidence of fraud where there was none. "These claims met all the conditions but clearly were not fraud by any stretch of the imagination," he noted. But even the more sophisticated systems depend on the data they are fed. The databases and modeling rely on historical determinations of fraud, but those determinations are suspect. Few of the alleged frauds actually result in criminal convictions, so the systems depend on the companies' own determinations of what is fraud. The alleged victim of the alleged crime—the insurance company—becomes the prosecutor, judge, and reporter of results, results that essentially require the accused to prove his innocence. The companies define the problem and then measure future cases against their definition. Disputes over the amount of a claim may be referred to the SIU, and then reported to state or federal agencies as evidence of fraud; even if no fraud is ever proven against the claimant, the database record remains. Likewise, if claims are referred to SIUs and the hardball tactics there coerce a claimant into giving up, that is evidence of fraud as well. And because of the comprehensiveness of the databases, the doctors and lawyers involved have now been linked to potential frauds too and can be flagged by the system in the future.

A bias in favor of finding fraud is in insurance companies' financial interest. They reinforce that interest by giving employees incentives or pressures to find allegations of fraud. From the early stages of Allstate's CCPR and State Farm's ACE, adjusters and claims offices were directed to find fraud, and were rewarded when they did and punished when they did not. ACE's quality indicators included the percentage of cases referred to the SIU and the percentage pursued by the SIU. A State Farm report on the "anti-fraud results" of a California-based SIU noted "the substantial BI [auto bodily injury claims] savings and the 29% closure rate with no payment when we 'play hard ball,'" results that were described as "spectacular."[35] Shannon Brady Kmatz, former Allstate adjuster and later a whistle-blower, testified that Allstate's Albuquerque claims office had an SIU referral goal of 6 percent of claims; when it hit that goal—the highest in the Western region—the goal for the next year was raised to 7 percent. There is no reason to suppose, of course, that the incidence of fraud increased by that rate in one year. She stated, "People making claims were to be viewed with suspicion. They were all thought to be potentially someone who would cheat Allstate in some way." An individual employee's performance development summaries—their annual ratings—included specific goals for SIU referrals. Farmers Insurance did the same. Personnel evaluations listed a "critical" "expected result" as "surplus enhancement"; adjusters were to enhance the surplus—the company's profit—by "increas[ing] referrals to Investigations by 10%." Employees who did not measure up were warned. One form includes the ominous statement: "You have submitted 2 investigation referrals in 1998. This is an area you need to improve on."

As with other elements of the claims process redesign, even when the particulars change the principles stay the same. A 2004 survey of participants in an insurance fraud management conference revealed that 97 percent of company representatives believed it would be useful to benchmark their SIU referral rate with that of the industry as a whole, and 69 percent were willing to share referral rate data with their competitors to set the benchmarks.[36] Eighty percent of companies calculate savings made through antifraud programs, and some of the rest have a particular reason for not doing so; as the SIU of a large company wrote in response to a 2003 survey: "We believe that tracking the outcome (of investigations), or dollars denied due to fraud, creates an unacceptable and unnecessary risk of civil litigation. . . . In the best-case scenario, this creates the perception that SIU investigators are compensated for denying claims and at worst it creates actual bias by the SIU investigator."[37] Although it is in the company's interest to increase the "dollars denied due to fraud," it is not in the company's interest to get caught at it.

The result of the campaign against insurance fraud and its integration into claims processing is predictable: Allegations of fraud will be used against policyholders as another means to delay, deny, defend. Cloteal and Alfred Cameron, Dallas homeowners insured by Texas Farmers Insurance Company, found that out.[38] Neither was home the night their house burned, and it was clear that arson was the cause of the fire. Farmers initially paid them for temporary living expenses, but then Tony Poncio, Farmers's branch claims manager, denied the claim, concluding that it was arson committed by them for insurance fraud. There were red flags: The fire was clearly arson, and the Camerons were not home at the time. They had only three thousand dollars in savings and had some credit card debts, and a fire marshal said Alfred had gambling debts, so they may have had a financial motive for fraud. Several years earlier they had filed a claim for fire loss to rental property they owned and for thefts of their cars. Their Farmers policy had been in effect for only three months before the fire. The house was for sale at the time of the fire, and the amount of the insurance policy was greater than the sale price.

Unfortunately for the Camerons (and ultimately for Farmers), the insurance company reflexively used the red flags as the basis for denying the claim without following the basic rule of claims practices: Investigate fully and fairly. Neither of the Camerons could have set the fire; Alfred was at a casino with a friend at the time and Cloteal was staying at her daughter's apartment to help her pack, because she was moving. But Poncio did not interview either the friend or the daughter, because "there was nothing else to look into about it." Their financial condition was not precarious; their annual income was ninety thousand dollars; they were current on their credit cards; there was no evidence of gambling debts except for the offhand remark of the fire marshal; the casinos where he played did not even grant credit; and they were financially secure enough to get a mortgage to purchase a new house. There was no evidence that their previous insurance claims involved fraud, and Farmers made no effort even to get the claims files to find the facts on them. They already had a buyer for the house and suffered a financial and personal loss by the fire; unlike the typical arsonist, they had not removed family photographs or other items of sentimental value beforehand. As the Camerons' expert in claims practices testified at the trial, Farmers performed the kind of investigation in which the outcome is determined in advance. The jury agreed; in a verdict upheld by the appellate court, it concluded that Farmers had broken its promise to act in good faith and deal fairly with the Camerons, and had violated the Texas insurance laws.

John Asmus, a claims adjuster for Shelter Mutual Insurance Company in Missouri, summed up the attitude that insurance fraud is rampant and a basis for denying claims when he told Jonathan Hensley, "You might as well get a lawyer because Shelter was not going to pay the house off."[39] Jonathan and his wife, Juanita, had purchased a one-story brick home near Steele, Missouri, but a year and a half later separated and ultimately filed for divorce. Jonathan remained in the house, and one Sunday afternoon, while Jonathan was out celebrating his birthday with friends, a fire began on top of the stove that destroyed the kitchen and dining room and spread smoke damage throughout. He stayed that night at his girlfriend's house, and at 5:45 A.M. the next day the house caught fire again, this time burning nearly all of the house to the ground. Over the next two days the fire department returned three times to put out rekindles of the fire.

Asmus met with Jonathan and gave him an initial check of two thousand dollars to purchase clothes and other necessary items. Shelter hired Chris Silman to investigate the cause of the fire. Asmus also contacted Cendant Mortgage, which held the mortgage on the house, to determine the balance owed on the loan, but Shelter never paid off Cendant as the insurance policy indicated it should. When Jonathan asked why, Asmus gave his regrettable reply.

Jonathan did get a lawyer. Jonathan, Juanita, Shelter, and Cendant eventually settled the claim under the homeowners insurance policy for $83,100 under coverage on the dwelling, but the settlement preserved

Jonathan's right to sue Shelter for other amounts. He sued for additional losses covered under the policy as well as under Missouri's statute that punished "vexatious refusal to pay" an insurance claim. The jury awarded him $58,170 for the personal property, $15,000 for additional living expense, $4,700 for debris removal, $500 for fire department services, $22,367 for interest, and, under the statute, a $15,713 penalty and $43,477 for attorney fees.

In upholding the jury's verdict the Court of Appeals pointed to many elements of Shelter's conduct that constituted vexatious refusal to pay. Up to the date of the trial, it refused to pay Cendant, even after it acknowledged that it owed Cendant the money. As a result, interest continued to accrue, and Cendant threatened Jonathan with foreclosure. When Asmus told Jonathan to get a lawyer, that statement effectively constituted a denial of the claim. By law, when an insurance company denies a claim it has to give reasons, but Asmus gave no explanation. Most important, for the allegation of fraud, Shelter's investigation was inadequate. Shelter suspected that Jonathan had set the fire, but it failed to fully investigate the situation and ignored evidence to the contrary. The company knew Jonathan had an alibi but never attempted to corroborate it. It relied on reports of a suspicious dark-color pickup truck driving away from the house the morning of the second fire, but it failed to consider that Jonathan's neighbors shared a driveway with him and drove a dark red pickup. Silman, Shelter's fire expert, took five debris samples from the house; only one of them tested positive for accelerant, but Silman failed to pin down where that sample came from, and actually kept changing his story as to its source, moving from the storage room next to the garage (where Jonathan kept a can of gasoline for his lawn mower), to the area of the front door, to the center of the master bedroom, to the wall between the bedroom and living room. Shelter said Jonathan's bad debts made the claim suspicious, but he had no such debts; in fact, at the time of the fire he made $85,000 a year, had forty to fifty thousand dollars in his 401(k), and owed no debts other than the Cendant mortgage on the house and a loan on his truck. Finally, whatever evidence Shelter had against Jonathan applied equally to Juanita, but it arbitrarily chose to exonerate her and focus on him.

Jonathan Hensley's case is distinctive only because of the frankness of adjuster John Asmus: "You might as well get a lawyer because Shelter was not going to pay the house off." The attitude is shocking but the openness is refreshing. Insurance fraud is a problem, but whether fraud against insurance companies or by insurance companies is the bigger problem and open to question.

11

How Consumers Can Respond to Delay, Deny, Defend

CONSUMERS BUY INSURANCE policies on their cars and homes to make sure that they will be protected if accidents happen or disaster strikes. Yet if you are in a car crash or have a house fire, it is more likely than ever that your insurance company will delay settlement of your claim, deny part or all of it, and aggressively defend the lawsuit you are forced to bring to collect the benefits to which you are entitled. This chapter provides some advice on how to reduce the chances of this happening and how to respond if it does.

The chapter is not a complete primer on buying insurance and filing a claim; there are other sources for that, many of which are described in the appendix. Instead, it converts the key points from the rest of the book on why and how insurance companies delay, deny, defend into lessons consumers can use to help themselves. Consumers cannot prevent or cure insurance companies' unfair claim tactics all by themselves; legislators, government regulators, and the courts need to step in, too, and the next chapter outlines a plan of action for legal reform. But consumers can do better in choosing their insurance companies and insurance policies and in pursuing their claims, and this chapter tells you how.

The most important lesson from this book is about the relationship between you and your insurance company. No matter what kind of warm, fuzzy feeling you get from your insurer's television commercials, the company is not your friend. State Farm is not a good neighbor; it is not even like a good neighbor. The cradling hands in Allstate's logo will not comfort and protect you like your mother's arms did. You can get wet under the Travelers umbrella. And so on. Your insurance company is a business, and its relationship with you is a business relationship. As a business, it has to make a profit. The way to make a profit is to keep costs within bounds. Because claims payments are an insurance company's largest cost, it makes more money when it pays less. Therefore, it has an incentive to pay you late, little, or nothing when you file a claim.

But just as your insurance company is not your friend, neither is it your enemy. As a business, it has to attract and retain customers. If it gets a reputation for failing to pay claims, it will have a harder time attracting customers. In the insurance business, repeat customers are a hugely important source of income; the company has an incentive to treat its customers well, so they will renew their policies. Like any other successful business, an insurance company has to be set up to perform its basic task—paying claims—pretty well most of the time, even if pretty well is not good enough and most of the time is not often enough.

The relationship between you and your insurance company is a special kind of business relationship. When you contract with your insurer you are buying the security of knowing that if something bad happens, the company will provide you a financial safety net. Because this relationship is special, the industry and the law have defined special duties that your company owes to you when you submit a claim. These duties include acting promptly, telling you what your policy covers, helping you file your claim, fully and fairly investigating what happened, paying what it owes you without forcing you to litigation, and more.

The nature of your relationship with your insurer should guide everything you do in buying a policy and filing a claim. The company is not your friend, so you have to look out for yourself. The company is not your enemy, so you should look for ways to cooperate with it. The company has a special responsibility to you, and you should insist that it live up to that responsibility.

Begin at the beginning. The best way to deal with trouble is to avoid it, and the best way to avoid trouble in the event you have a claim is to pick a company that has a good record of observing customer-friendly practices. The number one recommendation for consumers by the Consumer Federation of America (CFA) is: "If possible, avoid doing business with a company that has a history of anti-consumer behavior."[1] That is a big if, because companies do not willingly offer good information on which consumers can make decisions, and government regulators either do not collect that information or do not make it public. But there are some places to start.

Some state departments of insurance collect and post on their Web sites information about the number and type of consumer complaints filed against individual companies. CFA publishes a listing and evaluation of what information is available on those Web sites.[2] The National Association of Insurance Commissioners aggregates information from the states in the Consumer Information Source section of its Web site, and it allows consumers to search for complaint data on individual companies.[3]

This information about consumer complaints is incomplete and inexact at its best; it can only help in making rough identifications of particularly bad companies. Some experts have analyzed those data and other information to make assessments about individual companies. In a 2007 study, CFA looked at claims settlement practices, treatment of policyholders after natural disasters, profits, and other factors and recommended that consumers "avoid Allstate if at all possible."[4] Fight Bad Faith Insurance Companies, a Web site produced by a self-described group of consumers "who had legitimate claims that were denied by bad faith insurers," ranks The Hartford, State Farm, and Allstate as the worst in its claim practices "hall of shame" and Chubb, Amica, and Allianz as best in its "hall of fame," but the Web site does not explain exactly how the rankings were arrived at or who is doing the ranking.[5]

Another source of information is *Consumer Reports*, which periodically surveys its readers on their dealings with insurance companies. As the magazine notes, the surveys reflect readers' experiences, not necessarily those of the general population. Nevertheless, the results provide some guidance. In a survey of homeowners reported in the September

2009 issue, Amica, USAA, and Chubb policyholders had much better than average experience with claims and Farmers, Allstate, and Travelers insureds reported worse than average claim handling.

Because of the lack of complete information on companies' claim practices, each of these evaluations has to be taken with a grain of salt. And although State Farm and Allstate were criticized throughout this book, that shouldn't be taken as a judgment on them versus their competitors; they are just the largest players and the companies whose involvement with McKinsey & Company in the transformation of claim handling is the best documented.

A traditional piece of advice on choosing a company is to rely on an independent insurance agent who represents several companies. That advice also is becoming harder to follow, as more and more of the market is being occupied by companies that either sell directly to consumers or only through their own agents. Therefore, a good independent agent's advice, while sound with respect to the companies he represents, comes at the price of excluding many major companies from the search.

The bottom line on choosing a company, therefore, is to search for information, hope that the information reveals the best and worst actors, and recognize that the information is incomplete.

Being careful about the policy you buy is another way of preventing trouble if you end up filing a claim. Buy the right coverage, particularly the kind of coverage that avoids some of the most common claims issues. Companies increasingly sell policies on the basis of price, not coverage, and consumers buy the policies that way. Except for a few basic facts about the policy, notably its dollar limits, most consumers know almost nothing about its content. Instead, they rely on what they assume the policy covers, and the assumptions are often wrong.

Auto policies are relatively simple and standard. (Simple, that is, by insurance policy standards; a fifteen-page policy is common.) Most offer similar types of coverage, and the Web sites of state insurance departments and consumer groups often give explanations of them. Obviously you need to make sure you have all the coverage you need, both as to the type of coverage and the dollar limits. Many problems arise in auto claims, but few of the problems can be minimized or avoided when buying the policy.

Homeowners insurance is a different story. Many of the problems with claims come from inconsistencies between the fine print of the insurance policy and what the consumer thought she was buying. Sometimes this is unavoidable; as companies play follow the leader in limiting coverage through more exclusions and obscure clauses, it becomes difficult or impossible to avoid all of the traps. You can still avoid some problems by careful shopping. Know what you're buying; buy what you need.

Consumers often believe that their homeowners insurance protects them against losses from any source and will provide enough funds to rebuild in case the house is destroyed; after all, the most common homeowners policy is an all-risks policy with replacement cost coverage. As described in Chapter 8, however, all risks does not mean all risks, and replacement cost does not mean replacement cost. When buying a policy, be aware that you can reduce the risk of being surprised later by the lack of coverage.

An all-risks policy does not cover damage caused by a wide variety of risks, and the policy's anti–concurrent causation clause will exclude even some covered risks when they coincide with excluded risks. As catastrophes like Hurricane Katrina demonstrate, among the most important exclusions from the insurance company's perspective are the ones that enable it to deny payment to many people in the same area when they need it the most. The solution is to consider buying disaster insurance if you live in an area where a disaster is possible and the insurance available. This includes insurance for floods under the National Flood Insurance Program, earthquakes, and, in some states, wind. Disaster insurance is not a complete cure-all; flood insurance, for example, has a maximum value of $250,000 for a dwelling, which may not be enough to rebuild but at least is better than no coverage at all.

Read your policy and look for other risks that might be excluded. Often this requires creative thinking, as insurance companies will attempt to interpret exclusions aggressively to deny their liability for losses. In some cases it is possible to purchase a rider to cover a risk you might face (and a good agent will raise the possibility). If your heating system includes an oil tank in the basement, for example, the policy is likely to exclude coverage for the very expensive cost of cleaning up the oil if the tank should rupture, but an "oil tank endorsement" can fill that gap.

Even if a risk is covered, you need to make sure that the loss will be paid for in full. United Policyholders, the consumer advocacy group, reports that underinsurance after a total loss is a very common problem. Guaranteed replacement cost policies that, as their name indicates, guarantee the policy will pay the full cost of rebuilding a house are a relic of the past. Actual cash value policies pay only the depreciated value of the home and virtually guarantee that you will not have enough to rebuild. Replacement cost policies are the most common, but there are pitfalls that make it likely that the full cost of replacement will not be paid. To avoid this problem, make clear to your agent when you shop for the policy that you want full replacement coverage, so the agent doesn't try to sell you less effective coverage simply because it is cheaper. Get an accurate estimate of the cost of replacing your house from your agent or a local contractor and use it as the basis of the policy limit. For even more security, buy an extended replacement-cost endorsement, which gives you a cushion in case the cost to rebuild exceeds the policy limit. The insurance company also may argue that the policy only requires it to rebuild the house you had, which may not be possible if building standards have changed since your house was originally constructed. In some states the company cannot do this, but where it can, you should ask for a building code upgrade endorsement that would pay the added cost.

The same advice applies to contents coverage. Ordinarily the overall policy limit for contents coverage (furniture, clothing, and other personal items) is high enough for most people, but make sure it fits your situation. Read the limitations on contents coverage and see if there are any gaps. A typical policy will limit what the insurance company has to pay for loss by theft of "scheduled items" such as jewelry. If you have jewelry, silverware, antique family heirlooms, or other items of value, consider buying an endorsement to raise the limits of the coverage on them.

If you are lucky, you will buy insurance and never need it, your premiums purchasing you the peace of mind of knowing you are protected and nothing more. Inevitably, though, someone will suffer a loss, and it might be you. If you do, things might go smoothly, and your company will pay you everything you need, promptly and without fuss. Or you might enter the world of delay, deny, defend. If you have a loss, there are three basic lessons from this book to remember: Understand your coverage. Understand the claims system. Get help if you need it.

Understanding your coverage is easier said than done. The policy is long and complicated, it includes terms that have special meanings you don't know, and it can be understood only against a backdrop of decades of industry practice and judicial interpretation. But you can make a start. Professor Tom Baker of the University of Pennsylvania law school has outlined a five-step approach. First, survey the policy, checking such things as who is insured, what time frame it covers, and all of the forms and endorsements that make up the policy. (Make notes or an outline as you go.) Second, find out whether the loss is covered. Begin with the central promise about risks covered, such as all risks or named perils in a homeowners policy. Then look for definitions of terms, some of which are in a definitions section and others scattered throughout the policy, and for exclusions, which also are partly included in an exclusion section and partly in other sections. Third, look for additional kinds of coverage; a homeowners policy typically provides for additional payments for removing debris and the cost of renting another house while repairs are being made. Fourth, find out how to get paid. Determine how a loss is to be calculated; how, when, and where a claim should be filed; and what conditions there are for the claim (such as a requirement that an injured person submit to a medical examination by the company's doctor). Fifth, check your understanding by rereading the policy.

Understanding the claims system starts by understanding that the person on the other end of the phone when you call in a claim or the adjuster who comes out to your house is not an independent actor who will decide on the merits of your claim; she is part of the company's system of claim processing, and the system, not the individual, controls. The system is not designed to make the adjuster your friend; it is designed to make the company money. Nor is it designed to make the adjuster your enemy; in the long run the company can't make money if it denies every claim, because it will lose its customers. And the system operates against a backdrop of fair claim handling standards recognized by the insurance industry and written into law. Mastering the system gives you a considerable leg up in getting what is owed to you. You want to be like the customers of Bob Parr, the former superhero Mr. Incredible, who subvert the hard-hearted claims process at the insurance company where he works by "exploiting every loophole, dodging every obstacle, penetrating the bureaucracy."

To deal with this kind of system, unless the attempt to resolve your claim completely breaks down and you have to sue your insurance company, you should act as if the company will live up to its obligations while being on guard that it will not. Tell the adjuster (and maybe even write to the adjuster): I need your help, I expect you will provide me with every benefit I am entitled to under the policy and you will handle my claim promptly and fairly, and I will take all reasonable steps to cooperate with you in the handling of this claim. This approach sets a good tone for the relationship and lets the adjuster know that you are an informed consumer and will be an active participant in the process. If things fall apart and you end up in litigation, it also makes clear to the court that you tried to do everything you could to settle the claim amicably, so any problems must be due to the insurance company's violation of acceptable standards. The advice United Policyholders gives about complaints in claim handling is good advice throughout the process: Be polite, be prompt, be persistent.[6]

Information is the oxygen that the claim process breathes. The longstanding maxim of adjusters is more true than ever: If it's not in the claim file, it doesn't exist. Therefore, you need to fully document your loss and your interactions with adjusters. Understand what documentation is required of you and provide it, and respond to the company's reasonable requests for information. In a homeowners claim, for example, provide information, receipts, photographs, records, or statements that document the extent and value of your loss.

Also understand what information is not required of you and when you should be wary in responding to requests. The homeowners policy requires you to provide adequate proof of loss, but it does not require you to provide the actual receipt for the television set you bought five years ago. In a homeowners claim the company can require you to report for an examination under oath, at which you will be questioned on the record by an insurance company lawyer, and in a personal injury claim it can require you to undergo an independent medical examination by a doctor of its choosing. If you understand that the company often uses these procedures to gather information it can use to deny your claim, you will consult with a lawyer first, read up on how to behave at either examination, and come prepared to fulfill your obligation but not help the company deny your claim.

You are not the only one providing information in the claim process; the company and its agents provide information too. Their information may not be better than yours, and given the systems in place to limit claim payments, it may be worse. Their information will seem objective and indisputable, but that is only an appearance. This is particularly true of the information generated by the ubiquitous computerized claims systems. An Xactimate estimate of the cost of repairing property can vary greatly depending on how the adjuster assesses the loss, which boxes she checks on the software, and the accuracy of the prices built into the system. In most cases the cost estimate you get from a local contractor will be a better prediction of the true cost of repairs than the Xactimate estimate, so share your estimate with the insurer and demand that they take it seriously. A Colossus evaluation of general damages for injuries in an auto accident is largely imaginary, likely based on inaccurate medical information, an inadequate basis of comparison, and the insurance company's "tuning" of the system to produce the numbers it wants; you do not have to accept the computer's number as final.

To build the company's claim file, you also should take notes on every conversation you have with all insurance company personnel—who said what when—and send a note about the conversation to the adjuster and ask her to confirm its accuracy in writing. If possible (often it's not), have the adjuster document the conversation, too, and send you a copy. When you provide documents, send a cover letter describing what is included. And build your own claim file, with a copy of every document, note, and record.

You also should understand the hierarchy of claims departments and move up the hierarchy if you need to. If the first adjuster you talk to denies your claim after you have presented all the facts, your instinct may be to argue, persuade, or cajole her into changing her mind. All of that is likely to be of little use. The adjuster may have limited training and less discretion, and she is simply executing the instructions she has been given by the system. To move your claim along you need to go up the ladder to supervisors with more experience and more authority. The adjuster has a supervisor. The supervisor has a manager. The manager reports to a regional claims vice president. The regional vice president answers to the home office. To be most effective, state your case in writing and explain, don't complain. State the facts that make clear why your claim should be paid. Complaining doesn't help, and they have heard it all before. Keep moving up the hierarchy; you are trying to find the person who either will agree that the company should honor its promise to you or, as UP puts it, will "get upset that they are being troubled with such a minor issue" and will pay the claim to make you go away.[7]

Although not part of the insurance company hierarchy, your state insurance department can be helpful in resolving claim problems. The department usually has a complaint process, and the easiest way to get access to it is through the department's Web site. Complaints against insurance companies can be filed online or in writing, and a telephone help line is usually available too. The department does not always have the legal authority to force the company to resolve your complaint, but it can mediate disputes and persuade the company to review the problem. In very serious cases the department may also use your complaint as the basis for an enforcement action against the company if it has disobeyed the law. One cautionary note: The department's complaint office is usually understaffed and not always in the consumer's corner, so if you are not satisfied with its action, consider consulting with a lawyer to pursue your claim.

Another element of the claim system described in this book is the segmentation of claims. Not all claims are treated alike, and knowing how the system treats different kinds of claims enables you to better respond to what the company is doing.

Suppose you are in a low-speed auto crash and suffer neck injuries. Your insurance company may offer you what seems like a token amount of money to settle the claims, possibly even less than what you spent in medical bills. Understand that the company has categorized your claim as a MIST claim, and you can either take the money and go away or likely face protracted litigation that might be worth only a few thousand dollars. A first step is to remind the company of its obligation under the policy and under the law. For example, in most states a company is required by the uniform law that regulates claim practices to try to promptly and fairly settle a claim in which liability has become reasonably clear. It is also prohibited from offering you a lowball settlement that forces you to take them to court to get what you are entitled to. Letting the company know that you are aware of its obligation indicates that you are willing to enforce that obligation, either by suing for what is owed—and for other damages to which you are entitled because of the company's improper action—or by complaining to the state insurance department. That doesn't always work; companies have segmented MIST claims just because their small size can make it hard for you to find a lawyer to fight the denial, even if it is in bad faith. At least understanding what is going on puts you in a better position to make an informed decision about how you should proceed.

Segmentation also requires that some proportion of claims be treated as fraudulent and referred to a special investigations unit. The consequences can be serious. The investigation into your claim and your life will be searching, the probability that your claim will be denied (or that you will abandon it under pressure) increases, and there is even a small but real possibility that your claim will be referred to law enforcement for criminal prosecution. If this happens to you, take two steps. First, see this as just another part of the claim-processing system and don't assume that you have done anything wrong. Second, get a lawyer to help you through the process.

The ultimate step in segmentation divides claims into those in which the policyholder is represented by a lawyer or public adjuster and those in which she is not. If you choose to be represented, the claim process can become contentious as the insurance company moves into a more adversarial mode. At the same time, you are an amateur in the process of claim settlement up against a phalanx of professionals, and bringing in your own professional helps even the odds. Insurance companies usually discourage consumers from bringing in professionals. Allstate famously, and in some cases unlawfully, discouraged claimants from hiring lawyers. Today the Allstate Web site gives detailed instructions and FAQs about claims without mentioning that it might be in the policyholder's interest to hire a lawyer. As to public adjusters, it is similarly discouraging, stating:

> For their services, public adjusters charge you a fee based on the total value of your settlement. These fees may be considerable and are not reimbursable under your Allstate policy. As an Allstate policy holder, you don't need to hire a public insurance adjuster to settle your insurance claim. An Allstate claim representative, experienced in making claim settlements, will tell you what paperwork is necessary to finalize your claim. Of course, the decision is yours to make.

Will you be better off pursuing your insurance claim yourself or hiring a professional to work with you? For some claims the answer is obvious. If you are in a fender bender with a few hundred or a few thousand dollars worth of damage to your car and are sure no one was hurt, it doesn't make economic sense to hire a lawyer. (That doesn't mean you have to rely completely on the insurance company, however. Read up on your rights and how to protect them. Make sure the damages are estimated and the work is done at a repair shop you trust, not necessarily the one the company selects.) If you sustain serious injuries in a major auto accident and have to pursue a claim against your insurance company under your uninsured motorist coverage, you need a lawyer.

For claims in between these extremes, whether you get help depends on the claim and on you. Do you have the expertise, time, resources, and energy to pursue the claim yourself? If so, you don't need help. In many cases, one of those elements will be lacking. Many claims involve legal questions about the interpretation of a term of the policy or about the assignment of liability that only a lawyer can address properly. If you have suffered physical injury, you may be physically unable to deal with the stress of the claim, or you may be unable to detach yourself emotionally from the process to a sufficient degree to deal dispassionately with the insurance company. Scoping the extent of loss and estimating the cost of repairs after serious damage to a house requires more time, knowledge of construction techniques, and access to specialized experts than most people possess. When you are not sure whether to retain a professional, it usually pays to talk to one or several so that they can help you assess your situation. Often these consultations are free.

Professional help doesn't come free, and good professional help doesn't come cheap. Depending on the type of case and your personal circumstances, lawyers may charge either on an hourly basis or a contingent fee, in which they take a portion of the recovery if you win and nothing if you lose. Public adjusters charge a percentage of the amount you receive from the insurance company; their fees are regulated in many states, and the rate is usually 10 percent to 15 percent of the total recovery. In both cases, feel free to discuss what the lawyer or adjuster can do for you and how much it will cost, and then make the judgment about whether the value they add to your case is worth it.

If you decide you need help, get good help, from a professional experienced in the kind of claim you have. Insurance claims are as specialized as other areas of practice, so the lawyer who drafted your will may not be the best choice to help you pursue your insurance claim. Select a lawyer or a public adjuster the same way you would a doctor. Recommendations from the barroom, barber, or beauty shop are not likely to be reliable. Even if a friend or neighbor has had a good experience with a lawyer, he may not have enough expertise to evaluate that experience, and every case is different. Professionals know professionals, so better sources of advice are lawyers in other areas of practice, independent insurance agents, real estate agents, bankers, or others who may be similarly knowledgeable.

Whether you get professional help or not, you should become knowledgeable about insurance and the claim process to make you a better consumer when you buy insurance, and especially if you have a claim. This chapter gives you a start. The appendix lists some specific resources that can help. It's your policy, your claim, and your financial security that is at stake; take responsibility for it.

12

How to Stop Delay, Deny, Defend

THE PROBLEM OF insurance companies that delay, deny, and defend is big. No one—except maybe the companies themselves, and they're not telling—knows exactly how big. But the problem is big enough that thousands of individual policyholders and accident victims are not getting the benefits their insurance companies owe them. Big enough, too, that as awareness of the problem increases it may undermine public confidence in the insurance industry.

Consumers can take some steps to protect themselves against unfair claim practices, but they cannot prevent or cure the practices themselves. Bad practices persist because government regulators have failed to do enough to prevent and punish them. Lawmakers and regulators in every state need to do three things to protect consumers (and consumers need to push them into action). First, give consumers the information they need to take a company's claim practices into account when they shop for insurance. Second, make clear in the law that the rules of the road of claim handling are binding on insurance companies, and give regulators the power to enforce those rules. Third, make sure policyholders and accident victims filing claims have the ability

202

to hold insurance companies accountable when the companies delay, deny, or defend.

Here is a paradox: Insurance is the most highly regulated business in the United States, but the system of regulation has so far failed to implement these reforms and to protect policyholders and accident victims from unfair claim practices. Why isn't more being done?

The insurance industry, like other financial services such as commercial banking, investment banking, mutual funds, and stock brokerage, is dominated by large companies that operate across the country and even internationally. In the aftermath of the financial meltdown of 2008–2009, when the federal government bailed out insurance giant AIG, the Obama administration proposed instituting federal monitoring of the financial activities of insurance companies to prevent future catastrophes. For the most part, however, insurance is regulated primarily at the state level.

Insurance regulation in America began with the states, by way of conditions in the state charters that allowed the companies to organize and operate.[1] The first stock insurance corporation was the Insurance Company of North America, chartered in 1794, the predecessor of today's CIGNA; its charter required that its capital be invested in certain government bonds and its funds be deposited with the Bank of Pennsylvania.

The first broad attempt at regulation focused on making sure companies had enough money to pay claims, a particular issue because of widespread fires that threatened insurance companies' economic survival; the Great New York Fire of 1835 bankrupted twenty-three of the city's twenty-six fire insurance companies. Early efforts in Massachusetts in 1818 and New York in 1828 required insurance companies to file publicly available reports on their financial status in the fruitless hope that prospective policyholders would view the reports and possess the financial acumen to distinguish a financially sound company from a precarious one. The failure of that approach led to the creation of state administrative agencies to more directly regulate the companies, starting in New Hampshire in 1851. These early boards of insurance commissioners, later replaced by individual insurance commissioners, regulated policy forms, licensed companies and agents, and tried to prevent the frequent practice of collusion among the companies to fix the prices of premiums.

Insurance companies did not react well to these new regulations, and in 1868 tried to have the U.S. Supreme Court put an end to them. The National Board of Fire Underwriters, an industry group, argued to the Court that the sale of insurance policies was commerce within the meaning of the commerce clause of the Constitution, regulation of which was reserved to the federal government. That argument presaged the current debate over whether new federal legislation should supplement or supplant state regulation of insurance; the companies' preference for federal regulation was based on the belief that the federal government would be a less effective regulator and so leave the companies freer to go their own way, unchecked. In *Paul v. Virginia*, the Court rejected the argument, leaving the states as the primary regulators of the insurance industry.[2]

In the decades after *Paul*, state insurance commissioners expanded the degree of regulation, although, as often happens today, their efforts were as favorable to the industry as to the policyholders. Many states mandated the use of the New York Standard Fire Policy of 1886, a form so laden with conditions and restrictions on the policyholder that by one estimate insurance companies would be able to deny claims on more than a quarter of the policies issued. Only after scandals like the bankruptcy of many companies following the San Francisco earthquake in 1906 that spurred the work of the Armstrong and Merritt committees in New York did more significant regulation arrive.

Missouri's insurance commissioner took a particularly tough stance on rate increases, provoking litigation that was settled only with a bribe to the Kansas City political machine. The U.S. Department of Justice secured an indictment of the South-Eastern Underwriters Association, and its officers and member companies, for violations of the antitrust laws by fixing prices and monopolizing the trade in fire insurance.[3] In ruling on the case in 1944, the post–New Deal Supreme Court reversed its position in *Paul*, holding that insurance is interstate commerce and therefore subject to federal regulation, including the antitrust laws.[4] The insurance industry feared federal regulation would be more vigorous, and state regulators feared losing their authority, so they responded jointly by lobbying Congress to keep the status quo. The result was the McCarran-Ferguson Act, which directed that state regulation would only be preempted where Congress specifically said so. Recent proposals have been made to supplement or even supplant state regulation with federal control, but as of this writing (2009) it appears that due to political conflicts, state regulation of most of the insurance business is likely to be the norm well into the future.

Government regulation of insurance rests on two basic principles. First, insurance is not just another profit-making business; insurance affects the public interest. Insurance companies collect, invest, and distribute vast amounts of wealth, and the way in which they do that affects individuals and society as a whole. They serve as gatekeepers to the middle class; no bank will lend money for a mortgage unless the borrower qualifies for homeowner insurance. Auto insurance is mandatory in nearly every state as part of a state-regulated system for ensuring that victims of accidents are compensated for their injuries. All forms of life, health, disability, property, and liability insurance secure ordinary Americans' standard of living against catastrophic loss. Because insurance companies affect the public interest they are appropriately subject to control by the government in the interest of the public.

Second, markets do not always work well, and insurance markets, left to their own devices, work particularly poorly. The possibility of "destructive competition" has long been a rationale for regulation. Usually competition in an industry is a good thing. Competition in the restaurant business produces choices for consumers, who can be served beef in varied forms at different prices from McDonald's through Chili's to Morton's. Competition also keeps prices in check; McDonald's ability to raise the prices of its hamburgers is constrained by the presence of a Wendy's down the block. Some competition in insurance is good too; the ubiquity of television advertisements for auto insurance demonstrates the pressure on companies to keep prices low. But too much competition can drive prices too low, so low that the companies offering the cheapest policies will be unable to make a profit and become insolvent, leaving nothing to pay claims. The insurance market also presents consumers with more difficult choices than the restaurant market; an insurance policy is harder to read than a restaurant menu, and the trustworthiness of an insurance company is harder to evaluate than the quality of a restaurant. Finally, even if the insurance market were efficient, it might not produce results that are acceptable to society. Underwriters might use rational economic calculations to determine that some urban neighborhoods pose too great a risk to sell homeowners insurance there, but that form of redlining has racially discriminatory effects that society is unwilling to accept.

Regulating insurance in the public interest and correcting for market failures takes a myriad of forms: Insurance regulators license insurance companies; approve or disapprove mergers; mandate educational and other licensing requirements for agents, brokers, and adjusters; tax insurance companies; specify capital requirements; dictate the form and frequency of financial reporting; control the types of investments companies can make; create and force insurance companies to fund guaranty funds for the policyholders of insolvent companies; regulate the premium rates companies may charge; approve the forms of policies; create mechanisms to provide insurance that the market would not otherwise provide; bar discriminatory practices; limit commissions companies may pay brokers; receive and adjudicate consumer complaints; and more.

Thinking generally, however, regulators do three things, one very well, one reasonably well, and one only sporadically well. What they do very well is regulate the solvency of companies. What they do reasonably well is regulate the rates companies charge. What they do only sporadically well is regulate market conduct, including claim practices.

The regulatory problem of longest standing is ensuring the solvency of insurance companies; that is, making certain that companies have sufficient financial reserves to pay claims as they are presented. There is an obvious reason for the focus on solvency regulation: Policyholders are purchasing security, and they need some assurance that the security will be there if they need it. Less obviously, the failure of one company diminishes the public's faith in all insurance companies, thereby reducing people's likelihood of buying insurance and reducing the protection available to all. And the behavior that led to insolvency puts pressure on all companies; insolvency often results from collecting premiums that are too low or taking risks that are too great, and if one company does that, others race to the bottom in order to compete.

Regulators aim to prevent insolvency through a variety of techniques. Insurance companies must be licensed to do business, and the state reviews the company's capitalization and other measures of financial stability before issuing a license. Thereafter the company must report regularly on its financial condition. Regulators review the reports and, if a company's finances are questionable, will investigate further and take action. Insurers are required to set aside reserves in amounts and kinds related to the policies they have written. How capital and reserves may be invested is also controlled by the regulators; for property/casualty insurers, most of the funds are kept in debt instruments such as U.S. government securities and other high-grade bonds, and limited amounts are invested in stocks.

Solvency regulation works well in guaranteeing the safety of property/casualty companies. According to an A. M. Best report, of more than twenty-seven hundred property/casualty companies only seven went insolvent in 2008, and four of those were title insurance companies, not auto or homeowner insurers. The effectiveness of solvency regulation was tested during the financial crisis of 2008–2009 and generally passed. In September 2008 AIG faced collapse and had to be bailed out by the federal government. AIG was the largest seller of life insurance in the United States, and it sold life, property/casualty, health, travel, and other forms of insurance through a network of companies operating in 130 countries. What caused AIG's fall from being one of the world's largest companies, with assets before the crisis of a trillion dollars, to being a mendicant saved by the government only because it was "too big to fail" was its move into esoteric forms of corporate risk management, such as credit default swaps, far removed from traditional insurance. Through it all, however, regulators reassured the public that the property/casualty insurance companies that were the core of AIG's business remained financially secure. Several life insurance companies that essentially operated as investment firms with large obligations to annuity holders also lined up for federal bailout funds, but property/casualty companies were on sounder footing. Even though Allstate qualified for government funding, the company turned down the aid, citing adequate capital and liquidity.

Rate regulation, which state insurance commissioners do reasonably well, originally was related to solvency regulation. Insurance companies face what economists call a collective action problem. It is in the interest of all companies to keep rates high enough so that they collect enough money to prevent insolvency. It is in the interest of every individual company, however, to cut rates to attract more business. The typical results of the conflict between individual rationality and collective irrationality are price wars that prime the insurance underwriting cycle and make some insolvencies certain to occur. Government regulation solves the problem by imposing the discipline on the companies that the market makes impossible, and today regulators have a variety of mechanisms for regulating the rates companies charge.

Because the original purpose of rate regulation was to prevent insolvency, the initial focus of regulation was on adequacy of rates, or setting rates high enough so that the company's income is adequate to pay claims as they are presented. But because of the public interest that insurance serves, rates that are too high will deter some prospective policyholders from buying insurance and will cause others to be underinsured, with the adverse consequences that follow. Therefore, rate regulation is also concerned with making sure that rates are not excessive. Because of the public interest in insurance, rates also are regulated to ensure that they do not unfairly discriminate against some policyholders at the expense of others.

The area of state regulation that is only sporadically successful is the grab bag known as market conduct regulation. Here are included a variety of measures to achieve the fair treatment of policyholders. One form of unfairness is the sale of a policy that is incomprehensible or substantively unfair; regulators respond by requiring approval of the form of policies and requiring that they be written in language sufficiently plain to be understandable on the off chance that the policyholder actually reads it. Success has been mixed; most policy forms are standardized, produced by the ISO, and marketed and accepted around the country with little variation. The range of disputes about policy terms and the surprise policyholders express when they are denied coverage by some unknown or obscure provision demonstrate that regulation of policy forms is a sometime thing.

A second form of unfairness is the sale of policies by agents who are untrained or unscrupulous. States require agents to meet educational and character requirements in order to obtain a license, and they prohibit specific practices that benefit the agent at the expense of the consumer, such as persuading a policyholder to exchange one policy for another that pays the agent a higher commission but provides no benefit to the policyholder. Despite the regulation, the sale of policies that are unsuitable for their buyers and the receipt of unwarranted commissions by agents is hardly unknown.

A third form of unfairness is the subject of this book, opportunism through delay, deny, defend by the insurance company at the point when its promise obligates it to pay a claim. As the book demonstrates, here market conduct regulation has been notably ineffective. Claims practice regulation is typically an afterthought for regulators; a textbook coauthored by Therese Vaughan, former insurance commissioner of Iowa and now CEO of the National Association of Insurance Commissioners, perhaps inadvertently illustrates the problem when it notes, in only a single sentence between a three-page discussion of solvency regulation and a three-page discussion of rate regulation: "States have also adopted laws governing claims settlement and prohibiting unfair claims settlement practices."[5] Deborah Senn, former Washington insurance commissioner, puts it more bluntly: "Regulators have been nowhere on this. Regulation has really failed this issue."

With occasional exceptions when there is a public outcry about claims practices, as occurred after Hurricane Katrina, state insurance commissioners have always given market conduct regulation much lower priority than assuring companies' solvency and regulating premium rates. The allocation of resources tells the story. State insurance departments altogether devote less than 5 percent of their staffs to market conduct issues and 13 percent to consumer affairs issues, both of which encompass many problems in addition to claim practices.[6] As a result, department employees who assist the relatively few consumers who do complain about their insurance companies are overwhelmed by the volume of their work. A survey reports that in fifteen states, complaint handlers each have caseloads of six hundred cases or more, and in seven states, of one thousand or more. The result is predictable; nearly half of the states are unable to process all the consumer complaints they receive.[7]

There is a simple if cynical explanation why solvency regulation and rate regulation work well and claims practices regulation doesn't. Claims practices is the area in which the interests of insurance companies and the interests of consumers diverge most widely, and insurance companies have more clout with regulators. Cynicism is not an attractive character trait, and simple explanations are always partly wrong, but they are also partly correct, and being cynical and simple captures the essential truth about insurance regulation: The industry plays as big a role as do the regulators.

That is, if you can separate the industry and the regulators. Eric Gustafson of the Independent Insurance Agents of America expresses a common perception among insurance executives: "I view regulators as part of the industry. I don't view it as a separate entity."[8]

Indeed, today's regulator may become tomorrow's industry executive by walking through the revolving door between insurance companies and the government.[9] In a recent, much discussed incident, in August 2008 Alabama insurance commissioner Walter Bell resigned to become chairman of Swiss Re America Holding, a major reinsurer. A potential impediment was the Alabama law that forbids a former regulator from working for a company he regulated for two years after leaving the government. That restriction was deftly avoided because technically Bell was working for Swiss Re's holding company, not the subsidiaries that operated in Alabama. Bell's successor walked through the other side of the revolving door; Jim L. Ridling was former CEO of Southern Guaranty insurance companies.

Bell was a former president of the National Association of Insurance Commissioners, and his move was typical. In Senate testimony, former Texas insurance commissioner J. Robert Hunter ticked off the moves of five other recent presidents of NAIC: all to positions as lobbyists for the insurance industry except for the one who joined the board of directors of an insurance company. His litany could have gone further back; eleven of the last fifteen presidents have gone on to work for the industry. State insurance commissioners who do not ascend to the NAIC presidency have the same opportunity; an academic study of all state insurance commissioners serving over a seventeen-year period found that half went into the insurance industry after leaving office.[10] (Incidentally, the NAIC funds consumer representatives to attend its meetings, but they, unlike the commissioners themselves, are subject to a conflict-of-interest policy to make sure they are not subject to industry influence.)

There are exceptions, of course. The earliest was Webb McNall, a lawyer, journalist, farmer, and sometime vigilante who became Kansas's first superintendent of insurance in 1897. A month after taking office McNall suspended the licenses of New York Life, Mutual Life of New York, and Connecticut Mutual Life for failing to pay an eighteen-year-old life insurance claim; in an extraordinary predecessor of delay, deny, defend, the companies had refused the claim even though four juries had found against them.[11] In the early 1970s, University of Pennsylvania insurance professor and later consumer gadfly Herb Denenberg was Pennsylvania's insurance commissioner with the reported motto "*Populus Iamdudam Defutatus Est,*" loosely translated from the Latin as "The Consumer Has Been Screwed Long Enough."[12] After serving as insurance commissioner of Texas and Federal Insurance Administrator under presidents Ford and Carter, J. Robert Hunter has become a one-man truth squad on behalf of consumers, testifying before Congress, preparing reports, and serving as director of Insurance for the Consumer Federation of America. Deborah Senn served two terms as insurance commissioner of the State of Washington and was called by Ralph Nader "the best insurance commissioner in the United States" for her consumer advocacy. Jay Angoff was Missouri's longest-serving insurance commissioner and established competitive bidding processes for HMOs and workers compensation insurers that lowered rates for consumers. Florida insurance commissioner Kevin McCarty was the only insurance commissioner to take strong action against Allstate's refusal to comply with judicial and administrative orders to produce the McKinsey documents, resulting in their publication on the Internet. The list goes on, but not much longer; Denenberg, Hunter, Senn, Angoff, McCarty, and a few others are notable in part because their actions have been so rare.

Insurance companies have influence with regulators for all of the usual reasons and some unusual ones. The usual ones include money. For nine of the ten most recent federal election cycles, the insurance industry has been among the top ten in campaign contributions. (In 2008, despite contributions of $25.1 million from individuals and $21.2 million from PACs, it slipped to number eleven.) Because campaign contributions by industry donors are an investment more than an expression of ideology, the bets were placed across the board; in the 2008 presidential campaign, for example, Republican John McCain received $2.4 million and Democrat Barack Obama received $2.2 million.[13]

Campaign contributions at the state level are harder to track but potentially more important for the industry, because that is where most of its regulation occurs. The industry has been well represented in state campaigns, donating varying amounts as candidates and issues important to it come on the ballot: to candidates, $28.9 million in 2008, $17 million in 2007, and $58.7 million in 2006. Ballot measures attracted another $1.8 million, $13 million, and $9 million respectively, in each of those years. Money buys influence. The state legislative committees that write insurance legislation tend to be heavily stocked with legislators employed in the industry or friendly to it.

Influence also comes from organization, and the insurance industry teems with organizations that influence public policy: the American Insurance Association, the Property Casualty Insurers Association of America, the National Association of Mutual Insurance Companies, the Insurance Research Council, the Insurance Information Institute, and more. While the state tries to govern the insurance industry, the industry's trade groups "govern the government."[14] The groups' activities are both proactive and preventive, getting what the industry wants and forestalling regulation that it doesn't want, by continuously monitoring regulators' activities, maintaining close associations with regulators, lobbying, providing research, and promoting the industry's views to the public.

Industry influence is magnified by the unusual structure of insurance regulation.[15] An industry dominated by huge national and sometimes multinational corporations is regulated in fifty state capitals. The system is defended on the grounds of economic federalism; each state's needs are different, so each state requires a different regulatory regime. "We believe insurance is a local business by its nature," said Kevin Sullivan, assistant general counsel at Allstate, whose "local" businesses bring in $37 billion per year. Jay Angoff was closer to the mark when he explained the companies' desire for local rather than federal regulation: "They'd rather be regulated by fifty monkeys than one big gorilla."[16] (Unless the gorilla is weak and toothless; the Bush administration proposed optional federal chartering of insurance companies that would allow them to opt out of state regulation.) The multistate regulatory structure gives companies opportunities to whipsaw state regulators, threatening to support optional federal chartering of insurance companies or threatening to stop writing insurance in a state, as seems to happen regularly when regulators express any reluctance to allow companies to raise rates as they please.

Perhaps the most unusual aspect of insurance regulation is the role played by the National Association of Insurance Commissioners.[17] The NAIC was founded in 1871, shortly after the Supreme Court's decision in *Paul v. Virginia* made clear that the states would remain the primary controllers of the insurance industry. With a membership of the insurance commissioners of the fifty states, the District of Columbia, and five U.S. territories, offices in Kansas City, New York, and Washington, and a $70 million annual budget, the NAIC serves some of the functions that a national regulator of insurance companies would perform. It prescribes the forms insurance companies use in financial reporting, maintains national databases of insurance companies and agents, aggregates and publishes consumer complaint data, and otherwise provides technical support and coordination for the individual state regulators.

The NAIC has an ambiguous status as a private organization composed of public officials, a centralizing force in a decentralized regulatory system, and an entity performing public functions with major participation by private interests. Its CEO, Therese Vaughan, describes its interaction with state regulators as creating a "national state-based system."[18] The NAIC has long struggled to maintain an independent identity free of substantial industry influence. Through an evolving series of industry advisory committees, technical resource groups, liaison groups, and simply informal contacts, much of the work of the NAIC is accomplished only with industry participation. If the industry does not get what it wants through the NAIC, it switches its lobbying efforts directly to the state insurance commissioners or legislators who must approve and implement the final products.

The NAIC has difficulty maintaining its independence since most of its finances come from the industry that its members regulate, and financing has been withdrawn or threatened at key moments. In the 1990s the NAIC, with industry acquiescence, strengthened its financial reporting requirements for companies. But when the organization moved into other areas, including investigating redlining, illegal policy provisions, rates, and other market conduct issues, companies took a simple but effective measure in response. First State Farm, then Allstate, Farmers, and GEICO, refused to pay the fees accompanying their financial filings that made up most of the NAIC's budget. Trade groups hinted at an industry-wide boycott of the fees. Oddly enough, most states either had no legal requirements that the companies pay the fees or had loopholes that the companies could exploit. So a meeting at Nick's Fish Market restaurant near Chicago followed, arranged by Mark Boozell, director of insurance for Illinois (State Farm and Allstate's home) and including Maine insurance superintendent Brian K. Atchinson, who was then the NAIC's president, Robert Pike, general counsel of Allstate, and other NAIC and industry leaders. By the end of the meal the outline of a deal had been reached, and at the NAIC's next spring meeting it was agreed to limit the use of the funds paid by insurance companies to mostly solvency issues; the result was a cut nearly in half of the money available to investigate the companies' claims practices and other market conduct.[19]

The ongoing saga of the NAIC's market conduct project demonstrates how the industry blocks meaningful regulation of claim handling. An NAIC committee proposed that companies be required to report on their claim-handling practices annually, just as they are required to report on their financial condition. Among other information, a company would report: the number of claims opened during the year; the number of claims closed; the number of claims closed without payment to the policyholder; how long it took for claims to be processed; and the number of policyholders who were denied payment or who were forced to sue for what they were owed. The NAIC would aggregate and analyze the data so commissioners could use it to investigate companies with unfavorable practices, and consumers would have more information on which to base the decision to choose a company. The industry reacted uniformly and bitterly, devoting "immense energy and resources" to keep the data secret, as law professor and NAIC consumer representative Daniel Schwarcz described it.[20] The National Association of Mutual Insurance Companies, the Property Casualty Insurers Association of America, the American Insurance Association, America's Health Insurance Plans, the American Council of Life Insurers, and the Blue Cross and Blue Shield Association united in complaint. "We consider that proprietary information," said Deirdre Manna, vice president of industry and regulatory affairs for the Property Casualty Insurers Association of America.[21] Proprietary presumably because it would let everyone know what companies wanted to keep secret—which companies had better claims records and which worse.

The industry protests succeeded in drastically watering down the proposal. The one step that has been adopted so far is limited in two important ways. First, not all states participate. Second, because insurance companies had avenues of influence at state legislatures, the law in forty states cuts out a major part of it; by state law the insurance departments can share the information with the NAIC only on the condition that it be kept confidential, so the public will not have access to it.

Massive campaign contributions by the insurance industry, the power of insurance trade groups, and the multiple opportunities presented by the odd structure of insurance regulation make improving claims practices and stopping delay, deny, defend difficult. But difficult is not impossible, and as awareness of the problem builds, so too will pressure for action.

Expanding the NAIC's market conduct project is a needed first step. Regulators should require insurance companies to report and make publicly available information about claims practices that will enable consumers to shop intelligently for insurance. A consumer buying a car can go to car-crash ratings by the federal government, *Consumer Reports*, or numerous other sources to find out about the quality of the car and the reliability of the car company; the same consumer can't find that kind of information when shopping for car insurance. It's easy to shop by price; consumers can easily obtain price quotes from dozens of company Web sites, and a Massachusetts driver even can go to that state insurance department's Web site and obtain a list of sample premiums for minimum and standard policies. A Cambridge, Massachusetts, driver shopping for car insurance can quickly find out that Progressive offers a standard policy for $735. What the consumer cannot find out is whether Progressive's track record for paying claims is better or worse than State Farm's, which sells a similar policy for $177 more, according to the Massachusetts comparison site. She would certainly like to pay $177 less, but not if Progressive is substantially less likely to pay if an accident happens.

Some states require companies to report information on claims practices, and the NAIC has begun to collect the information. The data are currently confidential. Shockingly, the NAIC sends each company what it calls a "report card letter" with "information about the company ratios in relation to average industry ratios." That is, regulators tell companies what their competitors are doing, but consumers are kept in the dark. Every state should mandate that companies provide the information in a standard form. State insurance departments should publish the information on the Internet, the NAIC should aggregate it to provide statistics on the national performance of companies, and the raw data should be made available to groups such as the Consumer Federation of America and Consumers Union so that they can prepare reports for consumers.

The data collected by the NAIC are a good start. They include, organized by type of policy and type of claim: the number of policies in force; the number of claims open at the beginning of the year and the number opened during the year; the number of claims closed with payment and closed without payment; the number of claims settled in 30, 60, 90, 180, and 365 days, and longer; and the number of suits brought by policyholders. The required reports should also include the per suit equivalent of the pure loss ratio: for suits filed by type of claim, how much the policyholder or accident victim claimed; how much was the eventual settlement or jury verdict; and how much the company was assessed in interest, attorneys' fees, and penalties. The ratios and indices that could be computed from these would give consumers a ready guide to claim-handling performance: how quickly a claim will be paid; how likely it is that the company will pay anything; how probable is it that the consumer will have to sue for benefits under the policy; what kinds of cases go to court; and how realistic are the company's settlement offers.

The insurance industry has doggedly resisted any attempt at making information like this available to consumers. Technical objections abound; comparing the amount of a claim to the amount of a settlement could be misleading, because the policyholder might include items in a claim that are not covered, so paying less than the amount claimed is good, not bad. Robert Hartwig, CEO of the Insurance Information Institute, described statistics like these as "a naive way to think about the quantity of benefits that should be paid." Companies assert that information about claims practices is confidential, proprietary, and trade secrets.

This is nonsense on stilts. This information would be useful to consumers even if it is not perfect. If it can be improved on, insurance is an information-based industry and companies could produce useful, reliable information about claims practices with a fraction of the effort they devote to developing information on prospective customers for underwriting purposes. The opposition is based on the belief that ignorance is better than information. In fact, consumers benefit from information, and if insurance companies have something to hide, sunlight is the best disinfectant.

Markets, including the market for insurance, work best with information, but they still do not work perfectly. Even if consumers had adequate information on claims-handling practices, companies might not do the right thing every time. Moreover, because insurance is invested with a public interest, it is too important to be left to the vagaries of even a well-functioning market. Therefore, the second needed reform is to make clear in the law that the widely proclaimed but not always adhered to rules of claim handling are binding on insurance companies, and to make sure that regulators have the power to enforce those rules.

Nearly every state has made a good start by enacting into law a version of the NAIC's Model Unfair Claims Settlement Practices Act, which defines acceptable and unacceptable claims practices. Among other provisions, it speaks to delay, deny, and defend. For example, a company must act promptly on claims, reasonably investigate them, try to settle claims in which liability is clear fairly, and refrain from making lowball offers that force policyholders to sue to get what they are entitled to.

States need to adopt even stronger statutes spelling out the claims practices rules that companies must follow and providing realistic measures to enforce the rules. First, most of the adopted claims practices statutes state that a company can be punished only if it violates the rules "with such frequency as to indicate a general business practice." That is a bizarre qualification, like saying that a criminal's first offense is free and only repeat offenders or members of the Mafia should be punished. Every time a company violates fair claims practices standards the consumer who relied on the company is injured, and the violation of the law should be punished.

Second, some of the statutes cover "insureds" and some "insureds and claimants." If a statute only covers insureds (policyholders), an insurance company can do anything it wants when presented with a claim by an accident victim against one of its policyholders. These claimants need to be treated fairly too. Nearly every state requires drivers to carry auto insurance, because we recognize that insurance protects not only policyholders but also those people whom they injure. A company does not owe the same kind of obligation to an accident victim that it does to its insured, because the relationship between them is adversarial; the victim is likely to sue the policyholder and the insurance company will defend the suit. The company does owe the claimants some obligation to act fairly, however, such as by not making misrepresentations, by acting promptly, and by not dragging out litigation simply to browbeat the victim.

The claims practices required of insurance companies by law need to be enforced. Only public pressure will encourage more insurance commissioners to aggressively hold insurance companies to account. Aggressive enforcers need tools too. Under the Model Act and many statutes, there is a two-tiered system of penalties, with higher penalties for knowing violations and, remarkably, a cap on aggregate penalties within a specified period. Some of the penalties are laughably small. Connecticut, for example, has a penalty of $1,000 per violation and $10,000 in the aggregate per six-month period for lesser violations and $5,000 per $50,000 aggregate for more serious violations. These are not the scale of penalties likely to encourage a multibillion-dollar insurance company to obey the law. Others are more suited to the need. Illinois has a penalty up to $250,000 for a single violation with no aggregate cap. Tough penalties are needed, and a few statutes appropriately specify the factors the commissioner should take into account in assessing them: how much the policyholder or victim was harmed by the company's action; how much the company benefited; how serious the violation was; whether the company tried to fix the problem; whether the company is a repeat offender; and how big a fine is needed to deter the wrongful behavior in the future.

States could go even further. Insurance fraud is a crime in every state, but insurance companies have persuaded regulators and the public that the only real insurance fraud is that perpetrated against them. Insurance fraud perpetrated *by* insurance companies should also be prosecuted, and the companies punished appropriately. Only the most egregious violations of fair claims practices should be criminalized, but those would include violations that are part of a systematic corporate program to delay, deny, defend. Like the campaign against insurance fraud, a few prosecutions would have a salutary effect on changing the behavior of many companies; video on the evening news of the claims vice president of a company being hauled away in handcuffs would be an effective inducement for other executives to reexamine their companies' practices.

Insurance commissioners that are willing to enforce insurers' obligation to act fairly and have the powers they need to do so, still need to find out about problems. All insurance departments accept consumer complaints, but many need to act on them more effectively. The department should be recognized as the first place for consumers to turn when they think they have been mistreated. This is particularly valuable for claims involving small amounts that do not justify hiring a lawyer. In addition to helping consumers resolve disputes, the complaint process also helps the department, because it is a good source of information on which companies are generating the most problems and what those complaints concern, so the department has a better idea of where to devote its enforcement resources. A strong complaint process even helps companies. Not every complaint is valid, and having the insurance department tell the consumer that may satisfy her in a way that the company's explanation does not.

Even a beefed-up regulatory process will not always work. Policyholders and accident victims who are the targets of delay, deny, defend are the ones most hurt and the ones with the most interest in fixing the problem. Strengthening their ability to pursue individual claims against the insurers will compensate those who have been harmed and deter companies from behaving badly.

Every state gives policyholders the right to sue their insurance companies in some cases for what is known as "bad faith" claims handling, or violation of the accepted claims practices standards. When formulated well and applied rigorously, bad faith law works; academic studies have shown that claims payments are higher in states with strong bad faith law, indicating that the law induces companies to observe fair claims practices. [22]

The law of bad faith varies across the states as to who can sue for what. To fully compensate policyholders who are injured by delay, deny, defend, and to deter companies from engaging in that unlawful behavior, every injured consumer should have the right to sue for violations of fair claims practices. In cases involving liability insurance, the company acts in bad faith when it breaches its duty to defend or settle litigation against its policyholder. When the company unreasonably rejects an offer to settle the case against its insured within the policy limits, exposing the insured to a judgment in excess of those limits, the company acts in bad faith by gambling with the insured's money. In cases in which the policyholder files a claim against her own company, the company acts in bad faith when it fails to properly pay a claim within the scope of the policy. In cases involving claims by injured accident victims against policyholders, the company acts in bad faith when it violates fair claims practices in dealing with the claimant.

What constitutes bad faith needs to be better defined. Bad faith means that the company has violated claims-handling standards. The policyholder expected to be treated reasonably and fairly by the company. Therefore, those standards and the policyholder's expectation of reasonableness and fairness should define the legal standard for bad faith. Currently, that is not what happens in most states. To be found to have acted in bad faith, the company must have denied a claim without a reasonable basis, and must have actually known or recklessly disregarded the fact that it lacked a reasonable basis.[23] This test gives a company too much latitude to violate fair standards and then defend on the basis that it was only careless in doing so, not malicious. The test means that the company may resolve doubts in its own favor rather than that of the insured and may act carelessly in investigating a claim, determining coverage, and deciding whether and when to pay. No insurance company would advertise its policies on that basis, and no prospective policyholder would buy a policy from such a company. The company would never include a policy provision that stated it could negligently make a coverage decision or commit an improper claims practice with impunity, and no knowledgeable policyholder would accept such a provision.

Policyholders and victims should be given other ways to protect themselves against unfair claims practices, and creative legislatures and courts have shown the way. The New Hampshire and New Mexico courts, for example, have pioneered theories that aim at the problem of Rambo defensive tactics in litigation. They recognized the insurance company tactic of using litigation "to wear the mettle of the opposing party to reach a favorable termination of the cause unrelated to its merits" or as a "club" to wear down MIST claimants.[24] The purpose of insurance litigation is to adjudicate disputes, not to grind a victim into submission, and the victim should have the right to recover the economic and psychological costs of the tactics.

Establishing an action for bad faith or other wrongful behavior is important; making the action effective is equally important. Making the action effective requires that the policyholder or victim be fully compensated for the harm they suffered, and that the economic incentive for delay, deny, defend be taken away from the company. When a company violates fair claims practices, the harm and the incentive should be reflected in the damages. Many courts and legislatures have responded, and all should provide a comprehensive approach. When a policyholder sues for bad faith, the damages start with payment of the full amount of the loss that she was entitled to receive under the policy. If that's all the company has to pay, the company has an incentive to delay, deny, defend. More is required. As in many states, the policyholder should receive interest on the amount owed from the time it was owed, and the interest should be at a meaningful rate to make sure that the company doesn't benefit from the float. The policyholder had to hire an attorney to get the insurance company to honor its promise of security, so the attorney's fee and other costs of litigation should be repaid. In many cases the policyholder will have suffered other economic losses from not receiving the benefits on time, such as being out of work because medical treatment was delayed when the company refused to repay, and those losses need to be compensated. The policyholder also may suffer aggravation, distress, even physical upset because of the company's tactics, and those are real losses that should be compensated too. Finally, even more may be needed to prevent bad faith by the company, so some states allow damages to punish it for its wrongful behavior, either an amount set by the jury or treble damages—three times the amount of the policyholder's actual damages.

The point of all these measures is twofold. In the short run they provide a process that will better identify when insurance companies violate accepted claims practices standards and compensate consumers who are injured by the violations. In the long run they will mean fewer people will be injured, because there will be fewer violations. Good insurance companies will have nothing to fear. Substandard insurance companies will finally have sufficient incentives to act properly.

APPENDIX:

More Resources

WHEN LOOKING AT sources on insurance, either in print or on the Internet, keep one thing in mind: Everyone has a point of view. Industry publications have an industry slant, insurance company publications are trying to sell you something, and publications from policyholder advocates take their perspective.

MORE ON DELAY, DENY, DEFEND

David Berardinelli, the New Mexico lawyer principally responsible for the unveiling of the McKinsey documents, tells the story of how Allstate transformed its claim process in *From Good Hands to Boxing Gloves: The Dark Side of Insurance* (Portland, Ore.: Trial Guides LLC, 2009).

Delay, deny, defend by the country's largest disability insurer, Unum, is described in Ray Bourhis, *Insult to Injury: Insurance, Fraud, and the Big Business of Bad Faith* (San Francisco: Berrett-Koehler, 2005).

Law professor Jeffrey Stempel gives a complete account of the bad faith claim practices case against State Farm that went to the United States Supreme Court, along the way describing details of the litigation process in general: *Litigation Road: The Story of* Campbell v. State Farm (St. Paul: Thomson/West, 2008).

INSURANCE IN GENERAL

The National Association of Insurance Commissioners' Insure U Web site offers general information on insurance, including descriptions of typical policy terms, tips on buying insurance, and suggestions about insurance needs for different situations (e.g., young singles, established families, and seniors); go to www.insurance.insureuonline.org/.

The Insurance Information Institute is the insurance industry's principal public affairs arm. Its Web site (www.iii.org/) and publications offer a great deal of information on the industry, insurance topics, and consumer information, all from an industry perspective. Its annual *Insurance Fact Book,* available for purchase or in many libraries, is a basic resource for financial information and other statistics. The Web site's Facts and Statistics section and its Presentations section present information on many topics. Its Insurance Topics section includes FAQs for consumers.

Because insurance varies from state to state, state insurance departments are useful sources of more specific information. Every state's insurance department offers consumer information that may include lists of licensed insurance companies and agents, price data, indices of consumer complaints, explanations of policy terms, and buying guides. The NAIC Web site provides links to each state's insurance department Web site: http://naic.org/state_web_map.htm. The Consumer Federation of America published a report listing in more detail the information available from each state, also with links to the insurance department sites. J. Robert Hunter, "State Insurance Department Websites: A Consumer Assessment," Consumer Federation of America, November 2008 (www.consumerfed.org/pdfs/state_insurance_websites.pdf).

A great source comes from the group United Policyholders. Founded in 1991, UP advocates for consumers in legislative and administrative proceedings and in litigation, and it publishes many educational materials in print and online. Its Web site (www.unitedpolicyholders.org/) and publications explain what to look for when buying a policy, how to file a claim, when and how to hire professional help, and how to prepare for and survive natural disasters, and they refer to many other sources of information. It also lists sponsoring attorneys, public adjusters, and other professionals by state.

CHOOSING AN INSURANCE COMPANY

Some state insurance departments publish information on the consumer complaints they receive and the action they take in response. Check your state's Web site. Most states report complaint information to the NAIC. The NAIC Consumer Information Source section of their Web site enables consumers to search for complaint information for particular companies for all states or for individual states (https://eapps.naic.org/cis/). The Closed Complaint Counts by Code option displays information on the type of complaints filed. The Closed Complaint Ratio Report provides an index comparing a company's complaints to the premiums it received and national norms, giving a better basis for comparing companies than the raw complaint numbers.

Consumer Reports periodically surveys its readers about their insurance claims and provides advice on buying insurance and filing a claim. Its most recent report on homeowners insurance appeared in the September 2009 issue. Past reports are available on the Web site. (www.consumerreports.org) (Subscription is required for some information.)

Fight Bad Faith Insurance is a Web site produced by a self-described group of consumers "who had legitimate claims that were denied by bad faith insurers." The Web site includes news on insurance claims, consumer information and advice, and rankings of the best and worst companies for claim practices (www.badfaithinsurance.org/).

KEEPING UP TO DATE

Most of the news services, trade journals, and blogs about insurance are aimed at industry professionals. If you are interested, try National Underwriter Property & Casualty News (www.property-casualty.com/Pages/default.aspx) and Claims magazine (www.claimsmag.com/).

For consumers interested in insurance, consider these blogs:

Property Insurance Coverage Law Blog (www.propertyinsurancecoveragelaw.com/). William F. "Chip" Merlin, Jr., a leading policyholder attorney from Florida, offers consumer-oriented comments on legal issues and news items concerning property insurance.

A View From The Press Box (http://nusamsoapbox.com/). Sam Friedman, editor in chief at *National Underwriter*, is an industry insider who posts provocative comments on industry issues.

Terms and Conditions (www.iii.org/insuranceindustryblog/). The in-house blog of the Insurance Information Institute provides an industry perspective on current topics.

slabbed (http://slabbed.wordpress.com/). Detailed, often entertaining commentary on disaster insurance issues, particularly on the aftermath of Hurricane Katrina.

Tennessee Insurance Litigation Blog (www.tninsurancelitigation.com/). A point-counterpoint format featuring policyholder and insurance company perspectives on insurance law issues. Despite the blog's name, the discussion is often broader than Tennessee law.

OTHER SOURCES

Insurance companies share complaint data on their customers and insured property. You can find out what they know about you by getting a copy of your CLUE report from ChoicePoint (www.choicepoint.com/factact.html) and your A-Plus report from ISO (www.iso.com/Products/A-PLUS/Consumers-Order-Your-Free-A-PLUS-Loss-History-Report.html). You are entitled to one free report from each company every twelve months.

Acknowledgments

WRITING A BOOK like this is both a solitary endeavor and a collective project: Solitary, because of the hours sitting alone at a desk, but collective, because it depends on the years of effort by many people to develop information and ideas about its subject. While the usual disclaimer applies, and I am solely responsible for the facts and interpretations in the book, I am enormously grateful to those who contributed directly and indirectly to my understanding of the insurance claims process and the completion of this book.

Alan Casper, Lou Crisci, Steve Figlin, Richard Golomb, Allan Kanner, Frank Messina, Chip Merlin, Caitlin Palacios, David Ratcliff, Dan Schwarcz, Deborah Senn, Erin Taylor, and others who might prefer not to be named shared their time and knowledge. Jordan Rand and Anthony Fassano provided research assistance. Tony Roisman, Rich Halpern, and Risa Lower were helpful in many ways. Courtney Young strengthened the book with her editing. Scholars of insurance and insurance law and lawyers and experts who work and write in the field have produced a body of work that has broadened my appreciation for the subject. Ray Solomon and Anne Dalesandro and her corps of librarians provided tangible and intangible support. David Berardinelli's dogged battle with Allstate led to the publication of the documents that tell an important part of this story. Whitney Buchanan provided insight, hospitality, and an introduction to the world described here.

John Wright reprised his role as wise counselor and good friend. And very special thanks to Gary Fye and Charles Miller, who taught me so much.

JAY FEINMAN
Camden, New Jersey
July 2009

Notes

Introduction

1. Robert H. Jerry II, *Understanding Insurance Law*, 3d ed. (New York: LexisNexis, 2002), 21.
2. *Zilisch v. State Farm Mut. Auto. Ins. Co.*, 995 P.2d 276 (Ariz. 2000). See Chapter 2.
3. *Hamilton Mut. Ins. Co. of Cincinnati v. Buttery*, 220 S.W.3d 287 (Ky. App. 2007). See Chapter 2.
4. James Markham, Kevin M. Quinley, and Layne S. Thompson, *The Claims Environment* (Malvern, Pa.: IIA, 1993), 5–6.
5. Heckman, "Insurer Wants to Silence 2 Ex-Staffers," *Seattle Post-Intelligencer*, October 31, 2002.
6 Ibid.
7. Order sustaining plaintiffs' motion for contempt and sanctions against defendant State Farm Fire & Casualty Company, *Watkins v. State Farm Fire & Casualty Company*, District Court of Grady County, Oklahoma, January 12, 2007.
8. Order, *Hill v. State Farm Mutual Auto. Ins. Co.*, W.D. Okla., February 1, 2002.
9. Opinion and Order, Judge Thomas L. Clark, Circuit Court, Fayette, Kentucky, June 25, 2002.
10. News release, "Allstate Acts to Dispel Inaccurate Portrayal of Claim Practices." The documents are available at www.allstatenewsroom.com/media/terms_of_service.

Chapter 1: How Insurance Works

1. See Tom Baker, *Insurance Law and Policy: Cases, Materials, and Problems*, 2d ed. (New York: Aspen Publishers, 2008), ch. 1; Emmett Vaughan and Therese Vaughan, *Essentials of Risk Management and Insurance* (New York: John Wiley & Sons, 2001), chs. 1, 3.
2. See Baker, *Insurance Law and Policy,*, ch. 1, and Vaughan and Vaughn, *Essentials of Risk Management and Insurance*, chs. 1, 3.
3. Vaughan and Vaughan, *Essentials of Risk Management and Insurance,* 120.
4. Warren Buffett, 2006 Berkshire Hathaway Inc. Shareholder Letter, www.berkshire hathaway.com/letters/2006ltr.pdf.
5. Warren Buffett, 2008 Berkshire Hathaway Inc. Shareholder Letter, www.berkshire hathaway.com/letters/2008ltr.pdf.

6. "Judge Sentences 'Hit-and-Run Grannies' to Life in Prison Without Parole," *BestWire*, July 16, 2008.
7. David Dietz and Darrell Preston, "The Insurance Hoax," *Bloomberg* magazine, September 2007, www.bloomberg.com/news/marketsmag/mm_0907_story1.html.
8. Response of Defendant State Farm Fire & Cas. Co. to Plaintiff's Requests for Admissions Set 2, *Sheehan v. State Farm Fire & Cas. Cos.*, Calif. Super. Ct. (n.d.)
9. State Farm Web site, www.statefarm.com/about/2007year/claims/select_service.htm.
10. *Campbell v. State Farm Mut. Auto. Ins. Co.*, 98 P.3d 409, 415 (Utah 2004), citing *Holmes' Appleman on Insurance* 2d 8.7.
11. D. R. Jacques, "Society on the Basis of Mutual Life Insurance," *Hunt's Merchant Magazine and Commercial Review* 16 (1849): 153, cited in Baker, *Insurance Law and Policy*, 8.
12. *C&J Fertilizer, Inc. v. Allied Mut. Ins.*, 227 N.W.2d 169 (Iowa 1975).
13. Panko, "Extra Effort Pays Off," *Best's Review*, July 8, 2008, 39.

Chapter 2: How Insurance Doesn't Work

1. *Zilisch v. State Farm Mut. Auto. Ins. Co.*, 995 P.2d 276 (Ariz. 2000). See L. Laughlin, "Snake Killer," *Phoenix New Times*, November 16, 2000.
2.. *Price v. New Jersey Manufacturers Ins. Co.*, 867 A.2d 1181 (N.J. 2005).
3. *Hamilton Mut. Ins. Co. of Cincinnati v. Buttery*, 220 S.W.3d 287 (Ky. App. 2007).
4. Editorial, "Insurance for the Next Big One," *New York Times*, October 1, 2007.
5. *Goddard v. Farmers Ins. Co. of Oregon*, 179 P.3d 645 (Ore. 2008).
6. *Dhyne v. State Farm Fire & Cas. Co.*, 188 S.W.3d 454 (Mo. 2006).
7. *Wilson v. 21st Century Ins. Co.*, 171 P.3d 1082 (Cal. 2007).
8. "Insurers Behaving (Very) Badly," on InsureBlog, http://insureblog.blogspot.com/, August 27 2007; L. Bennett, "Progressive Now Says Its Spying Was 'Reasonable,'" *Atlanta Journal-Constitution*, October 17, 2007.
9. John N. Ellison, Timothy P. Law, and Luke E. Debevec, "Bad Faith and Punitive Damages: The Policyholder's Guide to Bad Faith Insurance Coverage Litigation," in *Environmental Insurance: Emerging Issues and Latest Developments on the New Coverage and Insurance Cost Recovery* (Philadelphia: ALI-ABA, 2008), 159.
10. *Adolph Coors Co. v. American Ins. Co.*, 164 F.R.D. 507, 509 (D. Colo. 1993).
11. *Goddard v. Farmers Ins. Co. of Oregon*, 179 P.3d 645 (Ore. 2008).
12. *Nance v. Kentucky Nat'l Ins. Co.*, 240 Fed. Appx. 539 (4th Cir. 2007).
13. Herbert Kritzer, "The Commodification of Insurance Defense Practice," *Vanderbilt Law Review* 59 (2006): 2084.
14. Susanne Sclafane, "New Product Covers Legal Costs If Buyers Decide to Challenge Claim Denial," *National Underwriter P&C News*, August 2008.
15. Letter from Mike Fernandez, vice president, public affairs, State Farm, October 1, 2007, www.statefarm.com/about/media/bloomberg.asp.
16. Daniel Schwarcz, "Redesigning Consumer Dispute Resolution: A Case Study of the British and American Approaches to Insurance Claims Conflict," *Tulane Law Review* 38 (2009): 756.

Chapter 3: Moral Hazard, the Bottom Line, and the Origins of Delay, Deny, Defend

1. Kenneth Arrow, "Uncertainty and the Welfare Economics of Medical Care," *American Economic Review* 53 (1963): 941.
2. Mark V. Pauly, "The Economics of Moral Hazard: Comment," *American Economic Review* 58 (1968): 531.
3. Kenneth Arrow, "The Economics of Moral Hazard: Further Comment," *American Economic Review* 58 (1968): 537.
4. *Conn. Mut. Lif. Ins. Co. v. Union Trust Co.*, 112 U.S. 250 (1884).
5. *Baumgart v. Modern Woodmen of Am.*, 55 N.W. 713 (Wis. 1893).
6. K. Fosaaen, "AIDS and the Incontestability Clause," *North Dakota Law Review* 66 (1990): 267.
7. Tom Baker, "Medical Malpractice and the Insurance Underwriting Cycle," *DePaul Law Review* 54 (2005): 393; Seungmook Choi, Don Hardigree, and Paul D. Thistle, "The Property/Liability Insurance Cycle: A Comparison of Alternative Models," *Southern Economic Journal* 68 (2002): 530; Sean M. Fitzpatrick, "Fear Is the Key: A Behavioral Guide to Underwriting Cycles," *Connecticut Insurance Law Journal* 10 (2003–2004): 255; Gay Fung et al., "Underwriting Cycles in Property and Liability Insurance: An Empirical Analysis of Industry and By-Line Data," *Journal of Risk and Insurance* 65, no. 4 (December 1998): 539.
8. "Conservative Investing Keeps P/C Insurers Safe from Crisis in Mortgage Securities," *Best's Review* 109, no. 6 (October 2008): 64.
9. Karen Koehler and Michael D. Freeman, *Litigating Minor Impact Soft Tissue Cases.*§1.1.
10. Adrian Sainz, "Ten Years After Hurricane Andrew, Effects Are Still Felt," Associated Press, August 23, 2002; www.sun-sentinel.com/news/weather/hurricane/sfl-1992-ap-mainstory,0,913282.story.
11. *Emblem Flashes* 45, no. 5: 3 (Farmers Insurance Group of Companies), August.
12. Charles Miller, "Behind the Scenes in the Insurance Claims Industry: How Insurance Companies Have Revolutionized Claims Handling," *Consumer Attorneys of California Forum*, July/August 2007, 13.
13. Richard E. Stewart and Barbara D. Stewart, "The Loss of the Certainty Effect," *Risk Management and Insurance Review* 4 (2001): 29.
14. Charles E. Schmidt Jr., "Industry Executives Receive New Marching Orders," *Best's Review / Property-Casualty Insurance Edition* 96, no. 10 (February 1996).
15. Russ Banham, "Loud and Clear," *Reactions* 26, no. 9 (November 2006).
16. Robert E. Keeton and Alan I. Widiss, *Insurance Law* (St. Paul: West, 1988), 958.
17. *Pacific Fire Rating Bureau v. Insurance Co. of North America*, 321 P.2d 1030, 1034 (Ariz. 1958).
18. Dan Lonkevich, "Lower Cost, not Service, Drives Sales, Survey Finds," *National Underwriter*, October 21, 1996.
19. Robert I. Mehr, "Channels of Distribution in Insurance," *Journal of Risk and Insurance* 36, no. 5 (1969): 583.
20. Alice Schroeder, *The Snowball: Warren Buffett and the Business of Life* (New York: Bantam, 2008), 135–36,430–38.
21. Bowers, "State Farm: Behind the Veil," *Best's Review* 102, no. 3 (July 2001): 63.
22. B. Cahill, "Geico Faces Challenges After Grabbing Market Share," *Wall Street Journal*, January 27, 2000.
23. From the Press Box, Quotes of the Week, www.property-casualty.com/2007/11/quotes_of_the_week.html#more.
24. www.autoratecompare.doi.state.ma.us/.
25. *Harper's Weekly*, April 24, 1869, p. 272, available at http://advertising.harpweek.com/.
26. "TV Makes Strides While Marketers Experiment Widely," *Advertising Age*, March 24, 2008.

Chapter 4: McKinsey Redefines the Game

1. Haas Edersheim, *McKinsey's Marvin Bower: Vision, Leadership, and the Creation of Management Consulting* (John Wiley & Sons, 2004); Ethan M. Rasiel, *The McKinsey Way* (New York: McGraw-Hill, 1999).
2. A. Byrne, "Inside McKinsey," *BusinessWeek*, July 8, 2002.
3. News release, "Google claims #1 position after McKinsey's 12-year reign as the most desirable place to work for MBA students," Universum, (n.d.) www.universumglobal .com/CMSTemplates/Universum.com/files/USpressrelease/2007-MBAPressRelease .pdf.
4. David Bleakley, S. Gee, and Ron Hulme, "The Atomization of Big Oil," *McKinsey Quarterly* 2 (1997): 123.
5. Bing, "When McKinsey Comes," *Fortune*, November 13, 2006.
6. Rasiel, *The McKinsey Way*.
7. Warner, "The Incredible Shrinking Consultant," *Fortune*, May 26, 2003.
8. Ibid.
9. Ibid., p. 9.
10. B. Kaplan and Laura Murdock, "Core Process Redesign," *McKinsey Quarterly* (1991): 27.
11. R. Heygate, "Immoderate Redesign," *McKinsey Quarterly* 4 (1993): 73.
12. David Berardinelli, *From Good Hands to Boxing Gloves: How Allstate Changed Casualty Insurance in America* 2nd ed. (Portland: Trial Guides LLC, 2007), 56.
13. *Miller v. Allstate Ins. Co.*, 1998 WL 937400 (C.D. Cal., 1998).
14. *Allstate Now*, January 1997: 24.
15. "Summary Annual Report: 2007 At A Glance," *The Allstate Corporation, 2007 Annual Report*, 12.
16. Heygate, "Immoderate Redesign."
17. Affidavit of Christine Sullivan, April 13, 2007.
18. Hayes Weiser, "Allstate Says New Claims System Puts People in Good Hands," *Information Week*, April 13, 2007.
19. State Farm Divisional Claim Superintendents Conference, 1986.
20. Charles Miller, "Behind the Scenes in the Insurance Claims Industry: How Insurance Companies Have Revolutionized Claims Handling," *Consumer Attorneys of California Forum* (July/August 2007), 13.
21. Interview, "Advancing Claims Excellence—An ACE of a Program," *State Farm Auto/ Fire Claims Quarterl* (Fall 1995), p. 8.
22. Message points, State Farm ACE (n.d.).
23. Deposition of Steve Hassoldt, *Feldotto v. State Farm Mut. Auto. Ins.*, Colo. Dist. Ct. June 2, 2003.
24. www.statefarm.com/about/media/bloomberg.asp.

Chapter 5: Mr. Incredible Goes to Work

1. Jeremy Masys, "The Silver Screen's Seven Most Endearing Claims Adjusters," *Claims* 37 (December 2001).
2. H. Laurence Ross, *Settled Out of Court: The Social Process of Insurance Claims Adjustments* (Chicago: Aldine, 1970), 46–54.
3. A. Hoda, "The Times, They Are A-Changin'," *Claims* (September 2001), 26.
4. Chad Bray, "Allstate Cutting Loss Costs Through Innovations, Alliances," Dow Jones Newswires, April 1, 2002.
5. R. Jones, Ira Blatt, and Thomas G. Barger, "Keeping Customers and Employees Happy: Claims Best Practices," *Claims* (October 2001), 50.

6. Acclaim, Allstate, n.d.
7. Karen Koehler and Michael D. Freeman, *Litigating Minor Impact Soft Tissue Cases,* §2.3.
8. James Mathis, "Efficient or Malicious," United Policyholders Web site, May 2008, www.unitedpolicyholders.org/e_news/May08/article_Auto.html.
9. *Cheatham v. Allstate Ins. Co.,* 465 F.3d 578, 584–86 (5th Cir. 2006). The court concluded that the adjusters exercised "independent judgment"even though they could only make recommendations that required their supervisors' approval.
10. *Bell v. Farmers Ins. Exchange,* 105 Cal. Rptr. 2d 59 (Cal. App. 2001).
11. Koehler and Freeman, *Litigating Minor Impact Soft Tissue Cases,* §5.5.
12. Summary Annual Report, 2007 At A Glance, The Allstate Corporation.
13. Mary Hayes Weier, "The Good Hands People Want Better Hands," *Information Week,* April 21, 2007; Mary Hayes Weiser, "Allstate Says New Claims System Puts People in Good Hands," April 13, 2007.
14. Jones, Blatt, and Barger, "Keeping Customers and Employees Happy: Claims Best Practices."
15. Peter R. Kensicki, "Can Adjusters Earn Bonuses Ethically?" *National Underwriter Property/Casualty/Risk & Benefits Mgt. Edition,* January 7, 2002, 25.
16. Cal. Ins. Code § 816.
17. Peter R. Kensicki, "Are Performance-Based Incentives Ethical?" *National Underwriter Property/Casualty/ Risk & Benefits Mgt. Edition,* September 10, 2001, 57.
18. Affidavit of Shannon Brady Kmatz, March 10, 2003.
19. Questions & Answers from DCS Conference, June 5–9, 1995.
20. Affidavit of James Mathis, July 10, 2001; Affidavit of Grace Hess, March 12, 1998.
21. Expert report of Charles M. Miller, April 19, 2007.
22. Declaration of William R. Hurst, December 29, 2003.
23. *In re Farmers Insurance Exchange Claims Representatives' Overtime Pay Litigation,* 336 F. Supp. 2d 1077, 1096 (D. Or. 2004).
24. Geyelin, "If You Think Insurers Are Tight, Try Being One of Their Lawyers," *Wall Street Journal,* February 9, 1999.
25. Joseph P. Pettita, "The Way We Were," *For the Defense* (November 2000): 16.
26. Van Duch, "Allstate Faces Continued Criticism for Internet Bids to Attract Policyholder Defense Lawyers," *National Law Journal,* June 19, 2001.
27. Geyelin, "If You Think Insurers Are Tight, Try Being One of Their Lawyers."
28. Pettita, "The Way We Were."
29. Herbert Kritzer, "The Commodification of Insurance Defense Practice," *Vanderbilt Law Review* 59 (2006): 2053.

Chapter 6: Lawyers, Claimants, and Into the MIST

1. *Young v. Allstate Ins. Co.,* 198 P.3d 666 (Haw. 2008).
2. *Jones v. Allstate Ins. Co.,* 45 P.3d 1068 (Wash. 2002).
3. *Givens v. Mullikin,* 75 S.W.3d 383 (Tenn. 2002).
4. Ken Dornstein, *Accidentally on Purpose: The Making of a Personal Injury Underworld in America* (New York: St. Martin's Press, 1996):200–16.
5. National Institute of Neurological Disorders and Stroke, "Whiplash Information Page," www.ninds.nih.gov/disorders/whiplash/whiplash.htm.
6. Valerie P. Hans and Nicole Vadino, "Whipped by Whiplash? The Challenges of Jury Communication in Lawsuits Involving Connective Tissue Injury," *Tennessee Law Review* 67 (1999–2000): 569.
7. *Bonenberger v. Nationwide Mut. Ins. Co.* 791 A.2d 378, (Pa. Super. 2002).
8. Affidavit of Grace Hess, March 12, 1998.

9. Karen Koehler, "Top Ten Insurance Abuses in Musculoligamentous Injury Automobile Cases," in *ATLA Annual Convention Reference Materials*, vol. 1 (2001).
10. News release, "ADP Integrated Medical Solutions Launches State-of-the-Art Software for the Property & Casualty Insurance Industry," *Business Wire*, May 30, 2001, http://findarticles.com/p/articles/mi_m0EIN/is_2001_May_30/ai_75118710.
11. *Young v. Allstate Ins. Co.*, 296 F. Supp. 2d 1111 (D. Ariz. 2003).
12. 92 P.3d 882 (Ariz. App. 2004).

Chapter 7: "Insurance Company Rules" for Auto Claims

1. Health Care for America Now, "Insurance Company Rules," Web site: www.youtube.com/watch?v=ZOws2P78KrQ.
2. NHR Web site, www.propertyandcasualty.com/storefronts/claimres.html.
3. 45 P.3d 829 (Idaho 2002).
4. Karen Koehler and Michael D. Freeman, *Litigating Minor Impact Soft Tissue Cases*, ch. 20.
5. Memorandum, Everett J. Truttman, September 5, 1990.
6. Thomas B. Smith, "Alice in Discovery Land" (n.d.), at www.millerandzois.com/Judge-Smith-Discovery-Article.pdf.
7. *Hangarter v. Provident Life & Accident Co.*, 373 F.3d 998 (9th Cir. 2004).
8. *Metropolitan Property & Cas. Ins. Co. v. Overstreet*, 103 S.W.3d 31 (Ky., 2003).
9. Koehler and Freeman, *Litigating Minor Impact Soft Tissue Cases*, §20:1.
10. *Clack v. Allstate Ins. Co.*, 1998 WL 1997470 (Mich. App., 1998).
11. *Virginia Villegas v. Allstate Ins. Co.*, 2003 WL 21751489 (Mich. App. 2003).
12. *Hannawi v. American Fellowship Mut. Ins. Co.* 1999 WL 33430024 (Mich. App., 1999).
13. On Colossus, see R. Bonnett, "The Use of Colossus to Measure the General Damages of a Personal Injury Claim Demonstrates Good Faith Claim Handling," *Cleveland State Law Review* 53 (2005–2006): 107; "Colossus at the Accident Scene," *Wall Street Journal*, January 2, 2003; Aaron DeShaw, "Colossus: What Every Trial Lawyer Needs to Know" (n.d.); Candace Heckman, "Insurers' Use of Colossus, a Service to Judge the Worth of Claims, Comes Under Fire," *Seattle Post-Intelligencer*, May 15, 2003; Koehler and Freeman, *Litigating Minor Impact Soft Tissue Cases.*
14. Karen Koehler, *The Art of Negotiation in the Age of Colossus* (n.d.).
15. DeShaw, "Colossus: What Every Trial Lawyer Needs to Know" (n.d.).
16. *In re Farmers Insurance Exchange Claims Representatives' Overtime Pay Litigation*, 336 F. Supp. 2d 1077, 1102 (D. Or. 2004).
17. Affidavit of Maureen Reed, April 12, 2003.
18. Koehler and Freeman, *Litigating Minor Impact Soft Tissue Cases.*§2.3.
19. *Dougherty v. AMCO Ins. Co.*, 2008 WL 2556603, Declaration of Thomas J. Corridan (N.D. Cal. 2008).
20. *Kosierowski v. Allstate Ins. Co.*, 51 F. Supp. 2d 583 (E.D. Pa. 1999).
21. *In re Farmers Ins. Exchange Claims Representatives' Overtime Pay Litigation*, 336 F. Supp. 2d 1077, 1101 (D. Or. 2004).
22. *Libby v. Farmers Ins. Exchange*, 2008 WL 2421976 (Cal. App., 2008).

Chapter 8: The Risk of "All Risks" Homeowners Insurance

1. A copy of the policy is available on the Insurance Information Institute Web site. http://server.iii.org/yy_obj_data/binary/748905_1_0/HO3_sample.pdf.
2. Tom Baker, *Insurance Law and Policy: Cases, Materials, and Problems*, 2d ed. (New York: Aspen Publishers, 2008), 282.
3. Deborah Moroy and Dennis Martin, "A Box of Chocolates?" *Claims* (August 2007).

4. Hoopes, *The Claims Environment*, 2d ed. (Malvern, Pa.: AICPCU/IIA, 2000), 10.2, 11.1.
5. *State Farm Lloyd's v. Nicolau*, 591 S.W.2d 444 (Tex. 1997).
6. *State Farm Lloyd's v. Hamilton*, 265 S.W.3d 725 (Tex. App. 2008).
7. James J. Markham, ed., *Property Loss Adjusting*, 2d ed. (Insurance Institute of America, 1995), ch. 7.
8. Markham, *Property Loss Adjusting*, 212
9. United Policyholders, "Guidelines for Reviewing Adjusters' and Contractors' Estimates to Repair/Rebuild Your Home," www.unitedpolicyholders.org/pdfs/Guidelines_Estimates.pdf.
10. Kerr, "Xactimate: Property Loss Estimating in the 21st Century," http://ezinearticles.com/?Xactimate---Property-Loss-Estimating-In-The-21st-Century&id=1000509.
11. Markham, *Property Loss Adjusting*, 1.
12. T. Smith, "Home Team," *Best's Review* (June 2008), 61.
13. Conduct Examination of State Farm on Northridge Earthquake of January 17, 1994 (California Department of Insurance July 15, 1998)
14. Plungis, "Homeowners May Be Twice Burned as Insurers Cap Policy Coverage," Blooomberg News, July 16, 2008, http://www.bloomberg.com/apps/news?pid=newsarchive&sid=awYlZHEGHgAs.
15. Pulliam Weston, "Is Your Home Underinsured?" MSN Money, September 29 2008, http://articles.moneycentral.msn.com/Insurance/InsureYourHome/IsYourHomeUnderInsured8KeyTests.aspx.
16. *Dupre v. Allstate Ins. Co.* , 63 P.3d 1024 (Colo. App. 2002).
17. *Salesin v. State Farm Fire & Cas. Co.*, 581 N.W.2d 781 (Mich. App. 1998).
18. *Gilderman v. State Farm Ins. Co.*, 649 A.2d 941, 945 (Pa. Super. Ct. 1994).
19. *Tritschler v. Allstate Ins. Co.*, 144 P.3d 519 (Ariz. App. 2006).
20. *Anderson v. Allstate Ins. Co.*, 45 Fed. Appx. 754 (9th Cir. 2002).

Chapter 9: Hurricane Katrina and Other Insurance Catastrophes

1. *The III Insurance Fact Book 2008* (New York: Insurance Information Institute, 2008), 109ßff.
2. Benick, "The Flood After the Storm: The Hurricane Katrina Homeowners' Insurance Litigation," *Business Law Brief* (American University) 4 (Fall 2007): 51.
3. Peter J. Boyer, "The Bribe: How the Mississippi Lawyer Who Brought Down Big Tobacco Overstepped," *The New Yorker*, May 19, 2008.
4. Mississippi Department of Insurance, "Report of the Special Target Examination (Katrina Homeowner Claims) of State Farm Insurance Companies," October 17, 2008.
5. Quoted in Testimony of J. Robert Hunter Before the Committee on Commerce, Science, and Transportation of the United States Senate, April 11, 2007, p. 3, www.commerce.senate.gov/public/_files/Testimony_RobertHunter_CFA_Insurance_Regulation_Senate_Commerce_Testimony041107.pdf.
6. Tom Baker and Karen McElrath, "Insurance Claims Discrimination," in *Insurance Redlining*, ed. Gregory D. Squires (Washington: Urban Institute Press, 1997), 141.
7. Testimony of J. Robert Hunter, p. 11.
8. Howard Kunreuther, "Has the Time Come for Comprehensive Natural Disaster Insurance?" in *On Risk and Disaster: Lessons from Hurricane Katrina*, eds. Ronald J. Daniels, Donald F. Kettle, and Howard Kunreuther (Philadelphia: University of Pennsylvania Press, 2006).
9. *Pattern of Greed 2007: How Insurance Companies Put Profits Over Policyholders*, American Association for Justice (Washington), 3.
10. Appleman on Insurance Law and Practice (LexisNexis, 2009), §3083.

11. *Evana Plantation, Inc. v. Yorkshire Ins. Co.*, 58 So. 2d 797, 798 (Miss. 1952).
12. Subcommittee on Oversight and Investigation, House Committee on Financial Services, 110st Cong., 1st Sess., Hearing: Insurance Claims Payment Process in the Gulf Coast After the 2005 Hurricanes, at 65 (2007).
13. *Tuepker v. State Farm Fire & Cas. Co.*, 2006 WL 1442489, at *4 (S.D. Miss. 2006).
14. *Ruiz v. State Farm Fire and Cas. Co.*, 2007 WL 1514015 (S.D.Miss. 2007).
15. *Leonard v. Nationwide Mut. Ins. Co.* 499 F.3d 419 (5th Cir. 2007).
16. Ibid.
17. slabbed, http://slabbed.wordpress.com/about/.
18. Subcommittee on Oversight and Investigation, Hearing, 21.
19. Gene Taylor, "Federal Insurance Reform After Katrina," *Mississippi Law Journal* 77 (2008): 784.
20. Mississippi Insurance Department Bulletin No. 2005-6, September 7, 2005.
21. *Broussard v. State Farm Fire and Cas. Co.*, 523 F.3d 618 C.A.5 (Miss.), 2008.
22. The document is in the proceedings of the Subcommittee on Oversight and Investigation, "Hearing," at 71.
23. Expert Report of Charles Miller, April 19, 2007.
24. Ibid.
25. Report of the Special Target Examination (Katrina Homeowner Claims) of State Farm Insurance Companies, at 16 (Mississippi Department of Insurance, 2008).
26. www.statefarm.com/about/hurricane/archive/windflood.asp.
27. *Best v. State Farm Fire & Cas. Co.*, 969 So. 2d 671 (La. App. 2007).
28. Expert Report of Charles Miller, April 19, 2007.
29. Ibid.
30. *McFarland v. State Farm Fire & Cas. Ins. Co.*, 2006 WL 3071988 (S.D. Miss. 2006).
31. Hurricane Katrina: Wind Versus Flood Issues OIG-08-97 (Department of Homeland Security, Office of Inspector General September 2008).
32. Congressman Gene Taylor, "Evidence Of Fraud by Insurers Handling Katrina Losses with Both Wind and Flood Damage," www.taylor.house.gov/index.php?option=com_content&task=view&id=77&Itemid=36.
33. *State Farm Lloyd's v. Nicolau*, 591 S.W.2d 444 (Tex. 1997).
34. Anita Lee, "State Farm to Probe Haag Firm," *Sun-Herald* (Biloxi, Miss.), September 21, 2006.
35. Mowbray, "Same House. Same Repairs. Same Insurer. Why Different Prices?" *New Orleans Times Picayune*, May 20, 2007.

Chapter 10: Insurance Fraud and Other Frauds

1. William C. Lesch and Bruce Byars, "Consumer Insurance Fraud in the U.S. Property-Casualty Industry," *Journal of Financial Crime* 15, no. 4 (2008): 411, 413.
2. N.Y. McKinney's Penal Law § 176.05.
3. *Brief of Amici Curiae The Massachusetts Academy of Trial Attorneys and The Massachusetts Bar Association, Commonwealth v. Ellis*, No. SJC-07846 (Mass., December 2, 1998), 1998 WL 35031552, at 38 & n.5.
4. Tom Baker, "Constructing the Insurance Relationship: Sales Stories, Claims Stories, and Insurance Contract Damages," *Texas Law Review* 72 (1994): 1395, 1411.
5. Tom Baker and Karen McElrath, "Insurance Claims Discrimination," in *Insurance Redlining*, ed. Gregory D. Squires (Washington: Urban Institute Press, 1997), 141.
6. "Insurers Devise Anti-Fraud Plan," *Claims* (November 2001), 14.
7. Annual Report 2007, Coalition Against Insurance Fraud.
8. Figures are from the Coalition Against Insurance Fraud, the Insurance Information Institute, and the Insurance Research Council.

9. Richard A. Derrig, "Insurance Fraud," *Journal of Risk and Insurance* 69, no. 3 (2002): 271.
10. www.shopliftingprevention.org/TheIssue.htm. March 13, 2009.
11. For this and subsequent history see Ken Dornstein, *Accidentally on Purpose: The Making of a Personal Injury Underworld in America* (New York: St. Martin's Press, 1996).
12. Edward A. Purcell Jr., "The Class Action Fairness Act in Perspective: The Old and New in Federal Jurisdictional Reform," *University of Pennsylvania Law Review* 156 (2008): 1823.
13. Jerold S. Auerbach, *Unequal Justice: Lawyers and Social Change in Modern America* (New York: Oxford University Press, 1976), 127.
14. Segment Training, Special Investigations Unit, Allstate Insurance, July 1995.
15. Christopher Dauer, "Team Approach Sought to Stem Fraud," *National Underwriter*, December 14, 1992.
16. Coalition Against Insurance Fraud, "Communicating the Anti-Fraud Message," www.insurancefraud.org/communicating_fraud.htm.
17. Ibid.
18. See John Panneton, "Federalizing Fires: The Evolving Federal Response to Arson Related Crimes," *American Criminal Law Review* 23 (1985): 151.
19. *Daniels v. Liberty Mut. Ins. Co.*, 2006 WL 3239994, 2006 WL 2644949 (N.D. Ind. 2006).
20. Aviva Abramovsky, "An Unholy Alliance: Perceptions of Influence in Insurance Fraud Prosecutions and the Need for Real Safeguards," *Journal of Criminal Law & Criminology* 98, no. 2 (2008): 363; E. Hoyt, David B. Mustard, and Lawrence S. Powell, "The Effectiveness of State Legislation in Mitigating Moral Hazard: Evidence from Insurance Fraud," *Journal of Law & Economics* 49 (2006): 427.
21. McKinney's Insurance Law §§ 405-409.
22. Figures include all types of insurance fraud, including workers' compensation, disability, and medical. www.ins.state.ny.us/acrobat/fd07ar2g.pdf.
23. Abramovsky, "An Unholy Alliance: Perceptions of Influence in Insurance Fraud Prosecutions and the Need for Real Safeguards," 389.
24. Ibid., 396.
25. www.ircweb.org/news/200307242.htm. December 23, 2008.
26. P. Hans and Nicole Vadino, "Whipped by Whiplash? The Challenges of Jury Communication in Lawsuits Involving Connective Tissue Injury," *Tennessee Law Review* 67 (1999–2000): 569.
27. Lesch and Byars, "Consumer Insurance Fraud in the U.S. Property-Casualty Industry."
28. "Allstate Best Practices Guide, Identifying & Handling Potentially Fraudulent First Party Casualty Claims" (1992, 1994).
29. Richard V. Ericson, Aaron Doyle, and Barry Dean, *Insurance as Governance* (Toronto: University of Toronto Press, 2003), 319.
30. State Farm, "The Indicator" (Summer 1983).
31. Special Investigations Unit, Segment Training, Allstate Insurance, n.d.
32. Abramovsky, "An Unholy Alliance: Perceptions of Influence in Insurance Fraud Prosecutions and the Need for Real Safeguards," 392.
33. Regis Hyle, "Running Up the Flag," *Claims* (April 2007), 38; Maria Woehr, "Uncovering Crooked Claims," *Insurance & Technology*, July 1, 2006.
34. www.iso.com/Products/ISO-ClaimSearch/ISO-ClaimSearch-improve-claims-processing-and-prevent-fraud.html; Lesch and Byars, "Consumer Insurance Fraud in the U.S. Property-Casualty Industry."
35. Memorandum, Savings report on Westlake Anti-Fraud Results, January 24, 1984.
36. Fraud measurement survey, http://www.insurancefraud.org/fraud_measurement.htm.

37. Coalition Against Insurance Fraud, "Study on SIU Performance Measurement," www.insurancefraud.org/downloads/siu_study.pdf, June 2003.
38. *Texas Farmers Ins. Co. v. Cameron*, 24 S.W.2d 386 (Tex. App. 2000).
39. *Hensley v. Shelter Mut. Ins. Co.*, 210 S.W.2d 455 (Mo. App. 2007).

Chapter 11: How Consumers Can Respond to Delay, Deny, Defend

1 J. Robert Hunter, "Property/Casualty Insurance in 2008: Overpriced Insurance and Underpaid Claims Result in Unjustified Profits, Padded Reserves, and Excessive Capitalization," Consumer Federation of America, www.consumerfed.org/pdfs/2008Insurance_White_Paper.pdf, January 10, 2008.
2. J. Robert Hunter, "State Insurance Department Websites: A Consumer Assessment," Consumer Federation of America, available at www.consumerfed.org/pdfs/state_insurance_websites.pdf, November 2008.
3. https://eapps.naic.org/cis/.
4. J. Robert Hunter, "State Insurance Department Websites."
5. www.badfaithinsurance.org/.
6. http://uphelp.org/pdfs/Effective_Claims.pdf.
7. http://uphelp.org/claimtips/tip_claimdispute.html#effective.

Chapter 12: How to Stop Delay, Deny, Defend

1. Kenneth J. Meier, *The Political Economy of Regulation: The Case of Insurance* (Albany: State University of New York Press, 1988), ch. 4.
2. 231 U.S. 495 (1869).
3. Susan Randall, "Insurance Regulation in the United States: Regulatory Federalism and the National Association of Insurance Commissioners," *Florida State University Law Review* 26 (1999): 632–33.
4. *United States v. South-Eastern Underwriters Ass'n*, 322 U.S. 533 (1944).
5. Ibid. at 139.
6. Tennyson, *State Regulation and Consumer Protection in the Insurance Industry* (2008).
7. Daniel Schwarcz, "Redesigning Consumer Dispute Resolution: A Case Study of the British and American Approaches to Insurance Claims Conflict," *Tulane Law Review* 38 (2009): 735, 757
8. Randall , "Insurance Regulation in the United States: Regulatory Federalism and the National Association of Insurance Commissioners," 678.
9. Steve Piontek, "Stop the Revolving Door!" *P&C National Underwriter,* September 8, 2008, www.property-casualty.com/Issues/2008/33/Pages/Stop-The-Revolving-Door-.aspx.
10. Martin F. Grace and Richard D. Philips, "Regulator Performance, Regulatory Environment, and Outcome: An Examination of Insurance Regulator Career Incentives on State Insurance Markets."
11. H. Roger Grant, *Insurance Reform: Consumer Action in the Progressive Era* (Ames, Iowa: Iowa State University Press, 1979), 136–39.
12. www.badfaithinsurance.org/reference/HDenenberg/Herb_Denenberg_Bio.htm.
13. Figures from OpenSecrets.org.
14. Richard V. Ericson, Aaron Doyle, and Barry Dean, *Insurance as Governance* (Toronto: University of Toronto Press, 2003), 151.
15. Randall, "Insurance Regulation in the United States: Regulatory Federalism and the National Association of Insurance Commissioners," 670.

16. Scot J. Paltrow, "The Converted: How Insurance Firms Beat Back an Effort For Stricter Controls," *Wall Street Journal*, February 5, 1998.
17. See Randall, "Insurance Regulation in the United States: Regulatory Federalism and the National Association of Insurance Commissioners," 670.
18. National Underwriter *P&C News,* April 6, 2009.
19. Paltrow, "The Converted: How Insurance Firms Beat Back an Effort for Stricter Controls."
20. Daniel Schwarcz, "Differential Compensation and the 'Race to the Bottom' in Consumer Insurance Markets," *Connecticut Insurance Law Journal* (2009).
21. Market Conduct Proposal in Focus at NAIC Summer Meeting, *BestWire,* May 23, 2008.
22. Mark J. Browne, Ellen S. Pryor, and Bob Puelz, "The Effect of Bad-Faith Laws on First-Party Insurance Claims Decisions," *Journal of Legal Studies* 33 (2004): 355.
23. *Anderson v. Continental Insurance Company,* 271 N.W.2d 368, 376 (1978).
24. *Crackel v. Allstate Ins. Co.,* 92 P.3d 882, 890 (Ariz. App. 2004).

Index